ABUSE
of
TRUST

ABUSE *of* TRUST

HEALING FROM CLERICAL SEXUAL ABUSE

Allen A. Hébert

Broussard
Press

An imprint of Your Holy Family
Round Rock, Texas

AbuseOfTrust.org

Broussard Press
1-713-701-7007 ● www.BroussardPress.com
ISBN 978-0-9965980-3-3
Printed in the United States of America

ABUSE *of* TRUST
HEALING FROM CLERICAL SEXUAL ABUSE

Allen A. Hébert

Broussard
Press

An imprint of Your Holy Family
Round Rock, Texas

Published by Broussard Press
An imprint of Your Holy Family
603 Lime Rock Drive, Round Rock, TX 78681

AbuseOfTrust.org

Broussard Press
1-713-701-7007 ● www.BroussardPress.com
ISBN 978-0-9965980-3-3
Printed in the United States of America

So they defiled themselves by their deeds and broke their marriage bond with the Lord till his anger blazed against his people: he was filled with horror at his chosen ones.

Psalm 106:39-40
Office of Readings Saturday 6th week of Easter

TABLE OF CONTENTS

ABUSE *of* TRUST

Introduction

Unless you have been hiding under a rock for the past year, you are well aware that the Catholic Church has a major problem addressing the sexual abuse of minors by members of the clergy. I believe that the Church has made progress over the past twenty years in the area of prevention of sexual abuse, but it has not made much headway in the area of seeking out and offering healing for the victims of abuse. The victims and their families are hurting, the laity and leaders of the Church are hurting, hopefully this book will help to heal those wounds and begin to restore peace to the Church and her members.

In this book, you will meet several survivors of sexual abuse committed by a priest of the Catholic Church. Unlike the vast majority of victims, these survivors have received much healing from the Church that at one time harmed them. They are committed Catholics seeking to help other victims and the Church they love to heal. It is through recognition of the problem of sexual abuse of minors and the oftentimes uncharitable response of the Church to victims, that we can begin the healing process. By better understanding the suffering and needs of victims, we will more effectively minister to them.

My name is Allen Hebert. I was born and raised Catholic. I work in technical sales in the technology field, and my wife and I founded a non-profit ministry for families. I was sexually abused by a Catholic priest between the ages of twelve and fourteen, and I have been healing from this trauma over the past twenty one years. If you would have asked me a few years ago if I would ever share my story of being sexually abused by a priest with strangers, I would have died of fear at the thought. God has been gradually leading me towards acceptance of what happened and complete freedom from it. Interestingly enough, if the revelations of Archbishop McCarrick and the Pennsylvania Grand Jury Report in the summer of 2018 had not come to light, I would probably not be writing this book. I had not given much thought to my abuse since 2008. But all that changed, when our world started talking about the failings of the Catholic Church. I say our world, because I am a committed and active Catholic. My wife and I homeschool our children and manage a non-profit family ministry sharing the good news about God's plan for family life. We live across the street from our parish, and our community is our Church. In other words, we live and breath Catholicism, and we love our faith dearly. When all of our friends began talking about the clerical abuse scandal, we felt awkward to say the least. They would ask my wife and I how we felt about it and what they should and could do to help victims and our Church heal. Some of our friends even struggled to reconcile being a part of a Church in which some priests harmed children and then often treated the victims as adversaries rather than members of the Church who were very in need of love and compassion.

As the news continued during the end of the summer months and intensified as the year went on, it was apparent that God was calling me and my wife to share some very personal and intimate details of my childhood, how God entered into that suffering, and how He and His Church healed us. As I have pondered my unique perspective on clerical sexual abuse, I often wondered if I was the only victim who was still a committed, active Catholic. The victims that are in the headlines are usually anti-Catholic and even anti-religion. They often hate the Church and strive for its demise, and I don't blame them. These victims not only experienced sexual abuse, but also rejection by their Church, by their Father.

I have sought out and discovered that there are other victims like me. We all have very different experiences of abuse. We come from all walks of life: male and female, married, single, and cleric. The one commonality is the betrayal of trust and the injuries done to our sexuality, innocence, and faith life, and yet, we all found healing in the Good News of Jesus Christ as safeguarded and authoritatively taught by the Catholic Church. We all love the Church and desire to heal her of this great wound. We desire to help our fellow Catholics (the secondary victims) to receive healing and help our priests and Bishops to better understand how to seek out and offer healing to all victims of abuse, especially those harmed by a leader of the Church.

In addition to these witness chapters, we will also provide you with chapters written by experts sharing their wisdom and practical advice.

Elizabeth Terrill, LPCC, the Victim Assistance Coordinator for the Diocese of Gallup New Mexico, will help you to identify the warning signs of an abuser, as well as the behaviors exhibited by a child who is being abused. She will provide an overview of the process of healing and practical advice on the steps to healing, as well as what to expect when working with a Diocese.

Dr. Deborah Rodriguez, a pediatrician who is active in the Maria Goretti Network and the Catholic Medical Association, will explore the typical effects of trauma experienced from childhood sexual abuse and ways in which family, friends and the Church can help survivors work towards healing from abuse. She will also discuss ideas on how the Church can effectively seek out and minister to these victims. Her chapters identify key success factors in an effective outreach program and discusses how parishes and Dioceses can effectively assist in the healing process through Trauma-Informed Ministry.

Christopher West of the Theology of the Body Institute will present the beauty of the Church's good news about human sexuality based on St. John Paul II's Theology of the Body. This chapter seeks to untwist the lies that many victims of childhood sexual abuse were taught as part of their experience of abuse. It is through understanding the meaning of our bodies that we can throw off the shackles of the lies we have believed about ourselves and about our dignity as a beloved child of God deserving of respect.

Within these pages, victims of sexual abuse will know they are not alone and that others have felt the way they do; they will know healing is possible and that it is possible to find the peace that their abuser took away from them without losing their faith.

This book sheds light on a subject that is not often spoken about because it is so personal and so hideous. Yet, we can see the harmful effects of a culture of silence. It is only by showing the reality of the effects of sexual abuse and its cover up on the survivor, and also on the

Church, that we will enable the Church to once again evangelize the world.

Sexual abuse is not a Catholic problem; it happens everywhere. It happens in other organizations, communities, and it even happens in families. The Church has good news to proclaim to set the captives free from a world obsessed with sexuality, a world that hasn't been able to effectively prevent the sexual abuse of minors or adults in any meaningful way. The authentic teachings of the Catholic Church are life giving, but the scandal of sexual abuse by members of the clergy and the systemic cover up by leaders of the Church is preventing this saving message from being shared with the world.

I guarantee you know a victim of sexual abuse; the CDC estimates that 1 in 3 women and 1 in 4* men are victims. Do you want to help them heal? Do you want to use the words of compassion that will bring them peace and encourage them to seek healing? We all do. We are called to be the healing hands of Christ in this world. There are people in your community who are carrying with them the baggage of abuse and are wearing the chains that deprive them of the peace they deserve. They are afraid to talk to someone because they fear that you will judge them as harshly as they judge themselves. Read this book, understand the problem, feel empathy for the victims, and help our church leaders to do the same. The victim could be a member of your family, your church community, or your neighborhood, and you may be the person whom God has chosen to speak the comforting words of healing that they need to hear. Learn to share the peace and healing of Jesus Christ right now. Don't delay; someone needs you.

Victims of sexual abuse and their families, members of the laity, and leaders in our Church have all felt a sense of an abuse of trust. They trusted that their children would be safeguarded, they trusted that the Church would believe them when they reported their abuse, they trusted the abuser would be removed from ministry and punished, and their trust was betrayed. It is our hope that this book provides a beginning to repair that broken trust.

---

* https://www.cdc.gov/features/sexualviolence/index.html

Preface

Warning

This book contains disturbing content. What you are about to read concerning the actions of leaders in the Catholic Church is horrendous. While the stories do not contain any graphic language, you will encounter evil. Most adults should be able to handle the topic, but be warned that these stories may greatly trouble your peace. We have only included descriptions of the evil to help the reader to accurately understand the problem in order to compel you to action. We seek to motivate you and provide you with concrete actions that can be taken to heal victims, their families, and the Church.

If you choose to let your children read this book, we strongly recommend that you read it together. Many of the events that the survivors share are pure evil committed by ordained men within the Catholic Church. Your children will need your assistance to reconcile what they are reading with the faith that you are trying to pass on to them.

Goal of the Book

The primary goal of this book is to provide healing to victims, their families, and the Church (both the laity and the leaders). Sexual abuse harms more than just the direct victim. It harms the whole community, and left untreated, it will destroy that community. The goal of this book is healing, and in order to begin the healing process, honesty is needed.

Sacred Stories

As you read the witness chapters that follow, keep in mind that the words written here required a lot of hard work on the part of the restored victims and their editors. The process was grueling. When I first put out an invitation for other victims of clerical sexual abuse to contact me, I really had no idea what to expect. I only knew that there were other faithful Catholics out there who had suffered abuse and perhaps some of them, like me, desperately wanted to help other victims and our beloved Church heal from this grievous wound.

I didn't have an onslaught of people contacting me, instead I was timidly contacted by one here, one there, male and female. Some were strong in their resolve to share their story, others were cautious. My experience is perhaps unique. I received much of my healing without professional therapy, through unconditional love within my family, the authentic teachings of the Church, and the Sacraments. For most victims, the path is much more difficult. While it is still difficult and painful to think of my abuse and the effect it has had on my life and the lives of the people I love, I have been given the grace of a near miraculous healing in which the abuse no longer holds significant influence in my life. I hope and pray that every victim of abuse (whether the abuse was perpetrated by a cleric or other person) finds this same freedom, but unfortunately, this road to freedom is long and most never reach this point during their lifetime. Even those initial collaborators, who contacted me, found that as they wrote their stories, the pain came rushing back. A project they thought would be relatively easy to complete, turned out to be long and drawn out. The wounds they thought were healed still needed attention and further healing. My wife and I were no exception.

In addition to the personal difficulties experienced by the writers, many have been made to feel like they should just "move on" and stop dwelling on the abuse they suffered so long ago. I am sure that every abuse survivor wishes they could do this and some have. But, there are so many victims who have never experienced any healing, and some have never told another person about what happened to them. They suffer in silence and many continue to engage in destructive/risky behaviors as a result of the sexual abuse they suffered as a child.

One common motivator amongst all the contributors is a sincere desire to bring healing to victims as well as to compel members of the laity and the leaders of the Church to action. Every victim desires to hear words of contrition from their abuser, and if their abuser is incapable of providing this (either because they are deceased or unrepentant), they need to hear this from their family members, the Church. Not only do survivors need to hear it, they need to feel it. They need to hear more than empty words of apologies; they need to hear words of genuine concern for their complete healing and words and actions that condemn the perpetrator and his actions. Words are cheap; concrete actions speak louder than eloquent apologies.

The words written in these chapters are words written with much love: love for other victims and love for the Church. These are not the words of people who seek to harm the Church; we seek to heal it and to remove the cancer that has hurt so many. The initial sexual abuse was horrible, but the response from the leaders of the Church has often times been more hurtful and long lasting.

Imagine, if you will, being a victim (the survivor stories can help you enter into that). Something really awful happened to you as a child; you stuffed it away, vowing never to tell another soul. Then after years of risky, destructive activities, you recognize the root of the problem (the sexual abuse you suffered), and perhaps through counseling, prayer, or research on the subject, you realize that the only path towards healing is to tell somebody in your family. First you tell your spouse or best friend, they comfort you, and you feel a little better. Then, you decide to talk to the head of the family in which you were abused (in the case of clerical sexual abuse this is the Bishop). His response is to tell you how sorry he is that this happened; to tell you that they knew the guy who abused you had this problem, and they sent him to counseling but obviously it didn't fully address it. Perhaps they even imply that you may have contributed to his moral failure; or worse, maybe the Bishop accused you of making it all up because this priest is loved by everyone and has been in ministry for over thirty years with a spotless record. How would that make you feel?

Each of us has had unique experiences in this area (some have been good experiences, others absolutely horrible), but we have persisted and have found some level of healing. Despite the wound inflicted by the Church, we have retained our faith and have grown closer to Christ through His Church.

As you read the witness stories that follow, I encourage you to remember that each of these stories is unique and follows an individual's path from darkness to light. Along each path, many people helped the victim to heal and choose to return to, or continue embracing, their Catholic faith. In some cases, it was a kind word or a listening ear; at other times, it was a book or talk which spoke about God's unconditional love or the beauty of the authoritative teachings of the Catholic Church. In each journey, God was there providing what was needed to help each survivor choose to continue the hard work of healing and choose to grow in communion with our God. You may be that person for another survivor; God can, and does, use unworthy, imperfect, sinful people to heal and bring His beloved children closer to Himself.

Vulnerability

I told my Bishop that the Church needed to do the right thing and seek out the victims of clerical sexual abuse and minister to them to help them to fully heal. I know this is a big request. It involves not only admitting culpability, it also involves being vulnerable: vulnerable to being hurt by those who are hurting and vulnerable to financial responsibility for their healing. It involves spending a lot of time and resources to help others heal. Far too many leaders in the Church get caught up in thinking about these vulnerabilities and risks, and the victims know and feel it. They feel the Church doesn't care about their healing.

The Catholic Church is my Church too. We are all priest, prophet, and king, but each member plays a different role. Our Church needs to minister to and heal those whom wolves in sheep's clothing have harmed, and they need to do it now in a very visible way, with disregard for their own protection. If the Church can't show compassion to those wounded by their own, how can they show compassion to other victims of sexual abuse? If the Church can't be vulnerable and do the right thing, no one will believe the Church when speaking moral truths in other areas in which society needs to hear the good news of the Gospel. In other words, the Church's lack of compassion and desire to heal victims of clerical sexual abuse has an adverse effect on our mission to evangelize the world.

Reflection Before Reading

As we prepare to walk through a valley of tears,
we fear no evil for we know there is hope and healing
in these pages. Let us be strengthened and consoled
that there are warriors who are willing to fight to
bring mercy and justice to those who have suffered.

ABUSE *of* TRUST

The Truth Set Me Free

Allen A. Hébert

When I think back on my childhood, I remember two childhoods. One was similar to many of yours. I was born into a Catholic family, attended Catholic Schools, got in trouble with my teachers for talking to my classmates too much and disrupting class, played in the middle school band, went camping with the boy scouts, played little league baseball, football, basketball and soccer, had crushes on girls in my classes, tried and failed at many things, and had friends with whom I would do things we shouldn't have done.

My second childhood involved a priest I met when I was eleven and with whom I became friends and vacationed with in Europe. He taught me about a world that I was just beginning to explore: what it meant to be a man. He formed my understanding of Catholic morality, and eventually, I trusted him more than my parents. When I was at the cusp of adolescence, he won my complete trust, abused that trust, and abused me sexually. Not only was I violated physically, but also spiritually. The beautiful Truth, for which Jesus Christ gave his life on the cross, was taken away from me, for a time, by this unholy priest. He formed my morality to make me a slave of the flesh instead of a slave of the Lord. I was imprisoned by this devil, but the Lord set me free. The prayers of my family, coupled with the faithful witness of my wife and her family, saved me from a life of slavery to the flesh and spiritual death. I truly found a new life in Christ, and the Truth set me free.

A Typical Childhood

I was born in June of 1969 into a Catholic family. My father was one of four, and my mother was an only child. My parents both have family roots in the Cajun region of southern Louisiana where the Catholic faith is strong and ingrained deeply into the culture. I was baptized as an infant, attended Catholic schools throughout my whole life, and even attended a Catholic college.

My faith life was heavily influenced by my maternal grandmother, who was a daily communicant and member of the Blue Army (praying for the conversion of Russia). She also prayed the rosary and prayers from the Pieta Prayer Book. She gave me so many scapulars that I still find new ones in my photo albums and childhood memorabilia. She was very concerned about my salvation and often reminded me that she prayed for me regularly.

I grew up in Houston, Texas when the city was still relatively small. Dad started his own residential electrical service business, and most of my extended family worked for him at some point. I played all kinds of sports, and Dad was usually the head coach. He loved being involved in everything my brother and I did. We were a very close-knit family with strong ties to my Dad's siblings' families. I was an average student, who primarily got in trouble for talking and socializing too much during class. My childhood was pretty good: I had parents, aunts, uncles, and grandparents who loved me and were involved in my life.

I have vivid memories of sailing on Galveston Bay, flying in my Dad's twin engine airplane, taking family trips, and playing lots of sports at the Oaks Dad's Club. My maternal grandmother, MaMa, would often pick me up from school and make my favorite, unusual after school meals. I say unusual because I was a very picky eater. We would stop at Taco Bell on our way home from school, and I would

order two tacos, meat and cheese only, and a tostada with beans and cheese only. When she would cook, she would make blueberry muffins and make two or three special ones, without blueberries, for me. I also remember the summers with MaMa. Since my mother worked in my father's electrical service business, I would stay with MaMa and participate in her normal routine. We attended daily Mass, the Thursday Club (the over sixty-five social group at church), and I even took Gray Line tours with her and her friends to various historical places in Texas and Louisiana. We had a lot of fun and all her friends just loved having a young person around.

Grooming in Rural Texas

In 1981, when I was between eleven and twelve, our family took a vacation to Europe. During this trip, we met Fr. Andy Willemsen while staying at a hotel in Austria. Fr. Andy was traveling with his sister and her husband and a young man named John (real name changed). My brother and I started playing with John and discovered that he and Fr. Andy were fellow Texans.

After returning from our European vacation, our family connected with Fr. Andy, and he invited me to come visit him at the parish where he was serving, St. Mary's in Bremond, TX.

Over the course of the next three years, I would make regular weekend trips to Bremond to spend time with him. Shortly after I began visiting him, Fr. Andy invited me to accompany him on his yearly trip to the Netherlands in 1982. My parents and I both agreed that this sounded like a wonderful opportunity to experience a new culture with the locals as my guides.

1981 Trip to Europe, Where we first met Fr. Andy

While I don't remember exactly how he initially convinced me to enter into a sexual relationship with him, I do remember that in preparation for this upcoming trip to Europe, Fr. Andy told me that there was only one bed at his sister's home in Zundert, Holland. He said that most hotels in Europe were small and beds were usually limited, so we would need to share a bed. The last catch was that Fr. Andy slept without any clothes on, and since I was sharing a bed with him, I would also need to sleep without any clothes. Just writing these words makes me feel so stupid. How was I this gullible? Why didn't the red flags go up right away? Why didn't I talk to my parents or my grandmother about these conditions? The answer is that I had been groomed, I was the right age, and adolescence had kicked in. I was already beginning that phase of life when a young man begins to discover his sexuality and separate from being his parents' child to being a young, independent man. This is a natural phase, and, ideally, the parents are there to help their child through that interesting and deeply formative period. Unfortunately for me, there was someone else who I trusted and yet abused that trust by exploiting my innocence and adolescent curiosity and forming me into a willing participant in a sexual relationship with a much older man.

St. Mary's Rectory, Bremond, TX

The human mind is very powerful and protective. It appears that it continues to protect me from some memories that would probably cause much pain and suffering. I remember much of the abusive activities and some of the places where the abuse took place, but I cannot remember anything about the first time he molested me or specifically how he convinced me to undress in his presence.

Fr. Andy took on the role of a father: teaching me right from wrong and explaining to me that my parents wouldn't understand. He said that they were taught that sex is bad, but he knew better and wanted me to know better also. This alternate morality would adversely affect me and the young women I would date in later years.

During my days in high school, I distinctly remember a pervasive feeling of nervousness. It wasn't a lack of self confidence, rather it was a feeling that something bad was going to happen because things couldn't always be going my way. In retrospect, that feeling of nervousness was probably my conscience telling me what I was doing wasn't right and wouldn't make me happy or bring me closer to the Lord. After I decided to embrace the teachings of the Church in their entirety, I was genuinely amazed at how much peace I felt. Not a one time feeling but a general, pervasive sense of peace in my life.

> *"Peace I leave with you; my peace I give to*
> *you. Not as the world gives do I give it to you.*
> *Do not let your hearts be troubled or afraid."*
> *John 14:27*

Sexual abuse takes many forms. Sometimes it is forced upon a young person, and there is fear and coercion involved. However, in my case, I was groomed and accepted it as a completely normal activity. In fact, Fr. Andy told me about other boys with whom he had a similar arrangement. This included John, who I met in Austria in 1981 while he was traveling with Fr. Andy on his trip to Europe. I even told Fr. Andy that I was a bit uncomfortable with the homosexual aspect of the relationship, and he flat out told me that if he could have a girl he would. But he was a priest, and everyone knows that a priest cannot have sex with a girl. I asked Fr. Andy how our relationship would change over time, and he told me that as I grew up and eventually met a girl I wanted to marry, our sexual activity would cease at that time. As perverse as his explanations were, as a twelve year old boy, I accepted them completely without reservation. For around three years,

1981 to 1984, I visited the rectory in Bremond regularly, and in total, I accompanied Fr. Andy on two trips to Europe.

As I mentioned earlier, my maternal grandmother was praying for me. While she was a prayerful woman, she was not all-knowing, and to the best of my knowledge, the abusive relationship did not change the way I acted or have any effect on who I was other than accelerate my sexual maturity. In other words, I didn't start to withdraw; didn't go into depression; didn't start to abuse alcohol or drugs. I just continued to grow up and do the same things other kids my age did. Attending an all male Catholic High School was a near occasion for sin, but since I had been taught that sex was natural and normal for a young man, the activities that many of my classmates were engaged in with young ladies seemed perfectly normal and something that we just hid from our puritan parents for their own good.

As I grew older and began to date young women, I became increasingly uncomfortable with the homosexual nature of my relationship with Fr. Andy. Around 1984, I told him that I wanted to stop engaging in any sexual acts with him. He reluctantly agreed and the activity stopped. Every once in a while, he would try something, but I was firm in my decision and nothing more ever occurred. I kept in touch with him and even went to Bremond to visit on occasion. When I would get caught by my parents doing something wrong, I would avoid punishment by suggesting that I go visit Fr. Andy, and my parents were very happy to oblige because surely a priest would be able to set me back on the morally straight course. In reality, I would go up there, tell Fr. Andy what I had done, and we would laugh about it, and I would continue in my immoral lifestyle.

Despite the challenges in my young life, I matured, graduated high school, attended college, met a beautiful girl, got married, received a computer science degree, started a career, and was blessed with children.

Getting Married

My future wife and I met while I still believed and adhered to Fr. Andy's sexual morality. Fortunately, the love of a good Catholic woman, who knew and embraced her faith, was more powerful, and thus, I did what was necessary to win her hand in marriage. During our time of dating, most everyone we encountered supported Fr. Andy's sexual ethics or avoided discussing the subject, including our college's campus minister, Fr. Roger Temme. He has recently been identified as a credibly accused abuser priest in the Archdiocese of New Orleans. It is amazing that my wife held firm for as long as she did with all this negative pressure against the authentic teachings of Christ that she was taught and believed. One bright spot during our engagement was the couple who led our Engaged Encounter. They spoke the truth boldly and challenged us to live according to God's laws for the remaining time before we got married, and we accepted the challenge.

Fr. Roger Temme witnessed our vows

Sexual morality in our culture is very opposed to the life-giving morality of God, and it truly takes a heroic person (cleric or lay person) to go against the cultural tide. Those that do will be mocked and ridiculed, but I can tell you that at least one broken person was saved by those efforts. So, take courage, and speak the truth in season and out of season. The Gospel message truly does give light to those living in the darkness. Now embracing and living the truth of God's plan for human sexuality, my wife and I began our lives together, but I still had this secret that I hid from her.

A Light Comes On

After we got married, while on the road to accepting the teachings of the Church, I was still saddled with this huge secret that I didn't even know I had. I knew what I had done, but I just viewed it as a sin of my youth. The funny thing is, while I confessed all the other sins of my youth, I never confessed that one. Perhaps it was because a priest was involved, and so, while I then knew right from wrong, I somehow viewed that particular part of my life as outside of the rest of my life. Like a compartment inside of the rest of my life; it was there but not completely connected to the other experiences that I had growing up.

It wasn't until I was around the age of 28 that I recognized my relationship with Fr. Andy for what it truly was. I remember when I realized that I was a victim of clerical sexual abuse like it was yesterday. I had been steadily growing in my faith to the point that my wife and I began hosting a series of faith formation gatherings with fellow Catholic couples at our home. At the end of one of those meetings, we were visiting with one couple, and I mentioned that I had travelled to Europe with a priest, when I was in middle school. The husband made a joke about clerical sexual abuse; it was something to the effect that I was lucky that priest wasn't one of those priests *who abused young boys*. All I remember is that at that point I saw my childhood in a completely new light. It was like the scales were falling from my eyes; I could now see clearly and didn't like what I was seeing.

Knowing now what had happened to me, I needed to figure out what my next steps were, if any. At this time, I had made significant progress in my spiritual life. I had married the perfect woman, who came from a very Catholic family, and with her help, I was growing steadily in my faith and in accepting the teachings of the Catholic Church. I read Pierced by a Sword, a Catholic novel by Bud Macfarlane, consecrated myself to Jesus through Mary, and began wearing the Miraculous Medal. It is no wonder that the scales were falling from my eyes.

Miraculous Medal

After I realized I was a victim of sexual abuse during that encounter with my friend, I had to deal with it. It was around that time that one of the first clerical sexual abuse scandals made headline news. There it was, in my face, and I couldn't ignore it anymore. My first step was to share this secret with my wife. While on a Marriage Encounter Weekend lying in bed after a long day of talks, I told her. I think she was in shock; she couldn't believe it, and we talked well into the night about it.

Seeking Empathy

A short time after sharing this secret with my wife, around 1998, I recalled that Fr. Andy had told me that he knew Bishop John McCarthy. Bishop McCarthy was still the bishop in Austin, so I made an appointment with him about a confidential matter concerning Fr. Andy Willemsen. When I arrived at his office, he was pale white, and he didn't wait for me to start the conversation. He told me that when he read my message and saw that name, he got chills. I asked if he remembered Fr. Andy, and I told him that he sexually abused me as a child. He acknowledged that he knew him, and he never liked him. In 1988, someone had made a report about him in the Archdiocese of Galveston/Houston but didn't leave his name. He asked if I was that

young man. Unfortunately, I had to tell him I was not. I recently found out that my friend, John, was the one who made the report.

Bishop McCarthy told me that he was so very sorry for what happened to me. He also told me that back in 1988, when he received the allegation from the Archdiocese of Galveston/Houston, he immediately told Fr. Andy to pack his bags, get out of his Diocese, and go back to the Netherlands. This was a very different story than what Fr. Andy told me, but at that point in my healing process, I just wanted to know that someone else knew what had happened. I don't think I even wanted an apology, just knowing that someone knew what Fr. Andy did was enough.

Seeking Justice

In 2002, numerous cases of clerical sexual abuse and coverup in the Archdiocese of Boston made headlines, and once again, I had to deal with what had happened to me. I don't remember too much of how I reacted, but I do recall that I thought it was far-fetched for Cardinal Law to deserve to be forced to resign. So apparently, I didn't read too much about it. Clerical sexual abuse being in the news again prompted me to contact the Diocese of Austin's new Bishop, Gregory Aymond. This time, I was seeking justice. I asked about what happened to Fr. Andy Willemsen and was shocked to find out that not only did Bishop Aymond not know I was a victim of clerical sexual abuse in his Diocese, but he had no knowledge of Fr. Andy Willemsen.

After his office conducted some research on Fr. Andy, I was informed that he was still in active ministry. Bishop Aymond assured me that he would be contacting the Diocese in the Netherlands and that Fr. Andy would be removed from the priesthood. At a follow-up meeting, I was informed that Fr. Andy had been laicized. I asked what other punishment he received, and Bishop Aymond told me that he was no longer a priest. Bishop Aymond informed me that this was a very severe punishment. I said that it wasn't enough, but Aymond told me there was nothing else he could do due to the statute of limitations. Aymond did tell me that Fr. Andy was very angry when he was removed from ministry. At my request, he provided me with the mailing address for Fr. Andy. However, that piece of paper just sat in my night stand drawer, and I never did anything with it.

Bishop Aymond also offered his sincere apologies on behalf of the Church and encouraged me to go to counseling paid for by the Diocese. I attended a number of counseling sessions that helped me to deal with the guilt I had been carrying around for so many years. I blamed myself for the abuse; I was ashamed of what I had done and had profound fear that someone would find out my secret. The breakthrough came when the counselor asked me if I had told my parents. I had not. She asked how they would feel if they knew. I said they would be mad. She asked who I thought they would be mad at, and without any hesitation, I told her, "They would be mad at me." As soon as I spoke those words, the chains began to fall off my wrists, and I forgave myself and realized, for the first time, that I was the victim.

Healing my Wife

For a long time, I believed that I was the only one that needed healing. It wasn't until I joined the leadership team to conduct a men's retreat at our Parish that I realized, very painfully, that this was not the case. During the preparation for the men's retreat, each member of the retreat team gave a witness about their lives. Each person was encouraged to spend time in prayer asking the Lord what part of their particular faith journey they should share with the other members of the team. During my time in prayer, the Lord spoke firmly telling me that I needed to share about my abuse. My first reaction was an emphatic no. I began to argue with the Lord, saying, "I will share anything, but not that." It really caught me off guard; I never in my wildest dreams expected that God would ask me to share that part of my life with anyone besides my wife *and two bishops and a counselor*. After even more prayer and a continued strong feeling that God wanted me to share on this topic, I did it. When I got home that night, my wife asked me how it went and what I spoke about during my talk. This was not an out of the ordinary question, so I answered that I shared about my abuse. She was livid, almost hysterical, and for the next two weeks, we argued and fought. She couldn't believe that I would share that information with anyone. I told her God made me do it. I told her that every man is sworn to secrecy, but that didn't matter to her.

I shouldn't have been surprised. Scripture tells us that the two shall become one flesh, and thus, my history became her history too. While counseling helped me work through the shame, guilt, and fear, she had not received any of this help. I went back to Bishop Aymond and asked him if the Diocese would offer my wife the same counseling it provided to me, and he said no. My wife and I continued to dialog about why I shared it and about how it helped me to heal. I now realize that God told me to share it with my retreat brothers, not for them, but for me and for my wife, so that we would begin to heal from this trauma together.

Seeking to Heal Others

Another thirteen years went by without me thinking much about my abuse. Then, the movie <u>Spotlight</u> came out and won lots of awards. It was about the 'Spotlight' investigative reporting division at the Boston Globe that exposed the clerical abuse and cover up in Boston under Archbishop Bernard Cardinal Law. I saw it in my social media news feed, and I got curious. I wondered how I would do emotionally watching a movie about clerical abuse, so I rented it online and watched it while I was out of town on business. The movie is well done and shows in excruciating detail how the leaders of the Church covered up one abuse case after another, the deep pain the victims suffer, and the apparent callousness of the leadership of the Church in Boston. Emotionally, I was relatively unaffected by the movie, until the end. In the final scene, after the reporters, against all odds, published a lengthy expose of clerical abuse in the Archdiocese of Boston listing the abusers and detailing their crimes and the cover-up, the two main characters arrive at the Globe on a Saturday morning. The parking lot is relatively empty. They look at each other knowing that the work they did was a worthy endeavor and somewhat feeling like their job was done. But they were wrong. As they walked into the office, they noticed a lot of activity. Every person at work that day was answering phones. The phone lines were ringing constantly with calls from other victims telling their stories of abuse at the hands of priests.

It was in this moment that I recalled the young man that I met in Austria those many years ago. I wondered if he ever got help, if anyone helped him through his emotions, and if he felt that justice had been served. My abuser had not been publicly identified. I knew of at least three other victims of this man, and they were probably still suffering in silence like so many victims. I immediately called my spiritual director and told him what I had watched and how I was feeling. I told him that I felt called to help heal other victims.

It took another three years for the McCarrick and Pennsylvania scandals to motivate me to actually do something. It became apparent through my conversations with various priests that sharing my story would help them better minister to people like me. I scheduled an appointment with the new Bishop of Austin, Joe Vasquez. This time, I came offering to help the Church I love. I shared with him my story and what I believed victims want, and need, to hear from the leaders of the Church. I offered to help in any way I could to equip him and the priests of our Diocese to seek out other victims and show them empathy and do what I could to minister directly to other victims. Bishop Vasquez hasn't yet taken me up on my offer to help. Therefore, I discerned that I should seek out other survivors, who were just as committed to helping the Church as I was, and produce a resource to help victims of clerical sexual abuse in their journey of healing and provide guidance to the Church on how to seek out and help victims heal. This book is the fruit of that labor.

Reclaiming My Childhood

As part of my healing, I decided to research and find out all I could about the man who sexually abused me. It was almost like rediscovering a missing piece of my childhood. At the time, he knew everything about me, and I knew little about him. I knew he was from the Netherlands, had a married sister, had once taught in the seminary in Houston, was associate pastor and then pastor at St. Mary's in Bremond, TX, and knew Bishop McCarthy.

In my research in 2018, I reached out to the Vincentian Fathers and the Diocese of 's-Hertogenbosch, and I discovered the following:

Fr. Willemsen 1979

Fr. Andrew J. Willemsen, born March 12, 1928 in Zundert, The Netherlands, was ordained priest of the Southern Province of the Congregation of the Mission (Dallas) in 1954. After he finished his theological studies in 1955, he was assigned to the Western province of the Congregation of the Mission in the USA. The Provincial Superior of the Western Province, who resided in St. Louis, Missouri, sent Fr. Willemsen to study Canon Law in Rome.

He received a Licentiate in Canon Law from St. Thomas University (Angelicum) in Rome[1], and in 1957, he went back to the USA and resided for one year in Denver. In 1958, he was appointed to teach in California at St. John's Seminary, Camarillo[2]

In 1964, Andrew Willemsen was appointed to St. Mary's Seminary[3] in Houston, Texas and taught until 1981. During this period in the Seminary, he resided at the Vincentian Center, 1302 Kipling Street, in Houston, Texas and assisted with Masses in Parishes in the Houston area, including St. Mary Magdalene in Humble, TX. In 1982, the Vincentian Fathers withdrew from St. Mary's Seminary, and apparently, Fr. Andy wished to stay in the area. He was then incardinated into the Diocese of Austin and assigned to serve at St. Mary's Catholic Church in Bremond, TX.

Even though Fr. Andy Willemsen was a US Citizen, he returned to the Netherlands in 1988 and remained a member of the clergy of the Diocese of Austin. He contacted me just prior to his quick departure

and told me that Bishop McCarthy told him that if he wished to stay in the Diocese of Austin, he would be serving as a full time Canon Lawyer on the Marriage Tribunal. Fr. Andy told me that he had no desire to do that, so he was returning home to the Netherlands.

Transfer and Abuse Allegations

Father Andy Willemsen, C.M.
1981

In 1988, he returned to Holland. He reported to the Diocese of 's-Hertogenbosch for a possible appointment, after which the Diocese of 's-Hertogenbosch obtained references from the Diocese of Austin.

In December of 1988, Bishop John McCarthy of the Austin Diocese sent a very positive letter of recommendation concerning Fr. Willemsen. The correspondence I received from Mr. Vincent

Peters, Chancellor of the Diocese of 's-Hertogenbosch, provided this transcript of the recommendation and commentary:

> "I think your diocese would be fortunate to have Father Willemsen's services. He is extremely pleasant and an energetic and effective worker."
>
> Nothing was reported about possible sexual abuse on his part. Given the recommendation, he was then appointed as pastor in Steensel.
>
> In 2002, we received signals that Fr. Willemsen might have been involved in sexual abuse in Texas in the 1970s. Fr. Willemsen has been questioned by the diocese and research has been carried out by a number of canonists. Unfortunately, this did not bring clarity.
>
> The congregation in Austin also conducted an investigation. On January 8, 2004, we received the results of this study, which clearly showed sexual abuse by Willemsen.
>
> Willemsen was immediately fired as a pastor and the bishop has withdrawn all his faculties as a priest.
>
> Of course it is incomprehensible and shocking that the then Bishop of Austin wrote a positive recommendation and did not inform us about the sexual abuse. Had this been communicated, Willemsen would never have been appointed. The bishop of Austin knowingly caused a dangerous situation to arise in the diocese of Den Bosch. Fortunately, there are no signals that Willemsen in his time as pastor in Steensel has committed abuse.

He served in Steensel for eight years and was removed from ministry in 2004, and he died on April 20th, 2012.

Opening the Doors of My Mind

Shortly after visiting with our current Bishop, Rev. Joe Vasquez, my wife began counseling sessions. The Catholic therapist she began working with specialized in a relatively new therapy called Eye Movement Desensitization and Reprocessing (EMDR). EMDR is an integrative psychotherapy approach that has been extensively researched and proven effective for the treatment of trauma. Francine Shapiro, Ph.D, first discovered and developed EMDR therapy in 1987. At this time, I didn't think I needed more therapy, but the positive results my wife was seeing, along with the description of the therapy itself, piqued my interest. The thought of "talking" about what had happened to me with a therapist was not appealing, but EMDR was more than just talking, it was designed to help explore my own memories and reprocess them so that they no longer held so much control over me. I never thought I had flashbacks, but I did have memories of the abuse and other significant events in my life that I would think of often. I would recall the bedroom where most of the abuse took place. I would think about events during high school involving my parents and their disappointment with me after discovering that I had been engaged in immoral activities. When these memories came to mind, I didn't become incapacitated or incapable of functioning, which is what I always associated with flashbacks. However, they were unwanted, and I had no control over when these thoughts would pop into my mind. I came to discover that these memories were unresolved in my mind, and in order to keep them from constantly being thought about, I needed to "reprocess" them. That is what EMDR has helped me to do.

The work in opening the mental door to those memories is a bit scary, because there are often other memories that are suppressed that will be brought to the light. These memories are ones that were hidden to protect me. In my first EMDR session, I was asked to think about a person in my life with whom I felt love and protection from. This was easy; it was my maternal grandmother, MaMa (maw maw). I was given a device for each hand that would alternate vibrating between the left side and the right side. The therapist asked me close my eyes and recall MaMa's home, the furniture within it, and also me sitting with her. As I recalled this scene to my mind, she activated the left-right vibrations, and I began to dream while awake. I was transported back to MaMa's home prior to the abuse by Fr. Andy. I not only recalled the features of her home, but the emotions associated with it. I felt her love for me, and I felt safe. After the EMDR session, I was crying and very emotional in a good way. I was able to recall and feel her love for me that I had lost for a period of time. While I thought about MaMa often, until this session, I only had pictures in my mind of her and not the feelings of love from her. Now when I think of her, I once again have both. This is absolutely amazing.

This is what EMDR does. It is thought to simulate something similar to dreams, in what is referred to as the REM phase of sleep, while our brain is also fully awake. Our right brain and left brain talk to each other, and we reprocess any difficult situations we have encountered. The logical and creative sides of our brain work together to deal with and process traumatic events. Until we do this work, the trauma will continue to be unresolved and will pop up during times when something completely unrelated will "trigger" that traumatic event in our memory, and often, our response to the current event will be much more severe than the current issue would warrant.

As our sessions progressed, I was able to open the doors in my brain to resolve those painful memories that have caused me to overreact to current situations. I have been able to reclaim my emotions and not let these memories continue to exert control over my life. There are still parts of my abuse that I do not remember, and while I am curious about them, it may be for the best that I don't remember. It is my brain's way of protecting me from a memory I am not yet ready to process.

Why am I still Catholic

As I reflect on the effects that sexual abuse has on me, I am amazed that I survived. I not only survived, but I am happily married, blessed with nine children, and am a committed Catholic. I suppose

I fell in love with Jesus Christ and His Truth before I recognized the abuse I suffered by one of His ministers. The teachings of the Church are truly beautiful and life giving. They saved me from the lies that I was taught by Fr. Andy and lived according to for so many years as a teenager and young adult. The prayers of my grandmother were effective, and the faith and example of my wife and her family showed me there was a different way to be Catholic. Their witness was convincing and more compelling than Fr. Andy's abusive lies. Truly, the Truth set me free, and I was open to that Truth because I was supported by prayer and provided authentic teaching by courageous and faithful members of the Catholic laity.

I once put my faith in men who purported to be authentic teachers of the faith, but some of these men showed themselves to be untrustworthy and, in at least one case, selfish and criminally abusive. Does this mean that the Catholic Church and its teachings in the areas of faith and morals are untrue? No. Jesus selected twelve apostles, taught them for three years, and performed mighty miracles in their presence; yet, one of the twelve betrayed Him and the other apostles. One of the twelve Apostles, who spent three years with the Lord and was hand picked by Him to be one of his ministers from the beginning, still chose to betray Him and the Church. Why should we expect that the members of the Church today would be exempt from this level of corruption? Perhaps we should expect it even more, since priests and bishops today are chosen by fallible men. The Lord knew Judas would do all these things, and He chose Him anyway. Perhaps this was to show us that if in the future the faithful were to encounter a sinful, criminal, and corrupt priest, bishop, or Pope, our faith should not be shaken by their actions. We should seek refuge in the Lord and his Blessed Mother, as the Apostle John did at the foot of the cross. This may not be much consolation as we are going through the very real struggle that we are currently faced with, but it should be very instructive. We are not to put our faith in sinful human beings, but rather in God himself. The Church is part of God's plan. He established it, and it is His plan for salvation. He promised that the gates of Hell would not prevail against His Church. The Church can and will destroy the gates of Hell, but He never said that the Church would be spotless before the Second Coming. Jesus will return and He will sanctify His Church and She will be His spotless bride. But today is not that day. We have corruption in the Church, but let us blame those who are corrupt and not the Church nor the Lord. Jesus is perfect and yet he uses weak, sinful human beings to carry out his mission of saving souls and communicating His truth on this earth. We, as the laity, should demand justice from the leaders of the Church. We should, with due respect, demand that the ministers of the Church act with justice and teach the truth, and nothing but the truth, to the faithful.

I love the Church, and because I love the Church, I wish to protect her from harm. I believe that the Church was established by Jesus as His church on earth and is the primary means in which God communicates His truth and distributes supernatural graces to the faithful. The enemies of the Church, led by the father of lies, the Devil, Satan, Lucifer, are trying to infiltrate the Church and cause scandal, in order to compel people to abandon the Church and the sacraments and

cease to believe in God and His commands. It is a brilliant plan. Discredit the Church's moral authority, severely harm the families who are the closest to the Church through sexual abuse of their children, and destroy the Church's moral authority by convincing the leaders of the Church to try to hide the scandal. I, for one, will not lay on the battlefield wounded or abandon the fight. Instead, I choose to do the hard work of healing and return to the battle as a warrior who knows all too intimately the tactics of the evil one. Perhaps I will encourage the faithful by my witness and my willingness to continue the fight.

So, it is plausible that the corruption and sins of some priests and bishops is an attack against the Church of Jesus Christ from Satan, and if this supernatural war is truly at hand, then when these horrible things take place, our response should be a call to arms rather than sounding an "abandon ship". Our response should be similar to the apostles with Jesus at Capernaum, "Lord, to whom shall we go, for you have the words of eternal life." With St. Michael the Archangel and our Lady, we should take up the spiritual armor of faith and fight this evil with every fiber of our being. For we are fighting for the bride of Christ, the Church. In the book of Revelation, we know who wins in the end, but the battle is fierce and there will be many casualties. The Lord and His Church will triumph!

It is easy to condemn the Catholic Church. Not only are there bad, criminal priests that harm children, but there are bishops that cover up the abuse and seek to protect their image rather than protect children. And to add insult to injury, there is a dearth of convincing teaching in the area of sexual morality by the ordained members of the Church. The words that would eventually lead to my healing were delivered to me in large part by members of the laity, who taught the fullness of the faith (Christopher West, Tim Staples, Jesse Romero, Deacon Alex Jones, Bud Macfarlane Jr., Eric Genius, Doug Barry, Fr. John Corapi, Dr. Janet Smith) even while being persecuted. There are good priests in the Church, but they weren't key to my path towards healing the wounds of sexual abuse. Sexual abuse teaches us that people are just objects to be used for pleasure. The abuser, in my case, successfully convinced me that the official teachings of the Church were outdated, and he was going to teach me a better morality. Whether he believed these lies or was just saying what he needed to say to convince me to allow him to abuse me is irrelevant. For me, as a young person, I adopted his lies as truth, lived by that truth for many years, and taught it to my friends as well. Evil spread, and I was the one who spread it and encouraged my friends to live according to those lies. We all suffered because of it, and I hope and pray that my friends, girlfriends, and classmates discovered the authentic teachings of Christ as I did and that they have healed from embracing a life of sexual sin.

I am convinced that the Catholic Church is the answer to many of the worlds problems and that the clerical abuse scandal and subsequent cover-ups by the leaders of the Church are a brilliant way to prevent the Good News from being shared with the world. I, and other victims of clerical sexual abuse, have been severely wounded, but we have found healing in the Catholic Church and the teachings of Jesus Christ. The path to holiness is never easy, and yet, we are called to take up our cross, fight the good fight, run the race, keep the faith, and receive the crown of righteousness. The Truth has truly set me free, and it can set you free as well.

> *Draw your strength from the Lord ... Put on the armor of God ... to stand firm against the tactics of the devil. Our struggle is not with flesh and blood but with the world rulers of this present darkness... So stand fast with your loins girded in truth, clothed with righteousness ..., and your feet shod in readiness for the gospel of peace. In all circumstances, hold faith as a shield, to quench all the flaming arrows of the evil one. And take the helmet of salvation and the sword of the Spirit, which is the word of God.*
> *cf. Ephesians 6:10-17*

Endnotes

1 https://angelicum.it/
2 https://stjohnsem.edu/
3 https://smseminary.org/

The Two Shall Become One

Denae L. Hebert

*I used to live in Heaven on Earth. Oh, the age of
innocence, how I miss thee. Now I live in the Valley of
Tears where it takes a saint to have mercy for the wicked.*

- Denae Lynnette Hebert

Dreams Abound

When I met my husband, I saw him as the man I thought he
was—the man he should have been—and the man he would become.
Growing up, I had seen my parents' loving marriage and hoped that
someday I, too, would have my prince. I remember my parents saying
that they prayed for their children's future spouses, and I also would
think of, and pray for, my future spouse. I prayed on a regular basis
that God would bring me a loving, Catholic husband like the man I
saw in my father. I fondly remember blowing out the candles on my
birthday cakes while wishing for my future husband. Little did I know
how effective those prayers would prove to be.

My Background

> *"Shout joyfully to the Lord, all you lands;
> worship the Lord with cries of gladness; come
> before him with joyful songs." Psalm 100:1-2*

I was born in August of 1969 to devout Catholic parents in
the suburbs of Houston, Texas. I came from a long line of strong,
faithful Czech Catholic families. We were close to our relatives, and
I loved our frequent family get togethers. My faith journey began as
I witnessed the love that was modeled in the homes of our extended
family and through my parents' faith journey. When I was seven
years old, my parents went on a Marriage Encounter (ME) weekend,

and from that point on, our lives as "Sunday Catholics" completely changed. They started helping to give ME weekends for other couples, getting involved in Church ministries, and going to as many Church activities as possible. So, from as far back as I can remember, we were always actively involved in our faith. I learned to love the excitement of a busy and active life rooted in our Catholic community. My parents' friends became our family friends, and I developed close bonds with like-minded Catholics. I grew up loving to read the Bible, learning about the lives of the Saints, and even attending adult Bible study classes as a high school student. I started a high school prayer group and actively participated in giving retreats. Our family became involved in the Charismatic Renewal, and I loved the Praise and Worship First Friday Masses.

Getting to Know You

It was in January of my Senior year of high school that I met Allen at a lock-in for the youth group at my Church. He was hired by mutual friends to be the DJ for the evening. Not only did we have a natural attraction to each other, but there was also an almost instant connection. I loved his confidence and pursuit of me. He called me daily following the lock-in. We were so excited about

getting to know each other that we didn't want to wait for the weekend to go on our first date. So, I invited him over for dinner with my family and an evening at Church listening to a Catholic speaker, and he was not reluctant to have this be our first date. We made time to see each other every weekend and often during the week as well. He would travel across town to see me, and we always had so much fun together. We dated exclusively for a few months, and even though I invited and brought Allen to some Catholic events, I remember thinking, "I do not want to scare him away with my overly Catholic lifestyle." This caused my faith to take a quieter presence in my life as I tried not to share too much about all the faith experiences I had encountered.

Love is Blind

Allen grew up in an intact Catholic family and attended Catholic schools. His parents were very family-oriented, and I saw a boy very loved by his family. In my view, we had similar backgrounds and shared the same love for faith and family Although his family was not as involved in the Church as mine, they still seemed devoted to the faith. He had a godly grandmother, whom I adored. She seemed to be very pleased that we were dating, and she told me that she had prayed for him to find a good Catholic girl, like myself. He had, what seemed to me, to be the perfect background for being a fantastic Catholic. After our high school graduation, we each went our separate ways but both found ourselves in Austin, Texas for college.

Growing up, I remember longing to be able to be educated in a Catholic School and desiring to go to daily Mass. So, during my Junior year of high school and early into my Senior year, I naturally chose to attend a Catholic college, St. Edward's University in Austin, TX.

During registration, I selected my classes so that I would be able to attend daily Mass at least twice a week. My schedule began filling up with work and studying; I also was actively dating other young men. I became less involved in community life at Church. I still served as a eucharistic minister, but I no longer went on retreats or participated in prayer groups.

During our freshman year of college, Allen started to pursue me again, but he was still seeing an old girlfriend, who did not live in the same city as us. It was very difficult to rekindle a relationship that had once been exclusive knowing that we were both dating other people as well. I was still very attached to him and longed to reunite as boyfriend and girlfriend. This one girl from his past seemed to be his hesitancy. I did finally tell him that I could not see him anymore if he was still unsure of who he wanted to marry. I told him that I thought he was really in love with me but didn't even realize it. I moved on and made a new commitment with a young man I had been seeing. However, two months into that relationship, Allen came knocking at my door. He was done dating other people and wanted to know if we could try again. At this point, we were making the decision that if we were to get back together it would lead toward marriage.

With this change in status in our relationship, there was an increase in pressure that challenged my resolve to remain chaste. Allen shared with me early on that he had not lived life as chastely as I had, but I simply thought his history was no different than many of the friends

I had known who had failed in this area. I was very firm in preserving my chastity and tried to make it clear with him that sex was meant to be saved for marriage. Strangely, he just didn't seem to have the same view, and even though he attended Catholic schools and had a strong relationship with a priest from his past, he disagreed with this moral teaching. We continued to discuss this issue for the remainder of our dating relationship as we watched so many, friends and relatives alike, who clearly agreed with his point of view.

We filled our days with school, work, and spending time together. We each lived with roommates off campus, so we would often make plans to eat dinner together and discuss what we wanted to do over the weekend. We helped edit one another's papers and supported each other in our college studies. Because Allen had gone to small Catholic schools his whole life, attending the University of Texas was a bit of a culture shock. As we grew in our relationship, he started to explore the idea of transferring to St. Edward's, which he did during our Sophomore year. We could often be seen walking together on campus, and we attended the campus student Mass together on Sunday evenings. He even joined me in being a Eucharistic minister. We enjoyed exploring Austin, and he was very good at planning fun dates for us. During our sophomore and junior year, we would talk about when we could get married. He participated in a co-op program in which he would work a semester as a full time employee and then return to school the next semester. It was this full time work experience that afforded us the opportunity to get married before graduation. It was difficult to find friends that were in exclusive relationships, so most of our time was spent with each other. The other students in the co-op became our group of friends—even though most of them were single. There were, however, a few couples that were dating with whom we became close.

Once we determined that marriage was certainly in our future, but didn't feel like we had enough college or finances to start a life together, my resolve for chastity began weakening. He was relentless. He even had the audacity to state that "Adam & Eve never had a wedding," and to make matters worse, the campus priest at St. Edward's University seemed to agree with Allen. I felt alone in my resolve. How could I continue to impose the teachings of the Catholic Church on a Catholic that was being preached to by Catholic priests that premarital sex was fine? I remember feeling numb and dumbfounded that the priest refused to discuss this issue. He simply said, "we do not need to focus on this," as if it was the least of things to discuss when preparing for marriage. I was always taught to trust the priest, so for me, this was an assent, which caused me to believe that what he was telling me must be true. Unfortunately, I lost my battle for chastity due to the failure of Catholic priests to teach the truth. I rationalized that this was my husband, even if we were not married yet. This failure to be chaste before our wedding night was easier to accept since he too had not been chaste, but what I did not know was that his chastity had been robbed from him and indirectly mine was now robbed from me.

*"But whoever causes one of these little ones who
believe in Me to stumble, it would be better for him to
have a heavy millstone hung around his neck, and to
be drowned in the depth of the sea." Matthew 18:6*

No one should be taught a sin is normal and okay. This is a lie. Sin always has consequences even when individuals are not completely culpable. I remember wrestling with guilt once I started to understand that I had been duped or lied to by our university priest. I also remember feeling such remorse for the example I set, and I wondered how many I had led astray into this worldly view of sexuality. I was always very proud of how I was such a good example and how many people viewed me as the one to help them "stay on the straight and narrow" or follow the Church's teachings in other areas. Now, I had to admit that I probably encouraged others to embrace a sexually sinful lifestyle as others had for me.

I wish I could have been supported in my belief in chastity from my priest at St. Edward's. I wish I would have found people during college who could have explained the Church's teaching to my husband in a way he could have understood. The truth is, even if I had found that priest or person, he probably would not have been able to untwist the lies that had been taught to Allen for so many years. It would take a very long time for Allen to understand, and embrace, the Church's teaching on sex and marriage. Even when we went on our Engaged Encounter and discussed the Church's teaching, Allen still didn't fully embrace what we were told. We had been challenged by the witnesses who taught the Church's teaching on sexuality and decided to abstain until marriage. This was a definite blow to me for my choice in believing the lies that had been taught to us, but I was excited to think Allen was finally understanding my point of view. However, he confided to me later in life that he was just going through the motions, since he knew we would be married soon and didn't really believe the Church's teaching at the time.

The Man Shall Be Joined to his Wife

*"For this reason a man shall leave his father
and mother and be joined to his wife, and the
two shall become one flesh" Matthew 19:5*

While dating, we embarked on the endeavor of getting to know each other better, and the desire to know everything about each other increased as the relationship grew. It was always fun to learn new and interesting things about Allen's childhood. His family had vacationed at a ski resort during Christmas for years, and they had traveled overseas and gone on many grand adventures in their boat and airplane. He had so many different experiences than I did, and we would talk about what kind of life we wanted our children to have. As Allen and I embarked on our marriage, we were each taking turns working and going to school. First, he worked, so I could finish college. Then, I worked, so he could finish college. We also started to bank my salary, after he finished college, to learn to live on one income. We both wanted our future children to have a stay at home mom. Even though both of our mothers had worked on and off during our upbringing, for the most part, we had experienced stay at home moms when we were young. We were both excited about the idea of becoming parents, but we did want to wait until we were more financially stable.

As for our faith life, I remember praying my rosary at night quietly and wishing Allen felt comfortable praying together, but at the time, I just hoped that someday we would be able to pray together. Since we were no longer college students, we found a local parish to attend and began new routines of work, home life, and Sunday Mass.

After entering the Sacrament of Marriage, we encountered a deeper intimacy, and even though we embraced and lived a Catholic marriage, the wounds of sin were present in our bedroom. It took time and work to heal those wounds. I was completely blind to my husband's needs. I had no idea that traveling away from home for work could be challenging for him. I would learn years later that he had to train himself to turn off the television when traveling to help keep his mind chaste. The truth is chastity isn't just for the unmarried; it is for the married as well. If one doesn't learn to live chastely before marriage, it is presumably even more difficult to live chastely within marriage.

Our First Trial

"When you come to serve the Lord,
prepare yourself for trials." Sirach 2:1b

Shortly after our one year anniversary, Allen and I experienced our first real challenge. It would be a true testing of faith and sharpening of our commitment, not only to one another but to God. Allen had just started his career in the technology industry, when I suffered a complete mental breakdown. I had been an insomniac for days, and I was starting to speak irrationally. For me, the high I was experiencing during this time was very similar to the highs I had when I was involved in the charismatic renewal. I did not think I sounded irrational; it all made sense in my mind. I had difficulty accepting what my friends and relatives were telling me, but I knew I should trust them. It was with great sadness and fear that I signed the paper to check myself into the mental ward at St. David's. I was to be hospitalized for over a week and on medications for many months before I would become stable. For me, this moment was marked with great fear. I truly thought I might be locked away forever, and I was afraid I would never be comfortable praying again. I remember being in the hospital, clutching my rosary, as the nurse removed it saying, "You might use it to harm yourself or someone else." I was only allowed to check it in and out for certain periods of time. I was diagnosed with Bipolar or Manic Depression, and the only medication that would work for me was unsafe for children in utero. I was devastated. I so much wanted to start a family, and I was now being told that might not be possible. I was determined to get well and off the medication. My doctor worked with us, and praise be to God, my husband knew just what to do during this difficult situation.

Invoking the Treasures of the Church

"Is anyone among you sick? He should
summon the presbyters of the Church, and they
should pray over him and anoint him with oil
in the name of the Lord" James 5: 13b-14

Allen had arranged for the Anointing of the Sick upon my admittance into the hospital. I was not only showered with love and prayers from my community of friends and family but also our Church family here in Austin and the Church family in which I had grown up. God was gracious, and I was not only able to get well, but I was also able to stay well without medication, which is often not the case with Bipolar. Therefore, we opened our marriage to the possibility of children and were blessed with an easy pregnancy for six months. Then, God began to reveal why I had my first manic episode. It had simply been a preparation for something much harder.

We lived in the rent house Allen had in college during this time, and after only one year, we were able to buy our first home and put down roots. Allen was an excellent provider and a hard worker. He was paving the way to provide us with the life we dreamed of—where we could raise a family. When we moved into our first home, people thought we were overbuying because it was such a big house. However, we were pregnant with our first child, and we hoped more would come.

Blessings in the Midst of Trials

*"Consider it all joy, my brothers, when you
encounter various trials, for you know that the testing
of faith produces perseverance." James 1:2-3*

Only six months into the pregnancy, I started experiencing pre-term labor. I was hospitalized, and the doctor tried to stop labor. After four days, I was still progressing, and because the baby was breech, I had to deliver her by c-section. I was young and completely unprepared to deliver in such a cold environment as a surgical table. Rachel Marie was born 3 months early and weighed 1 lb. 14.5 oz. She had to stay in the hospital for three long months. Leaving the hospital everyday without our baby was one of the hardest things we had ever done. It wasn't long before the doctors said I had to go back on medication to stabilize my mental health. It was so disappointing to be unable to nurse my first born child, but God was very good. Our daughter would live, and I didn't need to be hospitalized for my mental health. Due to my first episode, we recognized my illness quickly, and I was able to get on medication. Needless to say, the first years of our marriage were spent fervently praying for our needs, as well as thanking God for the blessings He had given us not only to enjoy, but also for all the ways we had grown in our faith. Well, I soon found out that the type of c-section that was required to deliver Rachel would prevent me from ever delivering a baby naturally. Ever since I was a child, I had dreamed of having a large family. This made me feel that would be impossible, but we resolved to take one pregnancy at a time. Upon learning we would be expecting our second child, Ellen, we took all the necessary precautions. We watched for pre-term labor, as well as any signs of mental illness, but everything was fine and my mental health remained stable.

Living a Miraculous Life

*"Jesus looked at them and said, "For human
beings it is impossible, but not for God. All
things are possible for God." Mark 10:27*

Although delivered via c-sections, I was able to have my next four children with little to no incident: Victoria, Robert, Peter and Therese. I was thrilled to not only be able to have so many children, but truly felt God had granted me two physical miracles. I was able to have multiple c-sections, and my mental illness appeared to be completely gone. Bipolar is almost always a lifetime illness, and I have yet to have any more needs for medication. After the birth of our daughter, Therese, my doctor informed me that my uterus was thinning and I might need to think about not having any more children. However, he thought one more would be okay. So, we put our faith in God and ventured on. Henry came and the doctor said, "The uterus looks as good as it did after child number four." So, we proceeded to be open and along came James. When James was born, we were informed that my bladder had an adhesion, but the doctor was able to avoid it and could probably do the same again, if we chose to have another child. However, Joseph would be our last child, because I developed a dangerous condition called placenta accreta. I ended up being hospitalized for weeks before and after his early delivery; my full recovery took many months at home.

My faith during all these years was steady and growing. I tried various ministries at the parish, but I loved my involvement with Bible study the most. As God called us into homeschooling, I stopped going to Bible study, but I started to feel a strong pull from God to go deeper in my prayer life. I was already a daily communicant, but He wanted more. I longed to go to the chapel to pray. However, my time was so limited, and I couldn't see how it would be possible. Yet, I knew that was what He was asking. I prayed and prayed for the discipline to say yes to God. He finally answered me, but I had no idea how painful it would ultimately be to love God that much. I wanted to love Him, but I had to embrace suffering I did not want.

Learning About the Abuse

I prayed, "Please God" echoing Christ's words, as recorded in the Gospel of Matthew:

"My Father, if it is possible, let this cup pass from me; yet not as I will, but as you will." Matthew 26:39

In February 1999, eight years into my wonderful marriage, three beautiful children, and exactly six months before we would say a sudden goodbye to Allen's mother, Stephanie, Allen and I decided to attend a Marriage Encounter. I was excited to have Allen experience something I knew so much about. Prior to this retreat, we had attended a Life in the Spirit Seminar, but it was much too soon after my struggle with mental illness and did not bear any fruit that I saw. But this time, we were in a wonderful place in our marriage. Allen was wholeheartedly embracing the fullness of the faith, and we were praying together and always sharing wonderful intimacies of our souls. It was in this environment that a grave evil was about to touch my family. I was aware of the many evils of our world, but I was so blessed to be protected from them. They had never touched me in a personal way. I had little to no personal exposure to such heinous acts of man. It was on our Marriage Encounter weekend that Allen told me of the atrocities of his youth. The priest from his past that he had a strong relationship with had sexually abused him for an ongoing period of time. I was devastated. How could this be? I had not recognized any signs of this terrible abuse. I struggled for such a long time to understand this pain. He seemed to feel nothing from it. But I knew it must be there somewhere, and I worked hard to get him to share about it with me. Having been married for eight years already, I thought I knew all about Allen's past that there was to know. I needed to know that he was being fully open with me. When the secret was shared, I wondered what else I didn't know.

I believe marriage is built on trust. At the time, it seemed to me that this trust was broken. This new information made me wonder if he had ever trusted me at all. Had he even intended to be intimate with me for all of those years, and what type of marriage did we actually have? It shook the very foundation of security that our marriage was built upon. For our marriage to survive this grave offense, trust had to be regained, and I began to seek truth. At all cost, truth must be obtained. I desired honesty with nothing held back. To hold back is to say, "I do not trust you." In my mind, if you loved someone, you trusted them with everything. I wondered, "Does he love me enough to trust me with his secrets?" He still had great difficulty telling me everything. I really just didn't understand the pain and healing process that an abuse victim needs to go through before they can share. To share the whole truth with me would cause much more pain: pain for both Allen and me. Allen clearly did not want to inflict that on either of us, but there was already pain due to the many years of ignorance and living in the dark. I felt lied to; I felt betrayed; and there was a great disunity between us now. This disunity must be resolved for our marriage to survive. Surely we could endure the pain better, if we were open to one another about it. I believed that once he shared the abuse details with me, it would begin to lighten the pain we were both feeling, but Allen was not ready for a task like this yet. He wanted me to know that it happened and discuss it no more. He just couldn't go there, at least not yet.

A few years later, as the clerical abuse scandals in Boston became headlines in 2002, I was in excruciating pain. Then, the Church began to require all volunteers to attend the Ethics and Integrity in Ministry (EIM) training. To be told that if I wanted to still help out at Church, I must attend this training caused a new, deep, and profound pain. I was so angry with the Church for requiring my husband and I to attend such a program. I also did not believe this would have helped my husband be saved from such things. I believe if he had been catechized in the beauty of purity, he would have known what this evil was and run from it straight to his parents, who could protect him. I believe in teaching what is good, wholesome, and right or what I call the "Maria Goretti approach," and that if this approach is used, than anything contrary to truth will stick out. St. Maria Goretti did not need to be taught what grooming looked like; she refused any such thing. This concept takes me back to my thoughts when Allen first told me about his abuse. "Would I have believed the priest? Would I have been formed into this aberration of how sex is for one's gratification only?" I remember thinking, "If you are taught something different from what your parents would teach, why wouldn't you talk to them about it?" I remember having many long discussions with my parents, when confronted with strange behaviors. This included a childhood experience that caused me to immediately run home to mom and dad when a neighbor exposed himself to me. In my home, I felt completely safe and loved. I trusted my parents completely to tell me the truth. I wondered, "Did Allen not feel this way about his parents? Does a lack of feeling safe or a lack of feeling this mutual trust cause a person to end up in this situation?" I wondered why the Church didn't spend more time focusing on her beautiful teachings of chastity and Christian marriage instead of one type of sexual sin.

Confronting the Abuse

"Lord, my God, I call out by day; at night I cry
aloud in your presence. Let my prayer come before you;
incline your ear to my cry. For my soul is filled with
troubles; my life draws near to Sheol." Psalm 88:2-4

In October of 2005, I joined Regnum Christi (RC), a lay movement of the Church. It was like turning on a switch. I no longer had difficulty spending time in prayer; it was now easier for me to say yes to God. I needed the accountability it gave me, but little did I know how much the devil would attack my soul. I was almost immediately brought into a dark night. I was fighting temptations of depression and knowledge of a past pain came recurring in my soul. It was as if I was reliving some horrible experience, and I couldn't get it to go away. I was in such deep pain, and it was something private that I did not want to share. I cried out to God to help me in my anguish and felt like Mary at the cross.

It was during this trial that I know God was forging a deeper union with me. I do not know how to describe the experiences I had other than to say that it was not of this world. It was something on the order of supernatural. I truly believe the powers of Satan were influencing my soul. Again, I cried out to God, and he answered me. By some miraculous grace, our Blessed Mother, Mary, sent me a gift through a friend of my husband. I resolved to wear it on my upcoming RC retreat. God loosed the bonds of pain, so that I could approach Him in Adoration. Then, He truly purged the pain and healed my soul. During this time I had gone to Adoration, but I couldn't get close to the Lord. I would sit in the back and fight His pull to draw me in. It was so beautiful that, when on this retreat, I was able to go as close as possible to the monstrance, cry, and allow God to heal my soul.

My depression lifted for a time, but God was not done. The pain I was struggling with had been caused by my husband's involvement with a men's retreat called Christ Renews His Parish (CRHP), and I was angry that this organization had given my husband an avenue to talk of the abuse that we vowed to never share. I was familiar with sharing because of my family's involvement with the Marriage Encounter movement and knew it could be good. But, why did he need to share this? He didn't know. God just told him to share.

When I first learned of the abuse that had been in my husband's life, I wrote him a letter that stated my fear that he would be called to share this one day. However, he assured me that he was fine. He said it wasn't necessary, and we would keep it a secret from everyone. I was totally unprepared for how much this secret would eat at my heart. I had always been an open and honest person. I had felt that, when you have faith, there should be nothing to fear and no need to hide. But, this was truly something I was not prepared to ever tell anyone. My worst fear had come to pass, and I was completely devastated by it. A few months later, on my own CRHP weekend, I was still wrestling with God. What did He want me to do with this pain? What would He ask of me? My fear now changed to: Who else must we tell? How can you ask this of me?

Losing Trust

A few years after I joined RC, Fr. Marcial Maciel, the founder of Regnum Christi, was discovered to be an abuser as well. I had been an active member of Regnum Christi, and this was just another instance that the abuse of my husband's youth came back to haunt me. It seemed that there was no where I could go that these types of scandals did not follow me. I wanted to return to the innocence of my youth, when I trusted the Church and believed she was all good and Holy. These continued trials marked my soul with great sorrow. It was at this time that I removed myself from Regnum Christi, and I felt like I had been stripped of all my close relationships with other women, as well as my fervent prayer life. I remember feeling like a dark cloud had entered my life.

Over the next several years, there would be many joys and sorrows in my life, but the abuse of my husband's youth was something I wanted to bury and never talk about or think about again. However, he needed more healing, and I still didn't really understand what he needed or how much the abuse had affected him. He still had never completely been able to share many details with me, and I felt very left out of what he was going through.

When Allen chose to seek counseling through the diocese, I really wanted to be a part of his process, but no one invited me. We even requested counseling for me from the diocese but were refused. So while my husband was going through healing from his abuse, I was trying to bury the fact that this had even happened and trying to live my life as if it didn't affect us. We continued our lives by returning to the former existence of guarding this secret. However, every time I had to renew my EIM (safe environment) certification, it would open up this wound, and it really made me angry with the Church. I also learned not to trust Her, even though I still had a close relationship with Christ.

Abuse Harms More than Just the Abused

"If there is any encouragement in Christ, any
solace in love, any participation in the Spirit, any
compassion and mercy, complete my joy by being
of the same mind, with the same love, united in
heart, thinking one thing." Philippians 2:1-2

I remember going to my first Ethics and Integrity (EIM) training when the Diocese of Austin implemented the program. (Anyone serving in ministry in the Diocese of Austin must attend this training and renew their training on a regular basis. It includes a video interview of former victims describing the process of being groomed for sexual abuse, some details of the abuse, and the resulting trauma. The training then covers what grooming looks like so that ministry workers can watch for and report suspicious situations to the police and Church authorities.) I was nervous, apprehensive, and hopeful that something good might take place here. However, my soul was completely unprepared for the abuse I would experience this day.

I knew the beauty of the teaching of the Church on human sexuality and the sacredness of marriage, and this is what I expected to hear. Rather than teaching the goodness of sexuality and its rightful place, we were taught about one type of aberration of this truth. My thought was that any person in the room could be living in sexual sin, by watching pornography, cheating on their spouse, engaging in masturbation, etc., but not be convicted of doing anything wrong after watching the EIM training. They could think, "Well, I'm good, because I certainly would never abuse a child." I wondered why the Church would not take this opportunity to teach what our sexuality is for and why God made us this way.

Upon viewing the film and taking the courses for protecting youth, I felt completely violated. All of a sudden, I was entering into a truth that had happened to my husband that I had buried. I wanted to deny its very existence. I didn't want to see how his past affected him or why it should impact anything in my daily life, but the Church was forcing me to confront it.

To see abusers up close and personal talk about how they groomed their victims was like listening to someone tell me what they did to my husband. It pained me so and created huge questions in my mind. "Is this how it happened? What did your abuser say? What did he do? How did you feel?" It took everything in my power to compose myself in hopes that no one would discover my discomfort and suspect anything. As I wondered, "What will this be like when my husband sits here? He should not have to do this. Who are they to require this of him? It is barbaric to think of, forcing a victim to relive their horror."

I have lived my life knowing that it was a priest who stole my right to the innocence of the marriage bed. My marriage bed was defiled. I deserved to be the first one to explore sexuality with my spouse, yet this had been done by a priest. This damage that had been done created a lifelong journey of recovery, not only for my husband, but also for me and other members of our family.

I really wanted answers from Allen to my questions, so it became a topic of discussion between us. He was still not ready to talk about the details of his abuse. He knew it would hurt me and did not want to inflict that hurt, but, the truth was, it already had and only full disclosure could lead to full healing. When the two become one flesh, they begin the journey to know the innermost secrets of each other's souls. God intends marriage to provide a helpmate in our journey to Heaven. We are to bear one another's burdens. It is what makes the journey light. We must surrender our secrets to one another in order to be one. The vulnerability of exposing one's thoughts shows a complete trust in the other. If you love your spouse and believe your spouse loves you, then you hold nothing back. It is the path to oneness. The oneness the Scripture talks about, the oneness the Church teaches, which is the type of marriage I expected to have.

Seeking Healing

During the time that Allen was going through healing, he was growing in his faith life, and I, on the other hand, felt like my faith life had been deflated. I started to pull away from the Church, no longer going to daily Mass or weekly Adoration. It seemed that when I was there, I had to deal with my emotions of anger and hurt that I didn't want to experience. It became a struggle for me to pray, and I often only continued out of a sense of duty rather than desire. I also felt frustrated that my husband was so at peace with his abuse. I could not understand how he could forgive so easily, while I was still so upset by it. Nothing seemed right; all was unsettled. My world seemed to be turning upside down. While I had always been the one closer to the faith, now he seemed to have that role, and it made me very uncomfortable. Clerical sexual abuse damaged my soul, and it has been a challenging battle to regain the purity of heart and trust that I once felt as a Catholic. I suffered the same struggles that many abuse victims go through. My prayer life became a constant struggle, and I could not bring myself to open my heart to God. I felt that if I would allow myself to get close, He would only send me more struggles, and I didn't believe I was strong enough to handle anymore.

However, God continued to bless our lives. We would encounter many good and holy priests in our active Catholic faith life, but this secret would still always be ever present. Many times, if we had a difference of opinion with someone about the implementation of the faith in our parishes, I would often think, "If they only knew." My husband would never let our children go to an overnight retreat. Instead, we were always driving them there and picking them up, so that they could attend but never be left to spend the night. No one understood our rationale, and frankly thought we were crazy, overprotective parents. However, we were very strong in our resolve to raise children in the beauty of the Church's teaching without compromising their safety in any way. We took our job seriously in raising the kids in the faith, and we were determined to provide them with a strong family life where they could always turn if faced with anything contrary to the Church's teaching.

Many years would pass before God would ask us to tell our story again, but the knowledge that our closest friends and families did not know this about us still haunted me. Every time someone would share a difficulty or struggle with us, I would feel that we were almost being hypocritical by giving them the feeling that we were very close, when, in fact, I refused to share this struggle that we had. As my husband seemed to become at peace with his past, we even embarked on the founding of a family ministry, Your Holy Family.

The Abuse Haunts Me

When the latest scandal of 2018 came out, my husband was in a very different place than ever before. For the past three years, Allen had been telling me that he had this great desire to seek out a friend who also had a close relationship with Fr. Andy, the priest who abused my husband. Even though he began taking baby steps toward this process, he had not yet completely followed through with the idea. He was able to reconnect, but had not discussed anything about Fr. Andy with him.

We waited for our Bishop's response to the current scandal, and unfortunately, we were greatly disappointed. We felt no compassion from him, and thus, we chose to go visit with him. Before the visit, my husband chose to share his story with a few priests and discovered that they, too, had a real lack of understanding of the suffering experienced by victims. My husband wanted to share with the Bishop what he believed victims needed in order to facilitate healing, as well as offer his services to help train the priests. I, on the other hand, was very angry and didn't trust that the Bishop would care at all. We both wrote letters with specific actions requested, but my husband chose to meet with the Bishop alone. I was dealing with so much anger, and Allen didn't want my anger to put the Bishop in a defensive stance. Allen really hoped to change the Bishop's heart and to encourage him to step up and be a leader during this current scandal.

My letter to the Bishop began by encouraging him to know that he had the power, influence, and ability to affect change and healing for many harmed by clergy abuse. I shared with him how learning about my husband's abuse had introduced evil into my life that I had never experienced in my faithful Catholic upbringing and life prior to that point. I tried to help our Bishop understand that since I had never kept a secret of such gravity, a secret so dark and deep, that my husband had been unable to share his secret with me until after eight years of marriage. I explained that it was appalling to me that the Church did not have the resources available to help with my healing. While they had provided counseling for Allen, as primary victim, our Church did not provide counseling for those who were victimized by the ripple effect of clergy abuse. I told the Bishop that I had no one to talk to about it but Allen, who was wholly the wrong person to be helping me process and deal with the trauma that he was forced to live with every day of his life. I suggested three concrete steps of action that he could take to help victims and their families. First, allow spouses, and other affected family members, to receive counseling through the Diocese. The second action step was to allow those personally harmed by abuse, including spouses, to have an exemption from EIM courses. Finally, I encouraged the Bishop to train the clergy to minister to those affected by abuse, as healing is truly an ongoing process and priests will continue to need more resources to effectively serve their flock.

After two months of receiving no reply to my letter, I decided to write again. During these two months, it became apparent that Allen really wanted to share his story publicly in the hopes of helping other victims, and we began the painful process of telling our family for the very first time. Even though this was a painful process, it also brought some relief that now we had others who could share our burden and there was no longer a secret between us, but I still struggled with telling our minor children. I did not want to taint their innocence and really worried how this would affect their love for Christ and His Church, but they needed to hear it from us and not find out in some other way. The children seemed to receive the information as graciously as they could, and the older ones seemed to see the impact their father's story could have on others, which encouraged us in our resolve to begin the process of writing this book. I also knew that if we were really going to do this project that I needed help, and I needed help now. I was having difficulty sleeping, fear was creeping in, and I was simply not ready to bare such an intimate topic with others. So, I began the process of finding a therapist and contacted the Bishop again. I expressed the pain I experienced due to his lack of response, and I again outlined the same three steps for action that I was proposing.

After this letter, I received a reply that somewhat helped, but still was not completely satisfying. The Bishop apologized for his delayed response, and he agreed to pay for my counseling, which had already begun. He informed me of some of his current efforts that he had applied to educate his priests, and eventually, he allowed me an alternate path to satisfy my EIM compliance.

The Road to Healing

"...mourning and weeping in this
valley of tears..." Hail Holy Queen

I had many struggles and fears at this point. I really had not wanted to go to counseling, but I knew that if I did not do this, I would not be able to handle my husband's resolve to go public with his abuse. Because of our disappointment in the Church leader's apparent lack of interest in seeking out victims and helping them find healing, it became clear that we were called to help other victims and the Church through this book.

I was really struggling with the idea that the abuse didn't seem to cause my husband the same pain as it did me. I wondered, "If I shared the pain enough, would it no longer cause me pain, and could doing so diminish the evil of the event that caused the pain to begin with?" I believed it must never be taken lightly or dismissed. I believed it is right and just that the memory of the event causes pain. So, what is it when it no longer invokes that emotion? I believed to let go of the suffering from the memory is to lose empathy for the event. I wondered, "Has the Church become dead to the atrocity? Do they believe that it is so far away in the past that they cannot recognize the evil that was perpetrated? Do they not realize that people still suffer from evil that happened to them so long ago?" I believe if we try to forget about what has happened or if we refuse to talk about this grave evil, it will happen again. We must remember. But, how do I remember, yet let go of this suffering? The remembering continues to inflict my suffering. Must I choose to separate the emotion from the event? Is that really survival? To be fully human, one feels the effects of evil; to no longer feel the effects of evil is to kill one's empathy. To lose empathy is to lose the ability to love. Empathy reveals a love that understands and chooses to walk the road with you.

I have always had a great desire to love and feel empathy for others when they suffer. I often listened to friends' problems and difficulties, and many times, I suffered pain when they shared their struggles. Maybe my emotion of empathy is heightened, but surely God's is as well. Maybe only God has this ability, but are we not all called to be like Christ and love as He loves? To allow oneself to endure this feeling, is it not accepting the cross? The ability to bear the cross with the Lord and with others, without having it consume you, is surely a supernatural grace. Where is the Church's empathy? Only a handful of times have I felt it. I have felt it from a few courageous priests and Bishops. To them, I say thank you.

The main thing I have experienced as the spouse of a clerical sexual abuse victim is this need for empathy. I need people to see that this grave evil, this abuse that was perpetrated on my spouse, affects me also. Hopefully my words have explained how this is so. I humbly ask for your continued prayers, as we strive to be able to share something so intimate. Sharing something this intimate is a direct violation to our own right to privacy, but we share our stories because God asked us to. We do so in hopes that through our sharing, others may be helped. We do so in hopes that others, who have experienced this grave evil in their lives, will experience healing.

Wrestling With Acceptance

*"See to it that no one comes short of the grace of
God; that no root of bitterness springing up causes
trouble, and by it many be defiled." Heb 12:15*

This book project has brought to mind the many ways I have
been hurt by the people in the Church, which subsequently caused
much anger. I was angry that Fr. Andy abused my husband and hurt
that it took so long for Allen to tell me about it. I was angry that the
Church never took Fr. Andy out of ministry in the 1980's, when he
was first reported, nor in 1998, when Allen reported it. I was hurt by
the Church's refusal to provide me counseling in 2003. I was hurt by
the priest that married us, Roger Temme, when he failed to uphold the
Church's teaching on sexuality, and I was angry when he was also
identified as an abuser in the Archdiocese of New Orleans. I was hurt
that the Regnum Christi movement that I was involved in was founded
by an abuser. I was hurt when the Church insisted on my attendance
at EIM classes and when we found out that the Church never laicized
Allen's abuser. It feels like the list goes on and on. This gives me
cause to not trust the Church, but I want to trust the Church. I want to
love the Church, so with this project, we hope to inspire change that
will protect others from suffering similar grave insults.

As I come to grips with the production of this book and work on
my own healing, I am learning to integrate the knowledge of Allen's
abuse into my life. In the past, it was definitely something I wanted to
forget about and pretend it didn't matter. But, it does matter. It shapes
everything we say and do. We have learned how to better protect our
own children from experiencing this cycle of abuse in their own lives.
We have learned how to love each other in a deep and heroic way! I
love my husband, no matter what, even when his brokenness prevents
him from loving me rightly, just as my own brokenness sometimes
does the same. Many times, I certainly have had no idea what was
causing our disunity, but now, I believe that when we are torn apart
from one another, this great wound is the root cause. My trust remains

in the Lord as I have seen Him rebuild our unity many times, and I stand with my husband as we heal together.

My anger with the Church during this project has been very intense and volatile. I am often unable to control my emotions and find myself taking it out on family members. Because of my spiritual background, I took this struggle to prayer, and I began to contemplate God's mercy and God's justice. As a parent, I have seen the necessity to be just and discipline my children, in order to teach them right from wrong. I have also seen the times that I have been able to understand their failures and approach them with mercy, and I have been able to teach them in that way as well. It is hard to understand the mind of God and the lack of discipline applied to abusive priests which we have seen during this scandal. As I was spending much time in prayer over this issue without any results or resolution in my heart, I decided to go to confession and pour out this struggle to my confessor. To my utter surprise, grace touched my soul in such a profound way that day, and my anger toward the Church diffused. I am still mad about the atrocities of clerical sexual abuse, but it no longer evokes such a strong reaction of anger. I cannot explain it, but somehow, I was able to begin to feel compassion for the men, leaders that must be so broken to not be able to respond with love and compassion.

I have experienced many strong and difficult emotions throughout this healing process. At first, I wanted to deny the abuse, then I was extremely angry, definitely scared, but now, mostly sad. Sad that it happened, sad that it affects us so much, and sad that the evil continues. I want to feel the hope that I know God can provide, so I trust in his mercy as I work to maintain my relationship with Christ and His Church. I am thankful that through all of this, we have maintained a healthy marriage and family, and I know that this is only because God's grace has been healing these wounds.

However, this is not to diminish the great strain our marriage has suffered during this project. I still often feel angry towards my husband for wanting to do this project and pushing a very speedy time line for which I am clearly not ready. Yet, at the same time, I desire to rush and be done with it. This really pushes my emotions to the limit. I even question my ability to stay sane during all of this.

At times, the emotions are so strong, I have to check out from the project. By removing myself from any and all information related to it, I am able to recenter and balance myself. My Bipolar still causes stressful times in my life by instigating racing thoughts. I have to work very hard, with the help of my husband, to make wise choices to stay sane. I think I am often jealous of those who have a physical ailment rather than my own emotional ailment. It seems that they receive so much support from others, and there is no stigma to letting people know about their struggles. While I, on the other hand, feel the need to hide my difficulties so that others don't see a weakness in me.

It challenges me to admit that I need to ask others for support. This is very humbling and such a challenge for me, since I have always viewed myself as a very strong, trusting, and faithful Christian. It is very hard for me to admit that I need any support at all. I want to think that my reliance on faith and God should be enough, but the truth is I need more. So, I continue to spend time in therapy, and I thank God for the angels in my life that He sends to let me know they are praying for me. I am also thankful for my husband during this time, who has been my rescuer many times.

My faith life is still a constant struggle. I wonder how I can reconcile the two sides of the coin that Christ calls me to: the cross and the hope of the resurrection. I have always trusted God and known beyond the shadow of a doubt that He has my best interests at heart. He will see me through any difficulty, but this cross feels so unbearable. I often fight the temptation that if I get closer to Christ, he will only send me more suffering. Even when I choose to accept this particular suffering, my emotions take over, and I feel my Bipolar illness creeping in. I often wonder, "What would be better: to live in insanity and not know the truth of this reality or to live in truth and know the evil that man can inflict, does inflict, has inflicted, and that my own Church has participated in and covered up?" Yet, I do know it is men of the Church, not the Church. But how, how can it be so many, for so long? I truly relate to the cries of the Israelites in Egypt. When will the survivors of clerical sexual abuse be released from the bondage of this pain? Pain is a funny thing. When it is physical, it can often be remedied with modern medicine, but when it is emotional or of the heart, only God's miraculous grace can actually provide healing medicine. Just as it often is with a physical ailment, it can take a long time to heal. Sometimes, I even wonder if my emotional pain will not be totally healed until I reach heaven. I pray that is not so. I do desire complete healing here, and I know God can do it. I have experienced many such healings, but if it is suffering God asks of me, I pray that I may have the strength to not resent it.

Becoming One Flesh

*"See, I have refined you like silver, tested you
in the furnace of affliction." Isaiah 48: 10*

This suffering has drawn Allen and I closer to one another and profoundly closer to Our Lord. We believe that this experience was not only for us, but as suffering always is, it is for the greater glory of God. I knew God was with me, and it is because of this struggle, I can now say, "Thank you God for the gift of my husband's past that has brought us to such a deeper love." For I had, in fact, been beckoning God, since the beginning of our marriage, to give us that deep union of soul so that we would be able to truly worship Him together. I had no idea what that prayer would ultimately cost, but God has indeed answered my prayer.

No, it has not been easy. However, it has been such a joy to experience the love that God has for me, to experience the love that He intended for us to have for Him, and so, in turn, be able to also give Him that love. I love my God infinitely more today than I did yesterday. My prayers, devotions, and life are my way of saying thank you to my God, who has graciously and abundantly blessed me. All of my experiences have been a gift to me, even the difficult ones. It is these tough times that have caused me to dive ever deeper into prayer and stay close to our Lord. Through these embraces with Christ, I have been provided with the grace and strength I need to continue on the journey that God has planned for me.

Grace is Enough

"When the LORD began to speak with Hosea, the LORD said to Hosea: Go, get for yourself a woman of prostitution and children of prostitution, for the land prostitutes itself, turning away from the LORD." Hosea 1:2

Even though my heart has been hurt, broken, and crushed by the many abuses of my Church that I love, even though my mind has been on the brink of insanity many times in my struggle to reconcile the truths of God in his infinite goodness and the grave evils that befall the world we live in, and even though my soul screams out for justice, I choose everyday to accept, to love, and to pray for the mercy of God to penetrate my mind, heart, and soul. Victims choose to be called survivors, but I choose to be called restored. I have experienced God's love, and I have been restored by His grace. To God be all the glory, and I pray that you too may be touched with this indescribable grace: the grace that is beyond all understanding. It is inconceivable that anyone could thrive after something like this, yet my husband and I do. The only way this is possible is through some miracle that God has chosen to bestow on us.

Now, we continue to trust and pray for the miracle that will heal our Church, and we know it will happen. But it must begin with us. We must remove the anger and hatred from our hearts that this evil has caused and rechannel that emotion into action. We must be people of prayer and compassion, but it is not enough to just pray. God requires action; we must seek out the hurting and the lost. Then, and only then, will our Church be able to heal. We may not know the hour or day, but we know through faith that "the gates of hell" will not prevail. I pray that my action of sharing my suffering is an attempt at seeking out the lost, and I hope that He will be able to use this work to heal.

"You must return to your God. Maintain loyalty and justice and always hope in your God." Hosea 12:7

ABUSE *of* TRUST

But for the Grace and Mercy of God

Jim Field
co-written by Valarie Brooks

When I was three years old, my father moved us from Lafayette, Indiana to Farmington, New Mexico, a boomtown on the edge of the Navajo Reservation in the four corners area. My early childhood is full of many good memories. I remember a lot of love and affection and my mom bringing my youngest sister, Mary, home from the hospital. I wasn't sure exactly where she came from, but I loved her tiny fingers and toes! I also had an older and younger sister, but the new baby fascinated me.

We lived on Park Place, a cul-de-sac, and my best friend lived across the circle from us. Much later in life, I found out his family was Catholic, and he was an altar boy for Father Conran, who was a priest at Sacred Heart parish. Years later, my family would begin going to Sunday Mass there.

My dad bought one of the first televisions in the neighborhood. Our neighbors would come over with blankets and lawn chairs to watch the propped up TV inside the house. We could watch it through the front window and the side windows were cranked open for sound, while we were guzzling homemade root beer and munching popcorn.

I also remember watching the Navajos herding their sheep over the dusty hills a small distance from our backyard. I wanted to go over and see the sheep, but I knew I'd get in trouble for that!

Another pleasant memory is about the Navajo girls, who my parents had sort of rescued from the reservation. (Life for those living on the reservation was difficult, especially during winter.)

The first girl that lived with us was Minnie Rose, when we lived on Park Place. She was very nice, and she lived with us to help Mom with us kids and housework. The second one was Ella Mae, when we lived on North Wall Street. She often took me downtown. She tried to teach me the Navajo language and would tell her girl friends I was her little brother. During our downtown trips, I would see older Navajo women in their heavy, full length velvet skirts, with a lot of turquoise jewelry, and I would see funny looking horse-drawn wagons going down the street with automobile tires for wheels.

Not everything was perfect, though. New Mexico has frequent, unexpected dust storms. I remember leaning into the stinging wind, trying to walk home from school, and sometimes getting from one curb to the next with everything else hidden in the blowing dust. Tumbleweeds would pile up everywhere. Mom would stuff rags and rugs into all the cracks inside the house, trying to keep the dust out, but somehow it always managed to get in. We kids were also taught early on about being very careful about rattlesnakes and scorpions!

Later, while we were living in a bigger house on North Wall Street, I remember having rheumatic fever and a couple of concussions. I also stepped on a rusty nail more than once, while building forts from salvaged wood. My mom suffered frequent illnesses, and she would often have to spend time in the hospital. That was really difficult for us as kids, and we really missed her a lot during those times. Life was starting to become more difficult. My oldest sister did her best to take care of the three of us younger kids, because Dad seemed to work almost all the time or went to see Mom in the hospital.

When Mom was home, often Dad would take us on Sunday afternoon rides to the Bluffs, and we would trek over and around huge rocks and boulders, always being wary of snakes. Often, we'd see the unusual looking Navajo homes, called Hogans, with smoke coming out of a hole in the center of the roofs.

After a few years, when I was about nine years old, my mom decided she wanted our family to become Catholic. At this point, I have fond memories of the Franciscan Friars coming to our home, usually at night. They were funny looking to me, in their brown robes, but I liked them. They talked with Mom and Dad about God and stuff. There was often a lot of joy and laughter. I was intrigued with these guys. They taught us about big and little sins, but I had no real concept of who God or Jesus really were, other than Jesus was the Son of God. I had some vague idea that God was somewhere up in the sky, but I felt amazed by what little I did understand from the Franciscans. This was the sum total of my religious education as a little boy.

Just outside our orchard in the back, there was a huge, old cottonwood tree that housed many birds. I can remember thinking that God was probably in that tree. The day they cut it down, according to my mother, I became very upset and cried and cried because of the birds. She tried to reassure me they would find somewhere else to live. I was such a sensitive boy. Years later, my Dad said I always had my head in the clouds.

Our family didn't pray much, but I do remember that Mom would listen to the song "The Lord's Prayer" on the radio at sundown. It was very moving to her. That was the first prayer that I really began to understand.

We began attending Sacred Heart parish, which was about five blocks from our house, and I felt a really deep love for Jesus and being in the Church. During the summer I turned ten years old, I would wake up early on weekday mornings, bathe, comb my hair, and ride my bike to Mass. At first, I don't think my parents had any idea I was doing this.

After Sunday Mass, the priests would always tell me and my parents how special I was and that I was probably going to grow up and become a priest like them. I remember I really liked being told I was special.

I loved being in the church, and I loved the man, Jesus, nailed to the cross. I would gaze up at him and wonder how something like that could happen. I couldn't imagine such cruelty! I felt like I could really relate to how Jesus felt having those nails, which pierced his body, because I knew how much it hurt to step on a nail.

There usually weren't many other people in the church on those early weekday mornings, except I do remember a Mexican woman, who always dressed in black and wore a black lace mantilla. She would pray her beads in Spanish. She tried to teach me to pray the Rosary, but she only spoke Spanish. However, my Spanish was pretty limited, even though my best friend, Patrick Martinez, was Hispanic and spoke Spanish.

These memories about Sacred Heart Church and my childhood didn't surface until many decades later.

When I was 10 years old, during the fall of 1963, we abruptly moved back to Lafayette, Indiana. My religious education began, and I was taught privately at St. Mary's Cathedral rectory by a priest, Father Craycraft, who would later conduct my oldest sister's wedding. I was still attending Mass, but it was becoming very irregular. I do vaguely remember, toward the end of one of these private classes, there was a very heated fight with Father, and I stormed out of the rectory. I was very angry with him. (Just last year the old rectory was torn down, and I was glad to see it go! I stood and watched part of the demolition and felt very strange, but I was glad it was being destroyed.)

I was baptized at St. Mary's on July 25th, during the summer of 1964, when I was twelve. The priest was Father Joseph Voss, brother of Father Ron Voss, against whom I later made an

Fr. Ronald Voss

allegation of sexual abuse. He is on the list as a credibly accused priest in the diocese of Lafayette. He apparently molested many dozens of boys. Later, I had my First Communion and was confirmed on June 2, 1968. I'm not sure who the priest was; I think the records were lost by the Church. Mom probably knew but both parents have been deceased for years.

A couple of years after being confirmed, my father disappeared. He abandoned our family. Life seemed to turn upside down! We had known that their marriage was in trouble, because they had sat down with all of us kids and discussed dad leaving. I had begged my father not to leave, but a couple of days later, mom ironed all his clothes (even his handkerchiefs), packed up his suitcases for him, and he left. We had no idea where he was for four years. Mom was a real mess afterward and even missed the divorce proceedings. She clearly had her own emotional struggles and became emotionally unavailable for me and my sisters. Several relatives told me I was now the "man of the house." Inwardly, I would cringe, because I had no idea what exactly would be my job as "man of the house." Many nights, lost in confusion, I remember for a long, long time I would cry myself to sleep. I missed my Dad so much, and I felt so unsafe.

After Dad left, we didn't have much money, so I started working at different jobs. I had a paper route, shoveled snow, mowed lawns, and worked at St. Elizabeth's Hospital in the dietary department. I remember washing humongous pots and pans and delivering food carts to patients on the different floors. Looking back, I can't believe those nuns allowed me to work so dang hard! I also started skipping classes at school: I mean a LOT of classes.

When I was about 16, I left home a few times, hitchhiking to various places across the country, but I always ended up going back home. My obsession with sex had continued to grow stronger. I always dated the prettiest girls in school. I was very popular, but I had also started living a "double life" as a "closet" homosexual. It wasn't like I was making a conscious choice about all this. My life was an absolute mess. As a young teen, I was becoming obsessed with sex and was extremely confused.

It is all unbelievable to me now: how much I worked and how little I went to school. Sex was easy to find. I discovered that if I waited around a bit in various public places, sooner or later, some older guy would show up. Many years later, as a young adult, I learned these men were pedophiles.

I realize today that I was looking for a man to show some kind of genuine interest in me. Maybe someone who would ask, "How's school going?" or "How is life at home?". Life at home was horrible with my mother and sisters. Living with four females was really difficult. I think a lot of their anger about Dad's abandonment was misdirected toward me.

Strangely, when hitchhiking around the country during spring break, or during the summer, men who would give me a ride did seem extremely concerned about me. There was no sexual stuff. I would fantasize that one of them could somehow become my new father and life would be great. Often they would give me money or buy me a meal. Sometimes, they would ask about my parents and whether they knew where I was. I told them I didn't think that my parents were concerned. That's about as far as these men were able to express their concern.

At the age of sixteen, my Dad had reconnected with my family with occasional phone calls. He was remarried, with two young kids, and living in Colorado. Conversations were always awkward, and my feelings were a mixture of some happiness with a lot of sadness.

When I was seventeen, I attempted suicide for the first time. My emotional pain was an absolute torture, which I only realized many years later. I had gotten some Librium from a pedophile man I had seen for several years, and I took a lot of them. I couldn't stop swallowing them! Then, I drove myself to a mental institution. They admitted me for three days or so. When the psychiatrist eventually interviewed me, I was not open with how I was really doing. One question I remember to this day was he asked what I wanted in life. I told him that I always wanted to get married and have at least six kids, which was the truth. (However, deep inside, I was quite aware that I was way too messed up to ever be a husband or father.) He thought this was a great plan. My real life remained a very painful secret. He recommended me to a Transactional Analysis therapy group. That, as I recall, didn't last very long, and I just continued existing the best I could while still living at home.

At the age of 18, I was still looking for God, but I was no longer attending Mass. I had started going to an Assembly of God church, and was often praying to God to change me. God make me normal! Nothing changed. Right after I turned eighteen, I got very drunk one night and began running out in front of cars hoping that one of them would hit me and kill me. Someone called the police, and they put me in jail. At my court date, I reassured the judge it would never happen again. Shortly after this, as a sort of "church ministry," I got permission from the jail to talk to drunks about the word of God. I remember once going to a man and his wife to sort of counsel them and encourage them to read the Bible and go to church. I also quit drinking.

After the arrest, because I was eighteen, my name appeared in the newspaper's "police blotter" section. Some of the people at the Assembly of God church knew what I had done, and it didn't go over very well. I quit going to services. I resumed drinking. I felt lost and was becoming very angry.

In 1970, having barely graduated High School, I left Lafayette for San Diego with a friend I barely knew. We met while partying in Lafayette. This "friend" had plenty of money, and there were a lot of fun times with him. A few months later, in San Diego, he was arrested by the FBI. It was terrifying having agents staked out inside the condo and down in the parking garage. I had no idea what he had done wrong. The FBI said I had to maintain monthly contact with them.

Later, I found out he was involved with organized crime. He was arrested because he had come back to the condo to take me to a Lear jet, and we were going to fly to Chicago. I'll never forget the painful look on his face as he stared at me while being handcuffed. I felt so guilty and felt sorry for him. I never saw him again.

Immediately after the arrest, I was on the streets of Pacific Beach with no money. For a few days, I had sex for food or a place to sleep. After a phone call to Mom, she told me to find some Catholic shelter for men in San Diego that she had been told about. I think I considered it, maybe I even found it, but decided it probably wasn't a good idea. At some of these lowest points, I would turn to God, praying and singing songs I could remember from Assembly of God. There was no where else to turn but to God.

My Dad rescued me with a plane ticket to Denver. It had been six years since I had seen him. For a few months, I lived with him, my new stepmother, and my new half-brother and half-sister. After about a month, my stepmother didn't want me there, so I moved in with another guy I had recently met.

My life had become very scary, full of lies, secrets, and betrayals. It was during this time that I started realizing I had many "blocked out" memories as a child.

When I was 19 years old, I moved to Los Angeles with the man I was living with in Denver. None of my relationships ever worked, and shortly after, we split up.

Many years later, by now 27 years old and a very heavy drinker, I ran away from a nine year relationship with a guy who got into the business of making porn movies, and I wound up in New York City. I was hanging out at all of the popular gay clubs at the beginning of the AIDS outbreak in Manhattan. There wasn't a name for the disease yet. Many gay men were getting "spots" and/or pneumonia. They were dying very fast. How I never became infected is something I'll never understand.

By 1980, I had joined an alcohol recovery program in Manhattan, and my life seemed to be getting better. I returned to L.A.

I also became very interested in "new age metaphysics." I studied, read a lot of books, and attended lectures on various aspects about this and would wonder if Jesus wasn't also an example of a lot of what I learned. I was still away from the Church.

In the mid-eighties, I moved into a gorgeous, big home in Silverlake Hills with another man I barely knew. The house had incredible views and rental units that I helped operate. My partner died two and a half years later. He left everything to me.

Eventually, I had an established business selling antiques, furniture, and lighting. I began building custom primitive furniture and doing custom finishing. The rich and famous would come to my store. I had the things they wanted, and some of these clients even became friends. I never had to worry about money or needing anything. My self worth was becoming better, and I felt enormous gratitude. Occasionally, I would miss the Catholic Church, but I told no one.

From time to time, during a call home, my mom or my older sister would often harp about my not going to Mass anymore. Years later, they both recalled that I would go into a verbal rage, using lots of foul language, and make accusations about evil, perverted priests, and then I would quit speaking to them for a while. I have no memory of these episodes.

Around 1998, my mom had to have surgery, so I went back to Lafayette. During the surgery, my sister, Jennie, and I went together to the hospital chapel to pray before the Blessed Sacrament. I was struck by the beauty of that small chapel! It literally took my breath away! I thought it was very odd that, even though I had worked at St. Elizabeth's, I had no memory of having ever been in that chapel. I thought maybe I had blocked it out but couldn't imagine why. As we were kneeling there together, I suddenly knew that we were in the presence of Jesus. (I had always intellectually understood Christ was supposed to be in the Eucharist.)

I heard a soft, non-threatening voice speak, "Now you see my face darkly, as your faith grows it shall brighten." I turned to Jennie to see if she had also heard the voice, and she said, "See! He never really left; He's been here all along!" I visited the chapel several times over the next few days, but nothing else unusual happened. I couldn't stop thinking about that experience.

Mom came out of her surgery and recovered.

I went back to Los Angeles completely changed. I was obsessed with going to Mass as often as possible, and I began reading everything I could afford to buy regarding the Catholic Church, the saints, and the Bible. I started praying a lot, got a spiritual director, and sought pastoral counselling. I began attending a Bible class at Blessed Sacrament Church on Sunset Blvd. in Hollywood.

After asking many people where I might find Eucharistic Adoration, someone finally told me about the Monastery of the Angels in Hollywood, where the cloistered Dominican nuns had twenty-four hour perpetual adoration. They have a visitor side in their chapel, and I began to visit frequently. On almost every Friday at 2:30 PM, they had a Holy Hour of Reparation to the Sacred Heart of Jesus, which I attended faithfully. As a small group, we would pray many awesome reparational prayers from a little red prayer book. Next to daily or Sunday Mass, this was the most important event every week. Those nuns also made and sold pumpkin bread, which was absolutely delicious.

They also had a second hand gift shop where I would find holy cards, books about Saints of whom I'd never heard, and rosaries. I was told by a sister at the gift shop about a four volume set of books called "City of God" by Venerable Mary of Jesus of Agreda, for the encouragement of men. These books were translated from the original Spanish writings by Fiscar Marison, published by Ave Maria Institute, copyright 1971. The imprimatur was dated February 9, 1949 by Edwin V. Byrne, D.D., Archbishop of Santa Fe, New Mexico. The Sister told me about these books possibly being in the back room. She explained they were Mystical writings, and she would need to pray about whether she should allow me to purchase them. A few weeks later, she found the last set in storage and let me purchase them. I was quite happy and thanked her. (To this day, I haven't finished all four volumes; it seems I can only take in small amounts at a time and then pause for some time before continuing on.)

Life was great, sort of, except that I was gay. For quite a while, it had become very clear I was to live a chaste life. I kept having horrible images before, during, and after Mass. Horrible sexual images! And I couldn't seem to stop seeing them. I was faithfully attending daily Mass, Thursday night Bible classes, and even ended up going to a few Opus Dei meetings and events, which for some reason I found disturbing. I couldn't figure out what was wrong with me. I figured I must be doing something wrong. I would continually pray about this and quietly call out to God for help.

I was still in recovery and had about seventeen years of sobriety. As a result of Cardinal Mahoney, Blessed Sacrament Church started a "ministry for gays and lesbians" around that time, and so, in addition to all my other meetings, I began attending this group as well. I had not found any resolution with my "weird sexual images, thoughts, etc.", so I thought maybe other gays struggled with the same thing. Whatever was happening to me was getting worse. I started to become incredibly anxious and depressed. And in spite of everything, I felt powerless to stop these mental attacks. I actually went to confession so frequently that the priest told me to stop confessing every few days and just take communion no matter what! He said, in my case, the sin was mitigated, but why that was the case wasn't clear to me. I also realized the image of the crucified Christ was a "sexual image," and I believed everyone thought this way. Of course, this was just something no one would ever openly discuss. I was starting to think maybe this might not be the reality for others, and I began to take a very discrete poll with a few close friends, asking each one if they saw anything "sexual" in the image of a crucifix. To my horror, and judging from their look of horror, I realized I had this "really messed up in my head." I felt hopeless. No matter how much I prayed, I began to feel abandoned by God.

In late October, 1997, I returned to Lafayette. My oldest sister's daughter was going into the Cloistered Poor Clares Monastery on All Saints Day. I felt so honored when she gave me one of her most treasured belongings, which was a little crucifix that she would often hold near as she prayed. This trip home was particularly difficult emotionally because seeing my niece join this religious order reminded me that I was supposed to have become a priest. Years later, I realized I was subconsciously worried about her safety. She was going to be cloistered. I was happy for her and sad at the same time. I openly cried so much that week. I started thinking about the priests in New Mexico, who had told me and my parents that I was special. I was supposed to be a priest, but something had gone terribly wrong. My life and struggles with chastity were becoming very painful.

In August 1999, after eighteen years of continuous sobriety, I got drunk. I was still living in my beautiful home in Silverlake Hills, and work was better than ever. But my sober friends had seen it coming. My sobriety support person had even warned me to "knock off all that Catholic crap, or you're going to get drunk." I knew something with my faith seemed twisted! In spite of all the religious stuff I was participating in and meetings I was attending, at times, I just couldn't get the images out of my head. I drank periodically for about ten months, but even during that time, I still managed to work, go to meetings, attend Mass, and show up for the Friday afternoon Holy Hours of Reparation.

On Easter of the following year, I received the gift of sobriety once again. I was still struggling with obscene images and having weird thoughts, especially at church, or right after church. A few times, during those last few years in Los Angeles, I believed I even had opportunities to have sex with a couple of priests, but I resisted and prayed for them instead. It all seemed so absolutely crazy to me, and I could not sort it out. I was well aware that priests were sexually active but that they were active in a very hidden way. I couldn't understand why they weren't practicing celibacy.

After going through several failed gay relationships, I always felt betrayed, abused, or abandoned by these guys. Two relationships were especially painful because both of those men died from AIDS. So many of my close friends died so young. To this day, I know it is a miracle that I didn't contract that disease!

I struggled with staying sober, and I would drink, then get sober, over and over. So, I stepped up my attendance in recovery groups. I took a new accounting of past events, which I may have overlooked - events I had created and events I had experienced. Then, all of this was shared with another trusted recovery person. My life was pitiful. This personal inventory led me to list my assets and defects, which led to a lot of poor decisions I had made in my life. And through the process of taking this inventory, I discovered there were still a lot of missing pieces. There were still blank spots, where I could not remember anything. My recovery support person confronted me about these missing parts, but I simply couldn't remember them. He reassured me that I would remember them at the right time, if God wanted me to.

So I once again started therapy and discussed my missing memories. I wanted to find answers to questions such as: why had I attempted suicide twice by the time I was eighteen years old? Why had I ended up in a jail and a mental institution due to these suicide attempts? I couldn't even remember my oldest sister's wedding! After some time in therapy, the farthest I could get was to parts going back to when I was eleven or twelve years old, and it was around this time, when I had begun to struggle with sexuality. I have no idea how many times I started therapy and then would quit. Looking back, I think maybe I was getting too close to talking about things too difficult to deal with.

By January, 2001, I realized that I desperately wanted to move back to Indiana. I was sober now, and I needed to stay sober and to try to figure out what and why I had all these missing parts in my history. I wanted to sort out why I had continuous problems with relationships and acting out sexually. And I missed my family. I wanted to be back with them. I knew something was terribly wrong, because I couldn't remember why I'd left home in the first place or why I ended up moving as far away as possible.

So, I put my $650,000 house on the market, and it sold before it even hit the multiple listing, giving me just thirty days to pack and get out. I was very excited to be moving back and could hardly wait! My family was also excited. But a strange thing happened while I was packing. For the second time in my life, I heard a voice. It was soft and smooth. "What about the evil priests?" I actually turned around to see who was in the room with me, but there was no one there! I felt baffled but not really startled or scared. I replied out loud, "Well, they're probably all dead anyway." And as fast as it had happened, I put it out of my mind. I had become very proficient at blocking things out. It was years later before I remembered this.

As the time grew closer for my actual move, I became frantic about where I would live once I got back to Indiana. I started calling everyone in my family. To calm me down, they began to house hunt for me. I knew I couldn't live in Lafayette. I had to live in the country. Something was driving me crazy about that town, and I hadn't even left California yet. I also began really obsessing about where I would attend Mass.

On May 8, 2001, my mother's birthday, I arrived back in Indiana. I drove myself, three pets, and a few clothes, and in a short time, I bought a rundown farmhouse isolated in the middle of the country. Most of the time, I just didn't feel safe. Almost everyone in my family could tell that I had changed. I was deteriorating, both mentally and physically. I was still sober and going to meetings in Lafayette.

At this point, I was starting to understand some of the "clues" about the missing parts of my memory, and what might have happened to me as a boy...

Once, while attending Benediction with my sister, I was suddenly sure that the priest at the altar was abusing the altar boys! The service was attended by many parents and their children. At the altar, there were older altar boys on one side of the priest and younger ones on the other side. Fear, anxiety, and disgust ripped through my mind and body, and I turned to my sister and said with a loud whisper, "I hope someone is watching that priest!" She frowned at me and gestured for me to be quiet. At that moment, no one could have convinced me that the priest was not sexually molesting those boys! And the most bizarre thing is that I had no memory of any priest ever abusing me, and I had not yet heard about any clergy sex abuse scandals anywhere!

Afterward, my anxiety diminished, and I was filled with shame for having had such thoughts about the priest. Jennie must have understood what I was thinking and assured me that Father was a good and holy man. This experience made me realize, on a conscious level, that every time I was near a priest, I became preoccupied with sexual thoughts and was hypervigilant for signs about their sexual behavior, their private sex lives, and what they might secretly be doing. These were very secret thoughts that I didn't share with anyone but God.

I realized that every priest I'd ever met had always represented some sort of "secret sexuality," which resulted in enormous self-loathing for even allowing myself to think such things. I realized, in the past, I had a connection with many of my sexual encounters with thoughts about Jesus! Afterward, I would feel much shame and horror.

So, I approached the priest at my parish for pastoral counseling. I confided in him that I felt very unsafe, was filled with anxiety, and suffering from great sexual confusion. I even was developing a fear of going to Mass. I didn't share any of my private thoughts about priests and their sex lives. These feelings were about as close as I had ever come to having any ideas, memories, or recollections of the abuse that had happened to me. It was all buried so far down, for so long, so deep...like an old rusted box buried deep in the ground.

Father and I decided that it might be a good idea for me to purchase a gun for protection to make me feel safer. I bought a Mossberg shotgun and took it everywhere I went. And I did feel safer, for a little while. I had Jesus and my shotgun! Father also suggested that I do some volunteer work, which I did. He also recommended a psychologist if things didn't improve.

For volunteer work, I found out there was nothing available in the Lafayette area, such as a support group for people with HIV, so I started a Buddy Program. That lasted for maybe a year or so. My buddy was drinking too much and didn't want to do anything about it.

However, by Christmas 2001, I had fallen into a deep depression. I couldn't even show up for the family get-together at my sister's home. I felt like I had fallen into a black hole. And then, in 2002, the news broke about the sexual abuse scandal in Boston. I remember watching the news, this one little bit on CNN, and some guy was saying something about his childhood. He was crying, and it had to do with the Catholic Church. I don't even remember exactly what he said. He collapsed during the live broadcast, and then, I also collapsed to the floor, sobbing and crying. I suddenly knew this had happened to me, too. Now, I knew I had been sexually abused as a kid by a priest. At this time, I had no conscious memories of multiple abuses by priests. The logical thing - or the way this unfolded - was that I knew something "bad" happened at St. Elizabeth's Hospital the first time I worked there. I was absolutely going crazy, but I realized that there was stuff I had not been able to remember. This had to do with the missing pieces of my childhood. This was the stuff I would never have been able to deal with or process as a kid.

So, I began trying to figure it all out, trying to remember, and hoping to understand exactly what happened. My childhood memories were still missing big pieces, but I knew I had to report what had happened to me, even if I couldn't remember every detail. My memories were like watching a broken film, with a lot of "frames" missing at times. Then, there are some more visual "frames", and then, it would break up again. It's not like there were continually running clear pictures or memories. Some of my recollections are attached to a sort of intellectual type memory, not like a visual thing in my head. Some are visual, and a third sort of memory, well, it's like a "gut feeling". It is kind of like a feeling you might have of realizing that you forgot to do something very important; a sort of sinking feeling in the pit of your stomach.

These were some of the darkest days of my life, but everyday I would kneel before a little Crucifix and pray, "Most high and glorious God, cast Your light into the darkness of my heart. Give me right faith, firm hope, perfect charity, and profound humility with wisdom and perception, O Lord, so that I may do what is truly Your holy will. Amen." It was only during these moments that I could find some relief from the darkness that surrounded me constantly.

There was a deep conviction within that I had to cling to my faith and religion, because if I lost that, then they will have taken everything from me. This was a thought I repeated over and over to myself with great determination.

I remembered one priest, Fr. Craycraft, and I was thinking something might have happened with him, while I was working at St. Elizabeth's. I couldn't remember any details, but my mother and sister remembered plenty. My sister remembered thinking he had done something bad to me and that he had once been very close with our family. My mother remembered that he had personally involved himself with privately preparing us to receive the Sacrament of Confirmation. We would meet with him alone for religious instruction. He was also the priest who was going to perform my sister's wedding. Mom also remembered that years later, after Father Craycraft had moved to another parish, he had become very cold and distant toward my younger sister's family. Her grandson and his friends had told my younger sister they refused to be altar boys, because they didn't want to be alone with him.

I started to have more memories unfold. They were more deeply buried, from long ago, when we were in New Mexico. Memories I had locked away because I had been too young to understand what was happening, and realizing again, I would have had no way to process them. I remembered a priest who held me on his lap in the front of the church facing the altar, with my pants down, and his habit pulled up. I didn't like the way he smelled, and I didn't like how roughly he would hold me. I felt afraid of him. I just fixed my gaze on the crucifix and wanted to go inside it, but I seemed to somehow float above us while he would fondle me. It was like I was on the outside of myself and watching this. I didn't understand what was happening. I just knew that I didn't like him.

Eventually, my family and I went forward and requested a Review Board meeting with the Diocese of Lafayette. My therapist, who they provided, wrote a letter to the Diocese. The psychologist, Dr. Bonniello, wrote a "treatment plan" for me after about eight hours of testing and history taking. This was requested by the diocese. The Review Board meetings were a disaster! Monsignor Sell, who had sat in on several of my earlier therapy sessions, attended the meeting, and no matter what I said, I felt like they didn't understand and didn't believe me. Later, I received a letter from Bishop Higi, who said the Review Board had decided I was a victim of clergy sexual abuse. In the second paragraph of His letter, he wanted me to distance myself from the Diocese! I asked what he meant. Was I being excommunicated? Msgr. Sell was quick to say that no; the Bishop considered his office the Diocese, and it was a misunderstanding on my part. So, I requested a second letter for clarification. I never received one.

One of my closest sobriety support members also attended the meeting to advocate on my behalf. The whole Diocesan review was actually very abusive and left me feeling extremely angry.

After I reported that I was a victim of clergy sex abuse to the Diocese of Lafayette in Indiana, I was shown photos of priests from Farmington by the Franciscans. After several meetings trying to identify the priests at Sacred Heart and St. Elizabeth Hospital, I was looking at photos and was shocked to see a picture of Fr. Miguel A. Baca. In my memory, I had been thinking of Fr. Conran. But when I saw those photos, I

Fr. Miguel A. Baca

remembered that yes, there was another priest, who I had simply called "Padre". He would always greet me with a kiss and hug me tightly. He would hold me, kiss me on the neck, and sometimes rub my back. I remember liking him and wanting to be like him when I grew up. But I also remember him touching me, and I would become aroused. I remember the smell of his body, the wool in his robe, and other more specific details I won't share in this story but would be significant for my allegation. Part of the memory was that Padre was so nice to me. I remember, one time, when my mother was in the hospital, he promised to take care of me. I also remember that at one point he walked into the church and saw what Fr. Connie (Fr. Conran's nickname) was doing to me, and he seemed very upset.

After revealing some of what had happened to me with only a few members of my family, I found out my mother shared a couple of her own memories of Fr. Conran. She remembers him coming to our house and being very upset that he had never been invited to dinner. She also remembers that he would go to her friends' houses and get their boys out of bed early, dress them, and march them off to church. When she found out that I had been getting up early and riding my bike to church, she put an end to it. After telling Mom what I was remembering in New Mexico (I never shared graphic details), she exclaimed, "How could I have not seen what was going on?" All of this was very painful for my family members.

I also realized, as these memories finally started to surface, that when I was a small child, while I did not understand what was being done to me, I was not aware at the time of being traumatized by them. The priests repeatedly told me that I was "special" and that I was going to grow up to become a priest, like them. In my childish understanding, maybe I saw it all as some sort of game, that this was how you become ready to be a priest. Who knows? I'm really not sure exactly what I was thinking at that age. I'm not sure I could ever find the words to explain the "emotional disconnect". I don't know any other thing to call it!

I eventually remembered yet another priest, Fr. Frank Druehe, when I worked at St. Elizabeth Hospital. I was an adolescent by this time, knew what sex was, and was embarrassed by it. I was already living a double-life of having secret same sex attractions and relationships with pedophiles while also having girlfriends. I remembered this priest being bald, pudgy, and effeminate. Just watching him made me feel embarrassed. His habit was sheer, and I could see everything through it. I was old enough to know these men were supposed to be representatives of Jesus Christ. I remembered that he had come into a room I was in at the hospital and pulled up his habit to show me that he was very aroused. I ran and shut the door and asked him, "What are you doing?" I think I was trying to protect him or prevent anyone from seeing him or something. Somehow, I wasn't surprised that he wasn't wearing underwear, and he told me I could touch him. That's about as much as I remember during this incident.

So, it all totaled up to five priests who were abusive. Four of them sexually. I have no idea what happened with Father Craycraft. I just know I was upset, almost to the point of violence!

Eventually, I was referred to "Pathways to Hope" by St. John the Baptist Friary, where an outreach person named Jennifer Reed worked with me. They provided some assistance for me, like buying me a truck so I could attend meetings and therapy. But there was always a veiled threat that if I was to take legal action against the Church, all help would be cut off.

Eventually, I ended up filing lawsuits against the Diocese of Gallup, New Mexico, The Diocese of Lafayette, Indiana, The Franciscans in Cincinnati, and the Sisters at St. Elizabeth's Hospital. Throughout all of it, I often had terrifying thoughts that I was going to hell for speaking out against a priest and the Roman Catholic Church. I really didn't want to, but most of all, somehow I thought maybe they would tell me what they knew. Often, I was tortured by the thought that maybe I could be mistaken. However, with the exception of "Padre", other credible witnesses have come forward to accuse the same priests that I remember abusing me. I'm sorry there were other victims, but it presented evidence to me that these were deeply troubled men who had taken Holy Orders. In more recent years, I've wondered if clergy sexual abuse wasn't also part of their childhood or adolescent experiences.

My therapists, spiritual directors, and the Gallup Diocesan Outreach Person for Victims have reassured me that I have valid memories, but nothing about this has been or is easy. I made a decision that I didn't want to remember any more; I just wanted to move forward with my life. Yet, at times, I still struggle with these earlier memories. It terrifies me that I could have made a mistaken allegation. So I pray and go through the process again and again, with the end result being this is what I honestly remember. After three review board meetings in the Diocese of Gallup, all the members unanimously had declared my memories 100% valid.

After thousands of hours of therapy and a thirty plus day inpatient program in a trauma hospital in New Orleans, which was paid by disability insurance, I began to heal.

Survivors of Those Abused by Priests (SNAP) helped in the early days during the process of remembering all the abuse. Countless hours of conversation with other survivors gave me a voice and insight into the scope of damage as a result of clergy sexual abuse. My best friend, Sheila, who was also sexually abused in Boston, was a "gift" as a result of SNAP. We've spoken on a regular basis for years now. We participated as activists together, cried, laughed, and continue to be very close.

I consider all abuse of children or vulnerable adults as Satanic acts. The result to victims, and those close to them, causes grave physical, mental, and spiritual damage, which can lead to a lifetime of suffering. I've often wondered about victims who can't, or won't, speak up. How many are incarcerated or dead? How many died from suicide, AIDS, or addictions?

A very loving and supportive family was crucial to my survival and healing. They are great examples of faithful Catholics. Of course, the abuse I suffered has been very difficult for them, as well. My sister, Jennie, wrote this about how it has affected her:

> *"I am Jim Field's older sister. I feel privileged to share how I feel about my brother and what he has gone through with the priest sexual abuse. I love my brother and have great respect for him. Nothing that has happened to Jim has changed my love for him.*
>
> *As Jim began to put the missing pieces of his life together, it was very painful for our whole family. Because sexual abuse by priests happened in my family to someone I love, it makes me very angry and distrustful. When I found out what happened to my brother, I cried. My husband said to me, 'Don't worry, Jennie, Jesus will level the playing field.'*
>
> *My Catholic faith has not been shaken. This crisis in the Catholic Church has made me stronger in my faith. I have watched our Merciful God turn Jim's pain into good because he has stayed faithful to Him."*

Slowly, I was able to occasionally attend Mass. The Sacraments never became unimportant. Actually, they became even more precious and still remain the most important events in my life today. I've found a great amount of spiritual growth from frequent Confession with one priest, who I consider my confessor. Once again, in recent years, I've had help with spiritual directors.

All along this painful remembering, and even today, it's so clear to me that the Sacraments never abused me, which is so important about my survival. It was some really sick priests who abused me. Clergy cover-ups are abusive to all of us! It must stop!

I have forgiven my priest abusers and have requested a Mass intention for each. I pray sometimes for their souls. Maybe they repented. If I make it to Heaven after my judgement, I hope they are there too. I have no idea how all that works. I have also forgiven the ones involved with my allegations that made the whole experience an experience of further abuse.

Today, I focus on ways I can serve God. I attend Mass daily and confess weekly. I also attend an early morning men's Bible Study. The Holy Spirit has given me a deep devotion to making reparation to the Sacred Heart of Jesus for all of the abuses that have and continue to occur. I helped start a Holy Hour of Reparation to the Sacred Heart of Jesus at St. Mary of the Immaculate Conception Cathedral here in Lafayette. Each week, I help to set up for Adoration of the Blessed Sacrament. Sometimes, if the confession line is still long, at 4:20 I get to lead the Litany of the Sacred Heart of Jesus.

I also created an image of the Sacred Heart of Jesus, which I sent to the Diocese of Gallup as a gift to Bishop Wall for a way to help him in ongoing investigations of sexual abuse in that Diocese. He was very happy

One of the 12 promises made by Our Dear Saviour to St. Margaret Mary: "Those who propagate this devotion (to His Sacred Heart) shall have their names written in My Heart never to be blotted out." What a magnificent blessing! We can easily do this by spreading this prayer card among as many persons as possible, urging them to say these prayers daily.

Prayer to the Sacred Heart of Jesus

O most holy Heart of Jesus, fountain of every blessing, I adore Thee, I love Thee and with a lively sorrow for my sins, I offer Thee this poor heart of mine. Make me humble, patient, pure and wholly obedient to Thy will. Grant, good Jesus, that I may live in Thee and for Thee. Protect me in the midst of danger; comfort me in my afflictions; give me health of body, assistance in my temporal needs, Thy blessing on all that I do, and the grace of a holy death. Within Thy Heart I place my every care. In every need let me come to Thee with humble trust saying, Heart of Jesus help me.

Invocations to the Sacred Heart

Merciful Jesus, I consecrate myself today and always to Thy Most Sacred Heart.

Most Sacred Heart of Jesus, I implore that I may ever love Thee more and more.

Most Sacred Heart of Jesus, I trust in Thee.

Most Sacred Heart of Jesus, have mercy on us.

Sacred Heart of Jesus, I believe in Thy love for me.

Jesus, meek and humble of heart, make my heart like unto Thine.

Sacred Heart of Jesus, Thy Kingdom Come.

Most Sacred Heart of Jesus, convert sinners, save the dying, deliver the Holy Souls from Purgatory.

when he got it. That same image became a Holy Card at the Cathedral here, with prayers on the back: a Prayer to the Sacred Heart of Jesus and Invocations to the Sacred Heart. It was wonderful when Father suggested it, because it could encourage more Reparation to Jesus.

I try to understand how I can unite my suffering with the suffering of Christ. And please don't get me wrong, in no way does my suffering compare to His suffering. I try to remember to offer up little sacrifices to God for souls in purgatory or for whatever may be needed. Sometimes, I can almost understand this offering, and at other times, it's baffling. I know for certain I really love the Trinity and want to be pleasing to God. Life today is really amazing! I have moved beyond the abuse and the uncomfortable experience when I met with the review board. With my faith intact, there are still days that are very difficult, especially with the ongoing scandals that continue to unfold. I continue to pray for the Holy Father and all clergy, though often I find myself disappointed and angry with their behavior

Some of us, who experienced clergy sexual abuse, still do have our faith. Many have experienced far more traumatic events. Many can't go near a church or even pray. I have found great healing through receiving the Sacraments. They have always been, and always will be, holy. Remembering this helped me to survive those darkest years. The sacraments are the source for all of us to receive God's grace and mercy!

The Love of God Conquers All

Jess McGuire
co-written by Joanne C. Schmidt

*Love is patient, love is kind. It is not jealous, [love] is
not pompous, it is not inflated, it is not rude, it does not
seek its own interests, it is not quick-tempered, it does not
brood over injury, it does not rejoice over wrongdoing but
rejoices with the truth. It bears all things, believes all things,
hopes all things, endures all things. Love never fails.*
1 Corinthians 13:4-8

I spent a weekend preaching at a parish community in her
Diocese for their mission appeal program. It was here that I
first met the family of Jessica, who showed interest in my work
in interfaith dialogue. Despite the horror of her past, Jessica
and her family were in Church, and even though I was not
aware of her abuse at that time, Jessica has clearly been trying
to claw back from the ongoing trauma through the power of her
own faith for quite some time.

In our journey of spiritual direction together, she is fighting
to find the finger of God, not only in the abuse itself, but in
her journey toward healing, which has had its fits and starts.
Despite the deep pain, she is mining the resources of courage
and faith within herself that she is discovering in powerful
ways, and often in unexpected ways. She, like so many others,
are heroes of faith in this extraordinary crisis of the Church and
a powerful witness of hope that transcends the sinfulness of the
Church.

-Fr. Carl Chudy, SX

The phone was ringing, and it was my turn on the schedule.

I am a Trauma and Rape hotline volunteer, so my job, during the next 12 hours, was to respond to all kinds of trauma victims. Most of the time, the phone calls deal with everything from addictions to threats of suicide to domestic abuse to mental health issues. I know who to call, provide referrals, or offer a listening ear with the caller about his or her problem.

If there is a question or concern I can't address, a supervisor can be reached quickly.

This particular call, however, was from medical. A rape victim was at the processing center, waiting for me. My physical presence was needed to support her.

I knew the routine only too well. For six long hours, a specially trained doctor or nurse would conduct a forensic examination. The victim would give a complete medical history, detail what happened to her, and then be swabbed, scraped and photographed head to toe, while biological evidence was collected for a rape kit.

No matter how much care is taken, the process is humiliating and embarrassing. This victim of violence would have no time to absorb what had just happened to her, before submitting her body to further indignities.

Through it all, I would be there to reassure her and provide whatever comfort I could.

When I arrived at the processing center, she was alone in the room. Luckily, this time I would not have to deal with an over-emotional boyfriend, husband, or father, raging at the violation of a loved one.

"I just hate myself," she was telling me. "How could I have allowed this to happen. I have been so stupid. I'm just worthless."

"That's not true," I said in my most compassionate voice. "You didn't do anything wrong. You're the good person here."

I kept encouraging her as I'd been trained to do. I spent forty intense and rigorous hours of intervention instruction and rehearsing moments like this. You're trained one on one to give what they need, listen to them, and be there for them. I knew all the right words.

Hours later, she was still numb, exhausted, and wanting only to get away and go home.

"You're so sweet," she managed to blurt out. "You're amazing. Thank you for staying with me through all this."

"You're welcome," I replied, continuing to reassure her, patting her hand, and building her up.

"I really mean it. You're wonderful."

I was trying to be strong for her. Truth be told, however, I felt like a hypocrite. Feeling like a worthless human being after being victimized is common, and I was giving her advice I didn't always take myself.

But, being a hotline volunteer is my way of making a difference, of giving back.

You see, I, too, am a victim of sexual abuse. More times, and for more years, than I care to admit.

My abusers were not strangers, but the very persons I should have been able to trust the most: my biological father and the clergy who were entrusted with my care.

But I'm getting ahead of myself, so let me begin at the beginning.

I was born on December 19, 1973 to Catholic parents. We lived in an apartment on Beaver Street in a very dangerous part of Framingham, Massachusetts. From my earliest days, my biological father was very seriously abusive to my mom, my younger brother, and myself. He threw my mom down flights of stairs, was a drug addict, and extremely violent toward animals.

By the time I was three, I was completely traumatized.

I still have memories of hiding under the kitchen table and screaming.

My mother finally had had enough, and she whisked my brother and me away to live with my maternal grandmother in her ranch house in a better part of Framingham. My grandmother was a devout Catholic, so we attended church regularly at St. Patrick's Church in Natick.

Life was uneventful until we moved from Grandma's to a nearby apartment. While my mother wasn't looking to date anyone, a guy named Jim became interested in her. I've always loved dogs, so my brother and I jumped at every opportunity to visit Jim's apartment and play with the two black Lab Newfoundland puppies he'd snuck in. His landlord frowned on pets, but Jim won him over by helping with maintenance. He repainted, did yard work, and replaced carpeting—everything. He was very handy and liked to take care of everybody.

Still, two puppies were one too many, so Jim gave the female to his best friend and kept Clyde, the male.

It turned out to be a package deal when Mom married Jim in 1980, and Clyde, the puppy who would grow to 110 pounds, became a permanent and beloved part of our new family. Soon after the marriage, my biological father gave up custody of me and my brother, and our new Dad was only too happy to adopt us.

I was barely seven years old by the time all that happened, but the effects of trauma linger. My mom tells me I was withdrawn because of what I'd suffered at the hands of my biological father, but our adopted Dad did everything he could to make up for that, providing us the family life we'd never known before.

My dad was very strict, but the truth is that he spoiled us. I got everything I wanted: from waterbeds to you-name-it. Before I was ten years old, I was given diamonds.

More important, however, was the quality family time we spent together.

In the winter, there was ice skating and sledding at the iced-over pond close to our three-story home. Back in the Eighties, we could still trespass on that little pond and get away with it. My Dad knew the depth of the water and made sure we stayed within a certain range, just in case the ice broke.

In the summer, we would get a cottage for a week or two at Cape Code. At the beginning, my grandparents went down with us, but sometimes, there were other relatives and friends. We had so much fun swimming and boating. I still recall the first time I went on a boat, and my dad let me drive. He almost had a heart attack, when I went like ninety miles an hour, and my mother almost fell overboard. Luckily, my dad acted quickly and caught her!

To my mind, my dad was overprotective, but I recall a time I was ever so grateful he was. Dad's best friend was getting married. We were at a pool, but no one thought to bring bathing suits. The men were fooling around and throwing each other in the pool. Somehow, I was thrown into the pool too. When they saw me in the deep end, they panicked. They ended up coming after me, because I wasn't the greatest swimmer and didn't even know I was dressed.

Family time included barbecuing, particularly in the summer, when we didn't want to heat up the house. Our first barbecue of the season was on Patriots' Day, a state holiday celebrated on the third Monday of April to commemorate the Revolutionary War battles of Lexington, Concord, and the lesser known, but very important, battle of Menotomy.

Patriots' Day was also when the historic Boston Marathon was held. In recent years, it was in the headlines following a bombing at the finish in Boston's Copley Square, but during my childhood, it was simply the Mother of all U.S. Marathons. The 26.2 mile race started in rural Hopkinton just a few miles away, and the first half of the race began a descent, winding through the countryside village of Ashland across the rolling hills of Framingham. We had a front row seat in our yard, as the crowd of runners began to separate on the mostly flat terrain on West Central Street where we lived in Natick. Everybody came to our house to watch.

My brother Joe and I loved those holiday afternoons, because Dad would rent an ice cream truck and have it parked in our driveway. We could have all the ice cream we wanted all day.

On some days, Joe and I would jump the fence and play with the little red-haired boy next door, other neighborhood kids in between the three widely spaced houses, or chase after Clyde. Our parents put in a swing set to entice us to play in our own backyard.

My love for gardening probably developed around this time. Mom still teases me about planting watermelon seeds, then digging them up the very next day: typical child, I thought watermelons grew overnight! I also learned how tough it is to grow zucchini plants when you have a dog. When I accused my Mom of taking my zucchini plants, she told me Clyde had eaten them. Not only that, but for whatever reason everybody likes to pluck them.

I had more success with tomatoes, cucumbers, peppers, and green beans. My grandparents had a bigger yard, so that's where I planted pumpkin seeds, since we were there visiting all the time anyways.

Looking back, it all seems so idyllic, but behind these happy scenes was a parallel dark side my family had no knowledge of— and this time it had nothing to do with my biological dad.

It all started when my grandmother was babysitting me. Joe was with my other grandmother. The deacon at our church, Deacon Jimmy, who worked with my grandmother at Fenwal Electric in Framingham and was a close friend of hers,

Age 4 (when the abuse began)

was at her house. He knew my abuse history with my biological father, about the divorce, and that I had a learning disability. He saw a hurting child and knew that I was vulnerable.

He told my grandmother he would experiment to help me get over my fear of men. I think we were at a party, and I was really out of it. I have memories of two priests who were friends of the deacon.

"We'll just talk to her and spend quality time with her," they told my grandmother. I recall being led by the hand down basement stairs, being tickled, and touched. One of the young men wore a collar, but at that age, I didn't know he was a priest.

I now know that there is such a thing as secondary grooming. Parents, as well as kids, are manipulated. My grandmother was led to believe my hyperactivity and rebelliousness traced back to my biological father, not what was happening to me then. In that day and age, she trusted them. She was very religious and glad for the hour or two break she got while I was downstairs with the priests being "helped."

That was the beginning, and it magnified. Whenever the priests who were friends of the deacon were around, stuff would happen. The abuse happened on a regular basis over the next ten years, but they knew they could gain access to me at school or if I was on a church retreat. During religion classes (familiarly known to Catholic parents as CCD), I would be told by a teacher to deliver papers to the chapel, and one of the priests would take me into a confessional. They would tell me I was in sin and "now it's time to get the demons out of you." This had to happen to stop me from disobeying my parents, the priest would tell me after my "penance." Sometimes, before the penance, they would have me drink wine or vodka. I thought I deserved what was happening to me.

First Communion

I thought I was going to hell regardless of what I did. The priests lied to me and twisted the true meaning of the Sacraments. They would intertwine aspects of human sexuality with the Sacraments, such as equating semen with the Eucharist. Another Sacrament that was twisted was the sacrament of Reconciliation. They told me that there was evil inside of me, and to get the demons out of me, I needed to comply with the sexual acts they proposed. As you can imagine, many aspects of our faith reminded me of the abuse, such as the black clothing familiarly worn by a priest. When the priests vestments were red, I would remember the retreats when I was abused because of the red altar cloths and decorations at the church. A crucifix can trigger painful memories primarily because I would focus on a small crucifix while being abused in the confessional. There is much more that I could share, but I think you get the picture.

I suspect that other priests were aware of what was going on. One day at CCD, I saw a look of horror on their faces as they watched these two priests accompany some students to a classroom downstairs. I think they might have been aware but felt the need to keep their mouths shut.

When I was about ten, my parents were working and gave me permission to walk to CCD classes by myself. Over the last two years, I would skip CCD and go to the library instead. I only made about five classes. When the priest in charge asked why I was skipping and said that I might not be confirmed because of it, I dared him to tell my parents why I wasn't going.

"You know why I'm not going," I challenged. "Do YOU want to tell them why?"

He backed off, and I was eventually confirmed.

Even though the priests tracked my periods, I became pregnant in my early teens. I was given weird herbs and drinks to terminate the pregnancy, but the attempts failed.

Jess with Clyde

That was when I first saw Cardinal Bernard Law in person. Everyone knew the archbishop of Boston, and here he was with me and the deacon and two priests, consulting with a doctor. The doctor's ultrasound showed I was too far along to abort. On the pretense of attending a retreat, I was dropped off early one morning at the doctor's office. Over the course of several hours, the doctor gave me several shots.

"Inducing labor is not an abortion," the Doctor assured me.

I gave birth in a sacristy at a Church near the medical district. I won't go into the details.

The baby, thought to be a male 14 weeks along, was buried in a church courtyard near a statue of the Blessed Mother. I heard the clerics arguing in the sacristy beforehand: if seen in public, they would say they were burying a pet hamster.

One of them sounded scared, but I overheard the archbishop: "I'm the Cardinal," he bragged. "I can do whatever I want."

When it was all over, Cardinal Law was furious and screamed at me: "Because of your error in judgment, something evil came out of you." He told me it was all my fault that he had to move two priests.

But as horrible as the loss of the baby was, it ended the abuse. The two priests were transferred.

A year later, my grandmother passed away. When fourteen year old Clyde also passed, memories came flooding back: I remembered my biological father threatening to kill our family pet if I told what happened on our visitations. At the age of fifteen, I had a mental breakdown and was hospitalized for six months. Non-residential treatment continued over the next four years.

Age 13, when the abuse ended

All this time, I had blocked the entire period of clerical abuse from my mind just as I had the abuse by my biological father.

After graduation my parents moved to another town. I felt it was a new beginning for all of us. I worked at various jobs, including at a pharmacy and a restaurant. I volunteered to work in the church and had a healthy relationship with a priest. I helped sell Christmas trees for the church fundraiser and worked in the thrift shop. Fr. Kim was wonderful and sweet. He wanted to help me, but because of my past experiences, I was afraid to trust him. I left the church and got involved in a cult-like religious group.

Eventually, I turned to therapy once again to deal with my issues, but it was sheer torture. We got past the abuse by my biological father, but whenever the subject of the clergy abuse came up, I shut down and refused to even acknowledge it.

During this period, I met my future husband. I told Dan about the abuse, and he didn't think any less of me because of it. It seemed to have the opposite effect on him; instead of viewing me in a bad light, the thought of the abuse made him more amorous. While I didn't mind his reaction initially, it did have a negative effect on our relationship long term. He had a high-paying job as a computer salesman and took me to Paris and around the world. We were having a ball, and therapy was just too painful to deal with. When my therapist told me he was moving to the Cape, I didn't look to replace him. That was probably a mistake, but at that time, I thought I was okay.

Jess and Dan

After two years of dating, Dan and I became engaged. About two weeks before our wedding, Dan sold his condo and bought a house. My Dad had an inkling of problems to come when Dan suddenly turned on him and had a meltdown, but I ignored the warning signs.

Dan and I married in the chapel on a beautiful sunny day in May of 2001. All seemed perfect.

I was happy to have a brand new life, and I was even happier when I learned several months later that we were expecting our first child. During my pregnancy, we got our marriage blessed in the Catholic Church.

This happiness was short-lived, however. When my daughter was born, I hyperventilated whenever she cried. I wouldn't let the nurses take her away, holding her close to me for endless hours. I didn't comprehend it at the time, but I would later be told that despite suppressing my abortion experience, I somehow "knew" I had had another baby and feared losing her. I was kept in the hospital longer than normal, because Dan didn't want me home under those circumstances. Even after I did come home, I would pick her up the moment she cried and refuse to put her down.

Not long after my daughter's birth, more problems surfaced in our marriage. My husband had his own dysfunctions. Prior to our marriage, he'd taken a year off from work while his father was recuperating from colon cancer treatments. Shortly after our daughter was born, my husband had a hard time keeping a job. To make matters worse, his uncle, who suffered from schizophrenia, moved into our home when my daughter was two years old.

I was emotionally overwhelmed, engaged in unhealthy eating, and gained more than two hundred pounds. The weight gain limited my options, and I found myself unemployed. To maintain our home, we took in foster children. I needed help myself, but the older teens we took in had many issues that impacted our family.

To relieve the situation, I had a gastric bypass that improved my mental health and mobility. But as I was getting better, my husband was getting worse. He had told me when we were dating that he had had a nervous breakdown when he was at the by-then-coeducational Vassar College in Poughkeepsie and that he had a hard time dealing with stress. That became more and more evident when our daughter would act up or one of the foster kids got into trouble. When Dan was out of control, he would choke me until I was ready to pass out, and on a few occasions, he had outbursts in front of my daughter. For this and other reasons, I agreed with his wish to end our ten-year marriage.

Unfortunately, I soon found myself in an intense rebound relationship and got pregnant. When my son's father became violently abusive, I ended that relationship. I gave up the foster parenting and decided to return to Church.

I needed to replenish my spirituality and faith. I also felt the need to talk about my abuse within the church, hoping this would provide healing. I thought I could confide in the priest at our parish about what had happened to me, but the priest became defensive and thought I was attacking him. To my dismay, he shunned me. When I persisted, I was asked to leave that parish, along with my family.

What upset me the most is that the pastor broke my confidence and told my mother, before I could, that I'd been sexually abused by a priest. She assumed the abuse was recent, thinking I'd been abused by an innocent priest who'd been nothing but kind and wonderful to me. She was devastated when she learned later that it had happened during my childhood.

Meanwhile, my daughter, who was in chorus, which she loved, was extremely disappointed we were being evicted from the parish.

I was beyond hurt.

The next three months were the worst of my life. I had a hard time getting through each day. Flashbacks became incredibly intense. Heartbreaking pain surfaced. It was a living nightmare, and I cried the entire time. I had thoughts of suicide.

I needed a good therapist and a good spiritual director. The latter was important because my abuse involved confusion over the Sacraments. I had a very distorted view on Church teaching. Confession and Eucharist were twisted in my mind. I did research to find out what it was supposed to be like. I started reading Matthew

Kelly's books on Catholicism to better understand the Church and the Mass.

My daughter, who was about eleven, then asked about coming back to the Church.

I was hesitant. What if I was kicked out of the Church again? My son, James, has autism, which some people find disturbing. Being kicked out of the Church again would reinforce my feeling that I was not welcome. This is a direct cause of the abuse I suffered as a child and the way in which the priests twisted the Sacraments and told me that I had evil inside of me. But I realized that, no matter where you go, there will be gossip and backbiting and imperfect people. We needed, for my children's sakes as well as mine, to come back to the Church.

I'd been slowly following Kelly's suggestions in "Rediscovering Catholicism," starting with morning and evening prayer and Church every week. Around Easter, I started attending daily Mass. After a year and a half, I got up the courage to go to Confession.

"Is that IT for Penance?" I asked the priest.

"What did you expect?" he replied.

Looking for ways to blame the Church for what had happened to me, I complained bitterly to our new pastor that the Pope was at fault for the sex abuse crisis for not allowing priests to marry.

"You've been abused by a priest, haven't you?" the pastor retorted.

When I told him I had, he insisted I report it to the Archdiocese.

I tried to backpedal, but he insisted. "I will if you come with me," I said.

I attended the safe environment classes that the Archdiocese offered. I joined a survivor's group, and it was suggested that I find a spiritual director. Spiritual direction with a priest was not my first choice, but wherever I called, there were no female lay people or nuns who wanted to work with clergy abuse survivors.

One evening, in an attempt to have my ex-husband and daughter spend more time together, we attended an interfaith meeting. Fr. Carl Chudy and I planned to go out to dinner afterwards with the priest who'd conducted the session, but everyone else backed out. It was just Fr. Carl and I at Bertucci's that evening. Conversation got around to why people leave the Church, and I volunteered that my husband left because of the sex abuse crisis in the Church.

"I never said that," Dan interjected.

Fr. Carl responded to me directly. "I do a lot of work in this," he said matter-of-factly. "People just don't heal from that."

That was the last thing I needed to hear, so I got very angry. I would learn later that what he really meant was, instead of hopelessness, there could be transformation and renewal.

As it turned out, Fr. Carl was a priest at the very shrine that my daughter and my friends were urging me to go to. I did not initially like him, but there were roadblocks everywhere else I turned.

Was God making it very clear that he wanted this priest to work with me? Even my friends were encouraging me to consult him at the Fatima Shrine, where he conducted his ministry.

At the shrine, I wanted a different priest for a spiritual director, but I was told by his superior, "No, no. Fr. Carl would be best for you."

So, despite my fears, I did begin meeting with him. I was so scared I tried my best to get him upset, expecting to prove that all priests were out to harm me. I would overreact to just about everything and question everything. But as I was testing him, my plan backfired.

For the first year and a half, I fought him and nobody could put up with me, but Fr. Carl's persistence and kindness made a world of difference. This opened me to the fact that God was in complete control. For the very first time, I felt really safe with a priest. As we continued to meet, he clarified that sexual abuse victims don't really heal so much as they become a totally changed person.

That marked the beginning of my healing.

Still, it was very hard to talk about my abuse and the abortion. Things got vivid. As I got past each hurdle, there would be another one. Peaks and valleys. You go through the layers and the walls and the bricks, and slowly have them crumble. You grow each time and learn more about yourself. Prayer helps, but it doesn't always stop the memories. It's still very hard.

I had pushed down the memory of the abortion. I felt like losing the baby, reliving body sensations. It was very intense. To help deal with it, I went back to the spot where my baby is buried and took a picture there near the statue of the Blessed Mother-- even though it all happened more than thirty-five years before. To get some closure, I put a little garden in the back of my yard. I added figures of Mary and Jesus as well.

Three years later, I am only now beginning to understand the impact the abuse made in my life. I still look for any way to change the subject or to focus on small issues rather than myself, but with the help of Fr. Carl, I'm making progress. I am so grateful to him for opening the door to a different perspective on my abuse.

To help with my own healing, I observed how survivors like those in the Holocaust or the civil war in Africa's Sierra Leone could forgive unimaginable evils and still love the offenders.

I became more open to God's love, especially after exploring Julian of Norwich. In "Revelations of Divine Love," this fourteenth-century English mystic received assurance of God's unwavering love for man and his infinite capacity for forgiveness.

I needed that assurance after all that happened to me. I was mad at God and mad at myself. I questioned why this happened. Why didn't God stop it?

Fr. Carl recommended Fr. Henri Nouwen's books, "The Wounded Healer" and "The Prodigal Son." I began to forgive myself for the mistakes of my past, while comprehending the impact the abuse had on me. I had blamed myself for things that were the abusers' fault.

Another important influence was Fr. Richard Rohr. His writings helped me understand my anger, which would come out in unexpected and trivial ways—like getting hopping mad if I didn't get my coffee hot. Fr. Rohr writes that if we don't deal with our wounds, we take it out on others.

Fr. Carl assures me repeatedly that it's okay to be angry over what happened to me and that the anger is justified.

"Reflections" by Fr. Ron Rolheiser is what brought me to the Eucharist to be healed. In essence, in His suffering and death, Jesus took our wounds, our weaknesses, our infidelities, and our sins, died in them, and then through love and trust brought them to wholeness. Every time we go to the Eucharist, Fr. Rolheiser writes, we let that transforming event touch us and our emotional paralysis, bringing us to a transformation in wholeness, energy, joy, and love. The Eucharist is the ultimate healer.

Jess and her family with Fr. Carl

In fact, the Eucharist is key to me wanting to stay in the Church, regardless of the hurdles. Fr. Carl had the intelligence and insight to teach this to me not just once, but repeatedly. I make it a point to mention this, whenever I am teaching on the Sacrament.

I love the Eucharist now, although old images still creep into my head. I know you're supposed to fast an hour before taking Communion, but I often have to pop a mint in my mouth to remind myself I'm about to take the Body and Blood of Christ and not the abuse.

I also learned that quiet time is very important, as is daily prayer. Meditating on the Scriptures and listening to prayers before I go to bed has helped. I am thankful for family and friends in my life who have been a support system. I am grateful to my new parish in Upton, which welcomed my family and took an interest in my daughter, who was so hurt when we had to change parishes during her Confirmation year.

I've come to see that the impact of my abuse has had far-reaching affects not just on me, but on my family. Because I subconsciously pushed myself away from my adoptive father, who sacrificed so much for me, our relationship has been damaged. There was a lot of guilt in my family. When my mother finally learned of my abuse, she had a hard time accepting that this had been done in my childhood and that she had not protected me.

"How dare they!" I remember her saying. "I'd do all this stuff! I would be teaching CCD in the school, and they'd be molesting my daughter!"

Fortunately, Fr. Carl has been a mentor for them, too—my mom, my ex-husband, and my children. He's never broken my trust, and he goes the extra mile. He answers every email and every phone call. My family loves him and is amazed he could break through the emotional walls I have always had for protection.

We've established a connection. Fr. Carl knows immediately when I'm having a flashback or a bad day. He's been there through the whole thing.

"I've noticed a big change in you," my mother tells me. "He's the only one who broke through to you."

My daughter agrees. She told me I had always been cold and pushed people away, but I am now more loving, more open, and more expressive.

I've been asked if my brother had also been sexually abused, since he was an altar server at the same church in which I was abused. I asked him straight out, but he wasn't molested. When we were growing up, Joe, who is a year younger than me, spent more time with my adoptive Dad's parents and wasn't affected. He knows something happened to me, but not much about it. We're semi-close, but he lives in another state.

Things are coming along for me. Fr. Nouwen's books helped move me into the advocacy work I am doing at the Trauma and Rape Hotline that I talked about earlier. I believe when God puts you through something like I experienced, you learn to help others, but you have to be careful not to be manipulated. I made the mistake of taking in a homeless mother and her kid for about eighteen months. However, she took advantage of me and I had to ask her to leave.

I also Nanny, am a Eucharistic Minister, and teach religious education. I like the latter because I'm learning while I'm teaching and filling in the gaps from those CCD classes I skipped as a child.

After my parents decided to sell their house and move into a condo in Milford, we bought a house two miles away to be close to them. That worked out really well until last year, when my parents decided to move to Florida. They both still worry about me and didn't want to leave, but I convinced them they can't protect me any more. I stay in touch with them and talk to my mother on the phone almost every day. She still comes for visits.

A word to clergy: this healing process is very hard, so try to see the big picture. Everyone has been affected by this issue one way or another. Please do not reject the survivor because he or she is angry and asking questions. Bishops, too, please try to understand the unimaginable pain and rejection individuals have had to endure.

After my painful exit from our parish, I wrote to the Bishop. He never replied. I later saw him at a retreat about the sexual abuse crisis and confronted him; he supported the pastor.

In my experience, I was rejected by the Diocese and blamed by the Bishop. It's so hurtful. I say this not to blame them; I just think more understanding and kindness should be there and less blame. It is so hard to face this kind of abuse, especially in a church setting. Trust and healing is hard for all parties and blaming the ones who were abused just adds to the trauma.

The Church is still dealing with the clergy sexual abuse scandal as I write this, but hopefully, lessons will be learned and other children will not have to go through what I did.

I'm not sure what prompted me, but recently, I went online to see if the school where I'd been abused was still there. The website had pictures of the classrooms, and it immediately caused me to have flashbacks. I threw the computer down when I saw it.

To this day, I cringe every time I see a picture of Cardinal Law, who was directly involved in my abortion. It gives me no pleasure to know his pattern of wrongdoing was exposed for the whole world to see or that other victims came forward with their own stories that bolster my credibility.

After nineteen years as head of the Archdiocese of Boston, Cardinal Law resigned in disgrace in 2002, after his failure to remove sexually abusive priests from ministry was revealed. Sex abuse survivors were furious when Law remained a Cardinal, moved to Italy to serve at the Papal Liberian Basilica of St. Mary Major in Rome, and never faced criminal sanctions. When he died at the age of 86, in December 2017, Pope Francis attended Law's funeral Mass in Rome. No mention was made of the scandal he set, enabled, and covered up.

I learned from a family member that Deacon Jimmy, who orchestrated my abuse, died many years ago. I take some satisfaction in believing I saved my cousins from becoming his victims. My aunt moved into my maternal grandmother's house, while the deacon was still coming around, and I believe he was targeting my cousins. When my aunt told him I was saying bad things about the Church at that time and had left, he wanted nothing more to do with my Grandmother and her family.

I've yet to find out what happened to the priests who abused me for so many years. While I can't say for certain what ages the priests were, I do remember that some were young, some middle aged, and one was much older. Chances are that they, too, may have died. I've looked at the lists of credibly accused priests released by the Boston and Worcester Dioceses, but I can't be sure if the names are accurate or even all there. I'm not looking to hurt anyone, but I don't want other children to go through what I did either. To heal, the Church has a long way to go.

According to the Boston Globe, forty-eight priests and other Archdiocesan employees were alleged to have abused children, while Cardinal Law headed the Boston Archdiocese. The Globe's investigation of the scandal opened a Pandora's box about sexual abuse in the Catholic Church. The 2015 Oscar-winning film *Spotlight*, in which Cardinal Law's character is portrayed, epitomizes clergy sex abuse. It would lead to widespread scandals in other parts of the country and the world.

On the positive side, the Boston Archdiocese under Cardinal Law's successor, Cardinal Sean O'Malley, has tried to be there for me. They pay for my therapy and spiritual direction. They sponsor survivor retreats and an annual Mass for survivors. Cardinal O'Malley meets with survivor groups. He's trying, and I think he's one of those making a difference.

I recall Fr. Kim, the wonderful and sweet priest who was so kind to me before I left the Church that first time. Perhaps one day I will contact Fr. Kim so I can thank him, take him out to lunch, and explain what happened.

There are other good priests who are trying, but they are afraid to say the wrong thing with a survivor for fear of being sued. I recall a survivor meeting at the Boston Archdiocese where a speaker was being challenged from the floor. A priest went over and put his hand on the man's shoulder, suggesting it was not the time to be interrupting. The man pressed charges against the priest. He was eventually reinstated, but it explains why so many priests don't want to get involved.

It's so sad to have that mindset, but priests are our shepherds and need to guard their sheep from harm.

As for me, I get apologies all the time for the sexual abuse I suffered at the hands of clergy.

I tell them, "You're not the ones who did this to me. Please don't apologize."

I hope and pray that this book gives new insight to what the survivor has to face, and it's about facing that pain. Sadly, so many survivors can't, and it leads to addictions and even suicide. After being asked to leave the church in Hopedale, I planned to kill myself, and even set a date to do it. That day, I got forty Benadryl tablets and a bottle of 100-proof vodka and planned to consume them so that I would never wake up. But my son woke up and out of nowhere said, "Mommy, please don't leave today."

Thank God for that intervention.

When I first started going to Fr. Carl, he emailed me a prayer from Fr. Rolheiser he suggested I say every day. It is about bringing one's wounds to the Eucharist, and I'd like to share it with other survivors who may be reading this:

Bring your aching body and heart to God. Express your helplessness in simple, humble words:

Touch me. Take my wounds. Take my paranoia.
Make me whole. Give me forgiveness. Warm my heart.
Give me the strength that I cannot give myself.

In closing, I would like to add this ending prayer:

God Lord Jesus in heaven, thanks for my wonderful family and all the wonderful blessings you have given me to help me heal and see Your love. We all have crosses to bear, and it's so hard sometimes to see Your grace and mercy from this abuse situation. It has affected my life in so many ways, both positively and negatively. The impact of other people's sin can affect us all deeply, and it hurts so bad at times. I am grateful that You can take care of our wounded hearts and shape them in the palm of Your hand to anything You want if we allow You to work in our lives and mold us into Your vessels, if we surrender our lives to You. I am learning that You love us and want what's best for us, even with our hurts and woundedness. I have struggled so much with fear and insecurity, and it's a cross I will always have to bear. But as I experience Your love and grace and mercy, life is getting easier. Thank You for the many blessings of friendship and support I have. I know some days are going to be better than others, but I am grateful and thankful that I have You guiding me through it all. Thank You for these life lessons, even if they are hard to understand at times.

As I look at this healing garden in my backyard in Milford Massachusetts, I see the beauty in God's grace, love, and mercy. Healing is so hard, and the loss of this child was so hard. As Catholics, we value life, and the loss was so great to me that this priest took my struggle as a personal attack on him. He labeled me as a crazy person, and it is only by the mercy of God I moved on. I considered suicide over it, but by God's grace and love, I learned that my pain can hurt others too. My openness on this with a therapist or trusted friend has shown me that this is a time of learning and hope. I pray my story can be a learning experience for other priests. It is still so hard to even go to Mass, move on, and heal, but I am doing it.

ABUSE *of* TRUST

From my Cross to my Resurrection

Deacon Bob Henkel

*Blessed be the God and Father of our Lord Jesus Christ, who in His great mercy gave us a new birth to a living hope through the resurrection of Jesus Christ from the dead, to an inheritance that is imperishable, undefiled, and unfading, kept in heaven for you who by the power of God are safeguarded through faith, to a salvation that is ready to be revealed in the final time. **In this you rejoice, although now for a little while you may have to suffer through various trials, so that the genuineness of your faith, more precious than gold that is perishable even though tested by fire, may prove to be for praise, glory, and honor at the revelation of Jesus Christ.***

1 Peter 1:4-7

My name is Deacon Bob J. Henkel Sr. I was ordained in the Camden Diocese of New Jersey on June 11, 2005, and I still cannot believe the good Lord called me, of all people, to be His servant in the Holy Catholic Church Let me reiterate: His Holy Catholic Church.

The faith which saved me, taking me off a long, lonely victim's trail to the path of a victor under Jesus Christ our Lord! You might call it my "Road to Emmaus."

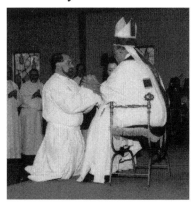

As I share my story, please understand I am opening myself up. I will become very vulnerable and very honest. In that vein, I will use exact circumstances and, most of the time, exact names (and will explain when I do not and why). What I am about to share is my history and my truth, and I wouldn't know how to share it any other way. It is also important to note that much of my history I am not proud of. More than this, I am very shameful and sorry and wish I could take it all back. Know there will be a lot of tears coming from my heart and my eyes as I am writing my account, because to share this with you is to relive every painful, shameful piece of it. However, there will also be tears of joy as my road leads to where I am today, still a sinner, but also a man of faith striving to be a better husband, father, friend, and deacon in God's Holy Church, one day at a time.

I am the second oldest of four boys, and as in many good Catholic families, we are all a little more than one year apart. We are cradle Catholics. We were baptized and received all of our Sacraments. We went to Church every Sunday and even went to Catholic school much of our lives; however, we didn't do this to increase our faith or to learn more about our Lord. We went through these motions so the neighbors would not talk about us. My mom and dad were, to me, the biggest fakes I had ever met. They had big egos, were self-absorbed, and had little self-esteem. We learned from a very young age that children should be seen and not heard. The worst thing we could do to our parents, especially my mom, was to embarrass her or the family.

My dad and mom were a working class, blue-collar family, much to their chagrin. They longed to be upper or middle-class. They wished to have nice material things and to 'keep up with the Joneses.' To my dad's credit, he kept working his way up the ladder no matter what it took. One of the ways he did this was by accepting transfers. I was born in Washington, D.C. We also lived in Maryland, North Carolina, South Carolina, Massachusetts, New Jersey, Tennessee, and Texas before moving back to New Jersey when I was about ten years old. We pretty much stayed there from that point on, which is why I always call New Jersey "home." All of our moving and learning to expertly put on facades to make everyone think we were happy and much richer than we actually were, taught us at a very young age that we could change our personality to suit whomever is in front of us so we would be accepted. This skill proved to be a handy tool, allowing us to easily assimilate to new schools and new locations.

Back in the late 60's and early 70's, moving up the corporate ladder meant business dinners, and these dinners always included drinking alcoholic beverages. As my dad kept progressing with each transfer, he attended more and more of these dinner meetings. The big problem was my dad was a bad drinker. Remember, the worst thing we could do, especially to my mom, was to embarrass her or the family. These meetings would always end the same way. When my dad came home, he could not walk to the door by himself, as he was too inebriated. His boss would be laughing along with my drunk father as dad was handed off to my mom, who was laughing with them until after the door shut and mom would hear the car drive away.

The laughing facade left quickly from mom's face, and the conversation turned very ugly, very fast. Raised voices escalated to physical abuse from both my mom and dad. I swore mom always got the best of the fights. There was pushing, slapping, choking, scratching, and knocking each other to the floor. Here we were, four young boys, ages 11, 10, 9 and 7 years old, trying to stop them.

"Dad just go to bed; take care of this in the morning."

"Mom, dad's drunk; just get him to bed, please!"

All of us crying and screaming to "please, please stop." When the fighting finally stopped, the four of us would return to bed, but be assured, we slept with one eye open, if we slept at all, those nights.

The next day would always look the same as well. My dad, obviously embarrassed he drank too much yet again, would sit at the kitchen table with a cigarette and a cup of coffee just staring into space with scratches on his face. My mom would be very busy, or at least looked like she was very busy, slamming cupboards, and putting laundry on. God forbid if dad tried to speak, he would be shut down immediately. Then, the phone would ring. (For those a little older, remember the phones that hung on the wall and had long cords so the person talking could roam around a bit). My mom loved to talk on the phone. She would pick it up, and it would be a friend or a family member. In an instant, mom's demeanor turned from anger and hate to laughter and peace: that is until she hung up the phone. The moment she did, her disgust, anger and hate returned. She wore this fake mask for the person on the other end of the line to make them believe everything was okay in the Henkel house. I heard a preacher once share a sentiment. He said when you ask someone how are you and they answer "fine," they are often not saying the truth. He said FINE is an acronym – Feelings, Inside, Never Exposed. This sure held true in our family, because what people saw of us outside our doors was nothing like the truth we lived on this inside.

"All the world is a stage..."

Throughout this masterpiece of theatre in which we lived through our early years, the four of us longed for what I believe the whole world longs. We wanted to feel like we were loved, as if we were somebody, and to receive affirmation. We would each try in our own way to get a little of this feeling from our parents. We learned pretty quickly, the best way to do this was to succeed in something. If the event making mom and dad most upset was to embarrass the family, we quickly found if we could turn it around, if we could do something mom and dad could brag about, we could feel a piece of this love which seemed too often to evade us. If we won in a contest, if our grades were among the best in the class, if we received any accolades in sports or school; we had a chance, for a little time, to get hugs and to hear our names mentioned on mom's many phone conversations.

I will never forget one time when I was the hero and the topic of conversation for weeks. Back then, the Sacrament of Confirmation was given in the sixth grade, when I was eleven years old. Mom talked to me about the big day. She said I would need a sponsor and would have to pick a confirmation name. She asked me to think about it and to get back with her and my dad. During this period, mom and dad had a great family friend named Fr. Claude Bender. Fr. Claude would often come by our house and go out to eat with my parents. One could see their friendship really forming and getting deeper. Another thing about Fr. Claude, we shared the same birthday, August 6. Confirmation was scheduled for May ,and as the date got closer, mom came to me and asked me about my sponsor and my confirmation name. I asked what she would think if I asked Fr. Claude to be my sponsor. You should have seen the joy in her eyes. This joy only multiplied when I also said I would take his name as my confirmation name.

She called Fr. Claude and put me on the phone, and he sounded excited as well. As I handed the phone back to mom, she immediately started sharing how proud of me she was and how this is a great moment for the family. It did not stop there; mom did not truly hang up the phone before calling at least six or seven people to tell them the great thing I had done. I was feeling the affirmation and love for which I longed. This feeling lasted for weeks. For a short time, it was as if I was the only child my parents had out of four boys. I was so happy and didn't want that feeling to ever stop. I thought, "So, this is what my friends have been feeling with parents who love them." Confirmation came and went, and so did the feeling of me being at the top of the sons' admiration and love chain.

The summer of that year (1973), we were getting ready to celebrate my twelfth birthday, which would be on a Monday. The Saturday before, our whole family was invited to Fr. Claude's brother's house in Pennsauken, NJ to celebrate his birthday. When father had off time from his pastoral duties, he would go over to his brother's house, who had built him an efficiency apartment in the backyard right next to  an above ground pool. It was nice. There was a sitting section, with a television, a wet bar, and a refrigerator, a bedroom area, and, of course a bathroom. Since it was going to be my birthday as well, Father Claude made sure there was also a small cake for me.

It was a hot summer August day with temperatures in the 90's. Before the party started, Father celebrated Mass in the kitchen with me as the altar server. After Mass, my brothers and I threw on our bathing suits and started swimming the day away. There was probably about forty people there, and everyone had a good time. As the day went on, people started to depart. Mom and dad called us to get dried off and get ready to leave. We begrudgingly hopped out of the pool and began getting ready.

Mom and dad had previously received a certificate for a romantic night at a hotel with dinner and champagne by some friends and were trying to think about who would take care of their four boys for the night. As one can imagine, trying to place one child for an overnight is difficult, but can you picture four boys? My parents were explaining their dilemma just as I came up and put my arm around my mom. Fr. Claude then said, "How about Bobby stay with me for the night, and I can bring him home to you around noon tomorrow?" First, my parents were surprised and asked if he was sure. My dad looked like he was thinking, "Okay, that takes care of one – three more to go." They asked if it would be okay with me. The Phillie's game was on, and I could swim more. I also never forgot how I was the hero when I asked Father to be my sponsor. I wanted to be the hero again. I looked at Father Claude, who said, "We will continue to celebrate our birthday." My family left with everyone else, and there we were, just Fr. Claude and I.

I was watching the Phillies, and it was still very warm outside. Father did not have air-conditioning but several fans, which helped a lot. He opened his refrigerator and pulled out an ice cold Rolling Rock eight oz. can of beer and asked me if I wanted one. It looked so good, and I asked him if I was allowed. He said, and I will always remember, "This will be our little secret, and afterall, it is our birthday!" I found something I was good at. That 8oz. can went down so smoothly and tasted delicious to me. Before the night was over, I had at least eight 8oz. cans. Remember, I was maybe 85 pounds soaking wet. I don't really remember going to sleep that night, but I will never forget waking up.

I woke up with his tongue in my ear, and as I looked at him, he had this really ugly smile on his face. He turned me over and said, "We are going to have some fun, and this will be another one of our little secrets." How is that for a birthday I only wish I could forget? When he took me home, he told my mom I was the perfect little gentleman. I excused myself and said I had to go to the bathroom. Mom tried to ask me more about the night, but I kept changing the subject and told her I wasn't feeling too well. I went to bed early that night. This began four years of sexual abuse. Until I was about to get married to my beautiful wife, I told absolutely no one what happened. I also know I wasn't Fr. Claude's only victim. On one occasion, he brought out a briefcase full of Polaroid's of young naked boys probably ages ten to seventeen. My picture, unfortunately, made it into the briefcase.

Life went on, at least on the outside. From this moment, I was

broken. I kept drinking at twelve-years-old and beyond. The drinks got stronger. I, from that first Rolling Rock, had a great tolerance for alcohol, and I hid it very well. As I progressed into my later teens and my early twenties, drinking turned into drugs and a lot of them. I never stuck a needle in myself, but if I could drink it, smoke it, pop it, or snort it, I did it. This progressed into becoming very promiscuous and a deranged gambler. However, through all of this, my childhood training kicked in stronger than ever. If you had met me then, you would have thought I was the happiest guy in the world, but on the inside I was F-I-N-E. During this time, I collected clowns. I probably still have close to a hundred clowns. To me, they represented my life, not just at that time but my whole life (up to about fifteen years ago). Clowns put all this paint and makeup on the outside and live their life just trying to make other people happy and to make them smile. They are hiding under all their make-up.

During the winter of my first year in high school, I had had enough hiding. I was tired of it all and could not take it anymore. At that time, my family lived on a very busy road, before streetlights and traffic lights were put in, at an intersection known for terrible car accidents. It was the beginning of February and it was cold outside – see your breath cold. Wearing my new high school jacket, I walked up and down the street. My plan was to wait for the right moment, and when a car came traveling too fast and close to the curb, I would jump out and finally finish the pain. The traffic was unusually slow for a Saturday night, so I kept walking. The road was dark and the trees were bare.

The only light on the street were a few stars shining, and a small light that hung over a big blue mailbox; they were bright enough just so people could see their mail drop in the box. I don't know what made me do this, but for some reason, I looked down and there on the ground was a piece of folded paper. Something drew me to this paper, so I walked over and picked it up. I unfolded it and here is what it said:

This is Me

This is me, accept me as I am. Please don't try to fit me into your stereotyped boxes. Don't label me a phony, because I am many people. There are many facets of my personality.
I do wear masks, however they are not all hiding masks;
some are very revealing masks but you may never know them all.

If you reject me or a part of me, I am hurt.
However, I could change that part of me to suit you but then that's not me, that's you.
Not everybody is going to like me and hey that's a fact hard to accept,
But if I change my life for everyone, then I am no one.

And if you can be happy with this new me, this plastic doll that you created,
Who thinks your thoughts, voices your opinions and feels your feelings,
then you are in love with you and not me;
I cannot be happy for me, therefore I cannot be happy for you
I am sorry for you!!

- Anonymous

Tears streamed down my face. I read that piece of paper over and over again. I hurried into my house and walked past my father, right into my bedroom. Since there were four boys, we never had our own room, but luckily, this Saturday night, my brothers were all out. I committed this piece of paper that saved my life to memory. Later in life, I thought it must have come from God, but there is no mention of God in the whole writing…or is there?

> *"But," said Moses to God, "if I go to the Israelites and say to them, 'The God of your ancestors has sent me to you,' and they ask me, 'What is his name?' what do I tell them?" God replied to Moses: I am who I am.* Then he added: This is what you will tell the Israelites: I AM has sent me to you. Exodus 3:13-14*

Back to that piece of paper that read - "This is me, accept me as I AM". God, my Father, I AM was with me all along, watching and protecting me.

Although this was a glimpse of good things, it was not enough to get me past my next encounter with Fr. Claude, or the next. As much as I tried to sidestep any possible meetings, it seemed I couldn't get away. Throughout my high school years, I put on my clown's face every day and dealt with whatever came my way.

Something amazing was happening to my mom and dad during this time. They went on a Catholic retreat for couples called Marriage Encounter. This retreat was the beginning of a true transformation for them. They met other couples who were real to their cores. These couples taught my parents they did not have to wear all the masks. They taught them God loves them so much, the way they are, and God has great plans for them. Mom and dad started hanging around these beautiful people more and more, and they changed right before my eyes. At first, I thought it was just another show, but time and consistency proved it was real. They went from people I never wanted to be like to people I wanted to emulate. I saw them reach out to those in need. I saw them take in people who were lonely or lost, feed the hungry, and truly live the corporal works of mercy. My dad, with my mom's total commitment and support, studied to be in the first class of deacons in the Camden Diocese. They began to realize the importance of the Eucharist. They tried to teach us receiving the true Body of Christ would give us the strength we needed to get through anything the world threw our way.

I guess for me a seed was planted, but I was still living my nightmare and still told absolutely no one what was happening. I managed to graduate in the top third of my class and received a little scholarship to attend a small college in Tennessee. I hopped at the chance and never looked back. This meant I was away from Fr. Claude, and I was so thankful. My trauma was buried inside me; however, the world would, at times, remind me it still had me in its grasp.

The next year of college, my scholarship money went dry, so I transferred to a state school in North Jersey: Kean College of NJ (now Kean University). I was delving more and more into drugs and partying, so I would not have to go to bed with my heart and mind reminding me of who the world told me I truly was. I sabotaged my relationships. When people would try to get close to me, I doubted their true motives. How could anyone love me? I'm damaged goods, and no one truly ever loved me before.

One young woman got very close to me, and I thought I truly loved her. I thought, for once, maybe someone could love me. I became so controlling, because I did not want to lose her. I believe I truly ruined a good part of her life. She was so smart, so kind, and had so much to look forward to. I just want to tell her I am SO sorry, and I wish I could take everything back. One of my very best friends in high school, who also shared my birthday and was an awesome friend and an amazing man, was collateral damage as he tried to help this young woman. I will not use their names, because I have yet to truly apologize to them. They were two amazing people. I have prayed so hard for them over my life and continue to do so. I truly hope they found all the happiness they deserve, and they deserve so much.

The following year found me at the same school but attending fewer and fewer classes. Another class of freshman came to campus, and with this class, an amazing young woman who would one day become my wife. Again, I was controlling hard and did everything I could to drive her away from me.

Something was different. This crazy girl wouldn't leave. Her name was Dana, and she was going to show me what true love was. We had a rocky go of it for a couple of years. Our good times were amazing but our lows were very ugly. She remained. I asked her to be my wife, and before we were married, I had to share with her my brokenness. I did not want to go into marriage with my awesome wife without her knowing how broken I was on the inside. I was afraid she would immediately leave me, but she told me the words I longed to hear, "Bobby, it wasn't your fault!" Dana continues to show me God and His Love everyday. God gave me this amazing example of His Love, and she continues to amaze me every day. Every day, I love her more and more. Thank you, Dana, for accepting me in all my brokenness and leading me to the path of goodness: the path of God. I don't believe I would have ever made it past my cross if it weren't for you!

God granted us two children, although we were still not going to Mass. Bobby was born in 1988, and Jennifer was born in 1990. With the responsibility of children, Dana and I realized we had to stop any use of drugs and had to be an example to our kids. However, I continued to try blocking out memories with alcohol. Mom and Dad continued to be awesome examples of God's Love and never moved backwards in their faith. They continued to be true servants and continued to lead my beautiful wife and I back to our faith by word and example. They told us we could find truth, and we can then truly be free. Lifting people up and showing Christ's Love was a daily activity for them.

At the beginning of 1993, mom was diagnosed with breast cancer that traveled to her bones. She fought hard until she went into remission. At that time, we transferred because of a job to Bayside, NY. It was 1994; our son was five and our daughter was three. My wife and I got together and thought, if we were ever going to teach our kids about God, we should do it now. We started going to a Mass within walking distance from our apartment. Once we entered the Sacred Heart of Jesus Catholic Church in Bayside, NY, we felt right at home. The community was welcoming, and the Pastor was amazing, a true shepherd of our Lord. All the kids at Mass would seat themselves as close to the aisles as possible, because when the Pastor would process in or out, he would make sure to high-five each child. We left Mass with our hearts on fire and with the beginning of an inside out renewal of faith for me and my wife.

We went back to Church for our kids and found it was really for us, too. We started getting involved in various ministries and sent our son and daughter to school there as well. I became a Lector and really loved proclaiming the Word of God, and I started to feel what the words communicated. As our faith started getting stronger, the world

was working to remind us how hard life can be. My job started to not only become uncomfortable, but I also felt I was being asked to act unethically. Right around that same time, I received a call from my mom, and she told us her cancer had come back with a vengeance. My wife and I looked at each other, and she said, "We have to go." I immediately went to talk with the landlord to break the lease. I called my brother, who was in the moving business, and asked my mom and dad if we could stay with them. We went to Easter Vigil Mass at Sacred

Heart and immediately drove home to Berlin, NJ to be with my family afterwards.

We were blessed to spend the last six weeks of my mom's life with her. Some of this time, she would need to be in the hospital, and I would spend the night. When we were alone, she would ask me to read the Bible to her. I remember one night, after I gave her a kiss, she asked me to read, and I opened to Matthew Chapter 6: 25-34.

"Therefore I tell you, do not worry about
your life, what you will eat [or drink], or about
your body, what you will wear. Is not life more
than food and the body more than clothing?

Look at the birds in the sky; they do not sow or reap,
they gather nothing into barns, yet your heavenly Father
feeds them. Are not you more important than they?
Can any of you by worrying add a
single moment to your life-span?

Why are you anxious about clothes? Learn
from the way the wild flowers grow.

They do not work or spin. But I tell you that not
even Solomon in all his splendor was clothed like one
of them. If God so clothes the grass of the field, which
grows today and is thrown into the oven tomorrow, will
he not much more provide for you, O you of little faith?

So do not worry and say, 'What are we to eat?'
or 'What are we to drink?' or 'What are we to wear?'
All these things the pagans seek. Your heavenly
Father knows that you need them all. But seek first
the kingdom [of God] and His righteousness, and
all these things will be given you besides. Do not
worry about tomorrow; tomorrow will take care
of itself. Sufficient for a day is its own evil.

After I finished, I closed my Bible and said, "Wow, mom, did you hear that?" I looked over, and my mom was sound asleep. I knew at that very moment, God meant this for me; He was talking to me, not my mom. Here I was, almost thirty-four years old, a college dropout without a job, a wife and two kids, and now living with my parents. I thought I was useless (as many in the world had told me over the years) and definitely not a man, by any means. When I got back to my parent's house, I shared the Scripture with my beautiful wife. There she was, looking in my eyes, almost gleaming and yelling, "Bobby, I believe in you. You are a good man! You are my man!" This passage, along with my parent's true conversion and my wife's deep love, was the catalyst for me wanting to study for the diaconate.

I dove into my faith. I wanted to learn more about the Word and kept reading the very Book that saved my life on more than one occasion. My mom, over the next few weeks, shared her deep devotion to Mary and Adoration with me. She was the first one who took me to Adoration and showed me the beauty of sitting in front of our Lord and Savior Jesus Christ. We talked a lot about our faith before she passed, and yet, I never told her about my abuse. I saw my mom, in the last week of her life and hardly cognizant, find out there was a family in need. She picked up the phone and started calling people until the family had their needs met, not just for the day, but for as long as they needed. She was my hero.

All during my childhood, I was living with parents I loved but did not like or respect. One weekend of diving into an understanding of their true Catholic faith on a Marriage Encounter weekend and meeting those who lived their faith changed these two people from those I preferred not to look at or be around to my heroes. Living the Gospel, sharing the Eucharist, sitting in Adoration and learning the faith made them stronger one day at a time. It is just more proof; it is never too late!

Over the years, I started to share my story to more and more sisters and brothers, especially if I found myself talking with others who experienced the same type of trauma. Many ask me, "Deacon Bob, how can you have such a deep Catholic faith after this priest did what he did to you?" I tell them, "It wasn't my faith that did this to me; it was one very sick man whom I now pray for and forgive. My faith saved me! My faith made me realize who I AM. I am not a victim; I AM a victor under my savior Jesus Christ. I AM a child of God. I AM loved and I AM forgiven."

We all need to work on all our relationships each and every day. I need to stay in prayer and to stay in the Scripture. I need to be around great sisters and brothers in Christ, who are continually lifting me and my family up and keeping us focused, not just reminding us of the Cross, but also to stay focused on the Resurrection. As Pope Saint John Paul II stated, "We are an Easter people and Hallelujah is our song!"

Father, I now see Your Hand guiding and protecting me in my darkest hours. I know how much You Love me, and I thank You for using my Crosses to bring about not only my resurrection but to also allow me to use my hurts to help others to mend. I thank You for my ministry in Your Holy Church! I thank You for the good people you put into my life: my parents, my brothers and sisters, awesome shepherds, my amazing children, and, most of all, my most beautiful wife, Dana of almost thirty-four years (Dana, I Love you SO much). Continue to guide Dana and I to be an example of Your Love to our children and all Your children You allow into our lives. Amen and I pray it again, AMEN!

ABUSE *of* TRUST

The Family is Standing

Letitia and Deacon Scott Peyton

I can vividly recall the day Scott came home and told me that he had signed up for RCIA (Rite of Christian Initiation of Adults) to become Catholic. I was baptized a Catholic, but my family was not actively practicing Catholicism. I attended Catholic schools and went to Mass with my family on the occasions that they went, mostly as a child. As we grew older and my grandmother passed away, we no longer went to Mass. Although my faith wasn't instilled in me as a child, I did want a Catholic wedding. At the time of our wedding, Scott was Methodist but was perfectly fine with a Catholic wedding. Even though we were not practicing Catholics until after our second child was born, we  did, from time to time, attend Mass. After we moved to Lafayette in the year 2000, we began attending Mass at Holy Cross. At Holy Cross, our lives changed very radically from a lukewarm faith, at best, to a faith on fire. It was at Holy Cross that Scott heard the call to become Catholic.

When Scott wanted to become Catholic, I guess you could say I was shocked. Scott was not the kind of person to take anything in life lightly and to make the decision to become Catholic was not just on a whim. I knew it was something he had given a lot of thought to. I wanted very much to share in his journey to Catholicism, so I went to RCIA classes alongside him. It was during this time that I realized my faith and my knowledge of my faith was, for the most part, non-existent. I was a terrible Catholic, and I had no idea! After Scott became Catholic, our lives changed quickly. We had four more children. Somewhere in between having children, I started to homeschool, and Scott heard the calling to become a Deacon. Our lives and our faith became the kind which gave us a peace and joy that

was beyond measure. Our children were a part of almost everything we did in our parish. We included them in most everything, and as a family, we enjoyed all that our parish had to offer to families.

Our two oldest sons, Alex and Oliver, have always been very close as brothers and best friends. They shared many of the same friends from a very young age, and participated in almost every aspect of their lives together, including Catholic sponsored events when their age difference allowed. They were inseparable from very young ages. They served as altar boys together in Mass. As our four younger children came one by one, they followed the same pattern. Since they came in pairs, two boys, two girls, and two boys, I suppose you could say God gave each of them a best friend who happened to be a sibling. The two older boys happily mentored their four younger siblings.

Our home was always filled with Catholic "things." If you were to walk into our house, there was no doubt as to our Catholic faith. We have statues, pictures, books, and rosaries everywhere. Our Catholic faith was being lived in our family in every way and through all of our senses. We went to Mass as a family, and we prayed the rosary as a family. Our faith was at the center of our lives and visible to all who knew us and those who came to know us. We loved our Church, our priests, and all those religious that we became friends with in our family journey. We even took family vacations to Benedictine Monasteries with the kids.

When our oldest son graduated from high school, he left home to attend Ave Maria University in Ave Maria, Florida. It was joyful and, at the same time, a bit sorrowful. We were happy to have him going to a wonderful university, but at the same time, our oldest was leaving home and was going to be seventeen hours away. When we left to bring him to Florida for his first semester, it was fitting that Oliver was with us. He was able to say goodbye to his brother and assume his new role now as the oldest son in the house. Being the oldest son meant he would now recite the last decade of the rosary and lead prayer during the day while Scott was at work, among other things. We seemed to settle in to a new family life while Alex was away at college for his first semester.

Then one day, a couple of years later, out of nowhere, Oliver said, "I'm not serving at Mass anymore." We were shocked. We couldn't understand. Why the sudden change? We attributed it to him getting older. We talked with family members, and the conclusion was that he was just being a teenager and losing his best friend and brother to college was causing the changes in his behavior. It didn't make much sense to us, since it seemed like a delayed reaction of over two years. We knew he was sad to see his brother going off to college, but it was the only explanation we had at the time.

Soon, he didn't want to go to Mass with us, and it was becoming more difficult to get him to participate in praying the family rosary. Each night, before we began to pray our family rosary, the kids each took a turn speaking their prayer intentions. When Oliver prayed with us, his intention was always the same, "For the spiritual and physical well-being of my family." As time went on, things continued in a downward spiral with him. We continued to look for answers. We knew something was wrong, but we could not get any answers from him and people continued to tell us it was just his age. While this seemed a plausible explanation, we weren't convinced. We knew our son well; we could see he was not happy, and something was bothering him.

In May 2015, Alex had decided that he felt called to enter the seminary. His decision didn't surprise anyone. People suspected he had a calling. He came home from Ave after a spring semester and went through the process to enter the seminary for our Diocese. Oliver was very upset to say the least. He did not want his brother entering the seminary. At the time, we could not understand why he was so opposed to his brother entering the seminary. None of it really made sense to us. I specifically remember a time when he told Alex, "You will become like them." As it turned out, a few weeks before Alex was to leave for seminary, he discerned that he did not have a vocation to the priesthood and decided not to go. At the time, Scott and I were praying that Alex was making the right decision and not just getting cold feet.

Oliver was now enrolled in the local community college for a technical degree in Diesel Technology. He was attending school and doing very well. Ever since he was a young child, he had been good at taking things apart and fixing things. He hated school but loved learning. He loved doing physical work and working with his hands. He and Alex always had a "project" going on. Oliver was always headstrong and convicted. I used to tease and say the book, *The Strong Willed Child*, by Doctor James Dobson, was written with him in mind. His strong convictions had always served him well. He was very much convicted to do what was right and loved his faith. He was the kind of person that was full of compassion for everyone around him. Since he was homeschooled, he had many opportunities to help people when other kids were not around.

Together with Alex, they would take our neighbor, who was a paraplegic, to his doctor's appointments and to the hospital when there was no one else to help him. Our neighbor had rods in his back and moving him could be very painful, if he was not properly handled. He trusted Alex and Oliver, and they became the ones who would carry him from his wheelchair to the car and out again, when his wife was not able to tend to him. They would go fishing with him, take him out to dinners that he was invited to, and keep him company. Our neighbor loved guns and would ask the boys to shoot guns with him. He taught them the skills that he knew. After Alex left for college, Oliver continued to help our neighbor. Oliver would do his school work around his doctors' appointments, so he could take him to the doctor, the pharmacy, shopping, or whatever he needed. He would tease Oliver and tell him he was the son he never had. Our neighbor passed away when Oliver was eighteen. This was another difficult time for Oliver, as he was so close to him.

Our neighbor wasn't the only person Oliver and Alex would help. They both helped our priest during the day, when their school work was done. After Alex left for Ave Maria, then Oliver became the sole helper. Sometimes, our priest would pick him up and bring him home when he was done; other times, I would drop him off. After Oliver got his driver's license, he would drive himself. Father always needed help killing ants around the church, the rectory, and the church hall, picking up limbs, clearing out the ditches that were not draining, fixing his phone, updating the computers, and other little odd jobs. There was always something that needed to be done for the Church, and Oliver was able to do whatever it was. Our parish Church was very small and very rural.

The Diesel Technician certification program that Oliver was enrolled in at the community college was eighteen months long. He had enrolled as soon as he graduated from school at the age of seventeen. It was something that he was very excited about doing. So, when he came home and said he wanted to quit school, shortly after receiving a scholarship for top student and with only a few months to finish, we were devastated. This was when the lowest of the lows began. He had just a few weeks left to graduate from school, and he had the promise of a full-time job with benefits already secured. He basically had everything an eighteen year old could hope for, and yet, he was so unhappy. He seemed so willing to just throw away the last year and a half and start something new, yet he didn't even know what that "new" could be. Scott and I were at a loss. He was doing what he liked to do, and yet, he was so unhappy.

Oliver seemed to be searching or reaching for something aimlessly, and now he wanted to quit school. We had no idea how to reason with him or figure out the root of his problem. We knew there was more than what he was telling us, but he wasn't willing to open up to us even though we are a very close family. We also had four younger children in the house, who were witnessing their older brother's sadness and our struggle to help him. We knew the value of family and the influence that grandparents can have on children, especially when parents are struggling. We also knew that we could not hide this problem that Oliver was experiencing. We knew there was a cause for his unhappiness, and we were not going to give up. We asked Scott's mom to talk to Oliver. She was very close to him, and we knew she could at least convince him to finish school, if nothing else.

During all these struggles, Scott and I were still very active in parish ministry. We led many different church groups. I led women's groups, he led men's groups, and, on occasion, we lead a couple's group. We taught marriage prep, CCD classes, planned the Sacraments, etc. for our parish. Scott would preach homilies on the first weekend of each month and at each Thursday evening Mass. He also led a perpetual rosary for Our Mother of Perpetual help for a local parish a few minutes away from us for a couple of years. We were always busy with family, as well as Church, activities, and most of the time, the two were inseparable. Father was always involved with or near to what we were involved in and our children were always with us. The community knew our children well, as did many of the priests in our Diocese.

Father would take us to lunch or to dinner after we finished a parish ministry or after a Sacrament had been administered in the parish. He would always tell us it was to celebrate all the hard work we did for the parish or to celebrate our birthdays, his birthday, or our anniversary, there always seemed to be an occasion. He said he wanted to make sure we knew how much he appreciated all that we did for him in the parish. We always went with Father to show our gratitude to him for trusting us with so much responsibility in the parish and because he always said he enjoyed being with us.

He shared a unique friendship with us because we were not just parishioners, but he and Scott were ordained clergy of the Church. Scott was able to attend many events in the Diocese and then report back to Father about what he had missed, when he did not attend. Scott, being a deacon, gave us particular insights into the Church and friendship with many of the priests of our Diocese. Since we were very active in our parish and in our Diocese, we were friends with many priests, deacons and their wives, and people in ministry across the Diocese. We  had even met people from different parts of the country who were very involved in the Catholic Church. We were living our faith with vigor and thought we were doing well as a family--until that Sunday night when Scott's phone rang.

• • • • • • • • • • • • • • • •

It was a Sunday night, and my phone rang shortly before midnight, but it only rang once. It was my oldest son, Alex, who when I went to bed was outside with his younger brother. The phone rang again, but this time, he did not hang up. He asked me to come outside. He told me "not to wake mom up" or let her come outside with me. As I walked out of the front door, Alex immediately came to me, and I could tell that he was upset. He told me that I had to promise him two things. The first was that I would not leave the house that night and the second thing was that I would not hurt anyone. I agreed and thought that between the two of them, one of them must have broken something of mine. When I walked under the carport, I immediately noticed a plastic Adirondack chair broken into pieces. I began to question them about what had happened to the chair when I noticed Oliver, he was sitting in another chair with his head down. I could see that he had been crying. Alex then told me to sit down because Oliver had something to tell me. Oliver first asked me again to keep my promises that I had made to Alex. I agreed, and then, he began to tell me what our priest had done to him. I was in complete shock. I was angry. I hurt for my son. I then realized why they had asked me to make the two promises.

I told Oliver that this had to be reported to the police and that we would go in person as soon as the Sheriff's Office opened in the morning, and he agreed. I also warned him that people would be upset with us for reporting Father. Even though I knew this, I didn't realize to what extent the people in our community would go to keep the "good reputation" of their beloved "priest". All I could do was hug my sons. As a father, I was helpless and devastated and realized this was what Oliver had been feeling for three years; I was hoping that this was a nightmare that would soon end. However, it wasn't.

After making sure Oliver and Alex were emotionally stable enough to leave alone, I returned to the house. I was dreading how I was going to tell Letitia. I knew she had woken up when I was walking out of the room. I knew this was going to be devastating for her too. This was going to be the most difficult thing I had ever had to tell my wife.

• • • • • • • • • • • • • • • •

I remember hearing Scott's cell phone ring and hearing him say, "Okay, I'm coming. No, mom is asleep." I suppose I fell back to sleep for a while after that. The next thing I remember is Scott waking me up. He was sobbing. I panicked! It was after midnight, and I had been awakened to him crying and trying to tell me something. I couldn't understand his words, and my heart was beating so fast. I wasn't sure if I just wasn't understanding or if he just couldn't speak. I told him to just stop. I needed a moment to pray and be ready for what he was about to tell me. I knew at this moment that there was something terribly wrong and that somehow it involved our sons. Scott just sat on the edge of the bed and waited for me to finish praying. I suppose it gave him a moment to collect himself too. After a few minutes, I told him to tell me. Then, he began to tell me. I was not in the least bit prepared for the news. I was in shock. I was stunned. I was speechless. I'm not even sure I was able to speak right away. After a few moments, I began to cry. How could our priest do this? How could we not have known? Why didn't Oliver tell us?

· · · · · · · · · · · · · · · · ·

Letitia didn't want to hear the details. She made me stop telling her what happened at the point where she knew she could no longer bear to hear it. I stopped at that point to allow her some time to regain herself before going on. I told her that as soon as the Sheriff's Office opened in the morning, I was going to take Oliver to file a report. She was so hurt, upset, and crying. She then asked me, "What are we going to do?" The only answer I could give her was to say, "We are going to have to practice what we preach. This is where we are going to be tested. We will have to rely on our faith." These are words that are very hard to live by, even today.

Dear God, what do we do, was my only thought. I think we just sat together in bed for a while and cried. Then, I needed to hold my son. I needed to talk to him. I needed to apologize to him for not knowing. I think I felt every emotion humanly possible for a mother to feel for the next few hours before daybreak.

At the time that we found out about what had happened to Oliver, I had been working for the State of Louisiana as a Probation and Parole Officer for nearly ten years. My job included working with people who had committed many different kinds of crimes, including sex offenders. I guess my law enforcement background began to present itself as Letitia and I talked, and I began to see more clearly that what Father had been doing for years was grooming us to gain our trust. He befriended our family, so he could molest our son. His cheerful attitude and constant joking were all part of his plan.

As the hours went by, it seemed like an entire lifetime before daybreak, Letitia and I began to reflect on the past few years with Father. What did we miss? How did we not see this? How could we, of all people, not see this coming? We had trusted Father, and Oliver trusted him too. Even the younger children, how would we handle this with them? What would we tell them about our priest? They knew and loved him as well. He had administered the Sacraments to them. What would we do with all the pictures we had with him. Do we throw them away leaving no pictures of First Communion? Do we toss them out and lose our photographs from Confirmation?

As Letitia and I waited for the sun to rise, I was recalling every moment that Oliver had told me about what had happened to him in the rectory. I recalled how his face was filled with pain and sorrow and how difficult it was for him to tell me the details of what Father had done to him. The look of betrayal on his face was unbearable. I was thinking about Alex as he had to hear this from Oliver and how painful it was for him. The sorrowful faces of my two sons that night will forever be etched into my memory. This was our priest, not some stranger! It was at this moment that I realized that I had been blinded by the "Roman Collar." This man, whom we trusted, had patiently groomed not only our son, but Letitia and I and our family as well, using his priesthood to gain our trust and to gain closeness to our family to allow him to commit this crime against our son.

As a father, this is one of the worst things that could ever happen to your family. I am prepared to protect my home from intruders, and I have over ten years of experience as a law enforcement officer. As a husband and father, I worked with Letitia to prepare our children spiritually. We did what "good Catholics" were supposed to do. We befriended priests, we invited them into our home, and we even encouraged our children to discern whether they had a vocation to the priesthood. I sacrificed time away from my children for over five years to discern and study to become a deacon. We wanted the best for our children spiritually. We homeschool our children, and we have always had a very close relationship with all of our children. Our four younger children all admire and look up to their older brothers. Before May 2018, we had never experienced such an attack on our family or our faith.

It seemed like this was the darkest, longest night that we had ever lived through, as we reflected on the last twelve years with Father. I started thinking about all the meals we shared with him, the times he came to our home, and the times I took my children with me when I went to the rectory and the Church. I began to think about all the Masses that I served with him at the altar and all the times my sons were present at the altar as servers. Did he ever think about what he had done to my son as I served with him at the altar? As he placed the Eucharist upon my tongue? It was as if a death had occurred in our family. A sudden death that involved a child and our faith at the same time. This was a kind of death like nothing else we had ever experienced. We had always turned to the Church for comfort in our times of trials, and now, this was the biggest trial we were facing and turning to a priest for help was the last thing we wanted to do. We began to wonder about every priest we knew. Was he capable of the same thing? Had any of them done this to anyone else's family? Finally, as the morning broke, Oliver and I left to go to the Sheriff's department, leaving Letitia at home with the rest of our children.

· · · · · · · · · · · · · · · · ·

I sat in a chair in my yard under my favorite tree while Scott and Oliver went to file the report. I prayed and prayed for help and understanding from God. I clearly heard the words of Jesus, "Are you going to leave me too?" I think I may have whispered out loud, "No, Lord. Where would I go?" I wanted to run but didn't even know where to run. I wanted to call someone but didn't know who to call. Scott had asked me not to say anything to anybody until he called me.

Since I was alone, I began to wonder how were we going to tell the four younger children? They were so young. Would they even understand? How much do we tell them if we tell them anything? What would this do to their faith? What would they think of us? Would they blame us for what happened to their brother? How would we tell Scott's parents, my parents, our brothers and sisters, and all of our cousins? What would our families think, especially those who had strong anti-Catholic opinions? Were they going to blame us? What do we say to our friends? What will our friends say? Do we even tell anyone at all?

We had lived very open Catholic lives to this point. We had six children; they were happily involved in all aspects of the Catholic faith. Scott was a deacon, and I was involved in ministry as well. Was this the reward for living out our Catholic faith? I was devastated. My husband was devastated. My oldest son was devastated. And, more importantly, our son had been hurt by a priest that we had known, trusted, and called a friend for twelve years. I had no answers! There was no plan that I could formulate in my mind to make things better. Where was the parent manual for how to handle this? Where was the list of numbers to call for help?

Finally, after a few hours, Scott called to say that Oliver had filed the police report. He shared with me the things that the detectives had told him. One of the things was that our local law enforcement didn't want us to inform our Diocese about the allegation because of the risk that the Diocese would send him away or hide him. We thought that was absurd! Why would our Diocese do such a thing? We belong to the Catholic Church. We are Christians! We could not conceive of the idea, in the very beginning, that our own Church would do such a thing or why the police would even think that. Despite having all trust shattered the night before, we knew we had to trust someone, and with Scott being in law enforcement, we agreed to trust them and let them do their job.

After our local law enforcement gave us the okay to inform the Diocese, Scott called our parish priest to inform him. It was about a week after Father had initially met with law enforcement. Scott met with our parish priest, and then, we both met with our Vicar General and another priest who had been a longtime friend of ours, who now worked in the Diocesan offices. I asked to step out of the room while Scott gave the details of what happened to Oliver. This was not something I could bear to hear. When I came back into the conference room with Scott, they asked more questions and seemed to have many concerns about the details of what had happened. Since this was the week of Alex's wedding, they offered to get us counseling before the wedding. This began the first of several meetings we were to have at the Diocese.

As a Catholic mother, I thought I was doing all the right things to instill a love of Christ and the Catholic faith into my children. We supported our priest and the priests of our Diocese. Was this to be the end result? Why would anyone else want to follow our example? No one had ever so much as hinted at the idea that being an active Catholic family could have resulted in this. What were we to do as parents? How was I going to get my son, my husband, and the rest of my children through this? What does a wife and mother do in this situation? No one had the answers to these questions.

· · · · · · · · · · · · · · · ·

As a husband, father, and deacon, my faith has been shaken to the core. The foundation of all that we believed in, regarding the institutional Church, has been shattered. Before May 2018, we had our Church and our priests to provide spiritual guidance. If we had something going on, we were able to find comfort and peace from the guidance of a pastor or a brother deacon. The hurt we are now experiencing is coming from the very place where we sought comfort. Out of fear of retaliation, some of my brother deacons and priests are admittedly afraid to even speak out against what has happened to my son. This puts me in the position of fighting a spiritual battle mostly alone and with little spiritual guidance.

· · · · · · · · · · · · · · · · ·

After each meeting at the diocese, we always left feeling completely physically and emotionally drained. I cried through most of the meetings. I dreaded each meeting but felt it was necessary for my son's healing, for my husband's healing as a father and a deacon, and for me as wife and mother. It was necessary to help us to get past this trauma. There was this hope that after any given meeting, all would just be resolved. There would be answers and healing. But, this was not the case.

Initially, we wanted to remain anonymous. I suppose most victims do, as well as their families. I just could not imagine having our son being subjected to this publicly. Only a handful of people, who we knew very well, knew about what was going on during the first few weeks. Oliver needed healing, and he needed privacy. We needed privacy as a family to protect our younger children.

· · · · · · · · · · · · · · · · ·

As time went on and we were meeting at the Diocesan Offices, we were encouraged by both the Vicar General and our Bishop to treat this situation as if we were a family and to work it out as a family would work it out. This was probably not the best analogy, as it turned out to be more like a very dysfunctional family. Letitia and I eventually met with our Bishop to discuss with him what happened to our son. A few weeks after we met with our Bishop, Oliver met with him to tell him about what happened to him. A short time later, our son Alex also met with our Bishop asking him to laicize Father as punishment for what he had done to his younger brother. Our Bishop assured Alex that Father would be punished by the Church for what he had done.

We continued to meet with the Vicar General, on a few more occasions, as a couple, and we also met with the Director for the Permanent Diaconate for the Diocese upon his request. We wanted to be as open as possible, since we were seeking answers and healing for our son and family. We were told that if we sought an attorney the Diocese would have to stop paying for counseling. Our main concern was for our son and getting him the help he needed. He was going to counseling and the Diocese was paying for his counseling, for our son,

Alex, and for ours as well. We were fearful, as parents, that we could jeopardize counseling for Oliver.

. . . .

We soon realized that our hopes of remaining anonymous were not going to be granted. Our Bishop knew that our son was getting married on the Saturday after we had informed the Diocese. On the day of Alex's wedding, our Bishop made the announcement to the Church parishes where Father was serving as parish priest that he was being removed from parish ministry because of an allegation. He made the announcements during the afternoon Masses at both parishes. He gave too many details about the family that had made an accusation against Father. The most telling detail he told them was that the family had moved from Morrow to a Church parish in Ville Platte. The parishes were so small that anyone who had left would have been known, but to say that the family went to Ville Platte, really gave us away. There were only two churches in Ville Platte and only one family that had recently moved to one of the parishes and that was us. Parishioners knew it was one of our sons, they just didn't know if it was Alex or Oliver.

Some of those who were at the wedding began receiving text messages from other parishioners and knew about what was happening as the wedding ended. At the reception, some of the deacons were checking their email messages on their phones and recognized that Scott had been deacon to the accused priest named in the email. They asked Scott about it at the reception. We had not yet told our families about what had happened to Oliver. The most important event in our oldest son's life was happening, and we wanted our family members to focus on the wedding, not this tragedy. We just prayed to make it through the night before our extended family members knew what was happening in our own little family.

I received a message that our Bishop was going to make a media statement on the Monday following the wedding and that we needed to be prepared. We decided to leave town on the Sunday after the wedding. We knew at this point that we needed to tell our younger children something about what happened and to have some time for ourselves to recover from the physical activities and emotions of the wedding and what we were dealing with within our Church. We took Oliver and all the younger children with us and left town for the week. Close friends offered to let us use their lake house that was remote and had no phone service. Our counselor thought this would be the best setting to tell the younger ones about what happened and that it was important to have Oliver present when we told them.

Scott had already dealt with telling his parents and told his mom to tell their family. I had reluctantly placed the burden of telling my family what happened to Oliver on my sister. She agreed to ask the rest of our family, my brothers with their families and my parents, out to lunch on the Sunday after the wedding, while we would be away, and tell them. This gave them time to find out what happened, and since we were in a remote place without phones, I would not have to try to answer questions or explain anything. I knew I would not be able to speak about this with my mom and my dad, especially after the wedding. I did not want them to hear me crying and in complete despair. I also did not want them to find out from the media, nor did I want them to find out from someone else now that the parish knew and the local media would be reporting on it.

• • • • • • • • • • • • • • • •

Some of the parishioners of St. Peter and Chapel of the Resurrection, the parishes that Father and I were assigned to, made up stories claiming that Alex and Oliver lied about the accusation and that our family did this because I had been transferred a year prior to the allegation from Morrow to Ville Platte. They even met one of our friends in the parking lot of a local store to discuss our family and how they thought the timeline of events did not "add up," so it had to be a lie. We were trying to figure out how they could be coming up with a timeline, since we were not talking to anyone about a timeline nor had we told anyone of the dates that Father had gone to the sheriff's department. But as it turned out, they were having lunch with Father at his house, and so, we had to assume that he was sharing the dates with them.

At some point after Father had been removed as pastor, there was a luncheon for him that members of the parish council organized for parishioners to come and help him pack and to say goodbye. Each day, we learned new things that became ever more burdensome and painful to us. We were beginning to feel this was going to be a never ending hell. We were realizing why so few victims ever came forward.

· · · · · · · · · · · · · · · ·

As a mother, I cannot comprehend the idea of my son having to heal from the abuse of a priest, fight for justice, defend himself from those who think he is lying, all while feeling alone and betrayed by his priest and wanting to protect his family from the hurt and sorrow he knew they would also feel. This is what clergy sexual abuse does to a victim and their family, those families that know of the trauma. This is too much even for a close family to have to heal from, so I cannot imagine a victim doing it alone. I made a promise to help purge the Church of this evil, so in fighting for my son, my hope is that our story will help other victims and their families heal.

My son is first and foremost the one affected by what happened. It pains Letitia and I to know that for three years he held this horrible trauma inside of him. For three years, he had to deal with this all alone. I just can't imagine. I have had such a hard time reconciling this with the Church's response. For three years, we spoke to him about becoming a priest, we prayed the family rosary, we pushed him to go to Mass, and we spoke to him about our faith and how important it is to us. For three years, we tortured him without even knowing it. During those three years, he saw us go out to dinner with Father. He saw me standing at the altar with Father. He heard us have conversations about Father and other priests. For three years, we put our son through horrible, torturous reminders of what had happened to him.

There are no words to adequately express how much I wish we would have never met Father and that this would have never happened to our son and our family. Unfortunately, we are not alone. Not long after Oliver came forward, the crisis in Philadelphia unfolded, and then, the flood gates were opened. The abuse was not just a Diocese of Lafayette problem but a worldwide problem.

We then began to feel some relief, not because we realized that the corruption was throughout the Church, but that hearing it somehow validated what had happened to our son. We began to feel relief, because the news was being made public and people could no longer discount victims of clergy abuse. The stories were all basically the same. With each new story continuing to come to light, comes the thought, "What are we doing here?" Do we fight the corruption in our church or do we run? I am still conflicted by the fact that I am an ordained member of the Catholic Church, the same Church that covers up crimes of sexual abuse.

It was a very difficult decision for us to file a civil suit. It was our son who expressed that he could no longer go to the chancery for meetings. He began to feel very uncomfortable in the meetings with the Vicar General. We wanted him to be in control and not feel forced to do things because his dad was a deacon, and I didn't want to be used in that way either.

· · · · · · · · · · · · · · · · ·

The day the civil suit was filed, I was contacted by members of the Diocese that first asked me if I was planning on resigning as a deacon and then told me that I may be removed from the clerical state. I could not believe what was happening. At this rate, I would be removed from the clerical state before the priest who molested my son. I spent an entire day waiting for the official decision. The next day, several members of the Diocese each called me claiming to have worked out a deal with the Bishop to keep me as an active deacon. This is when I realized that this whole process was not going to be a sprint, but a very long marathon.

Little has been done pastorally by our local church to help us heal. To my knowledge, very little, if anything, has been done to help the collateral victims like the parishioners of St. Peters and Chapel of Resurrection. They are torn between the collateral victims and a group of Father's followers, who continue to literally wine and dine him and believe that he could not have done this to our son, despite his full confession and now his incarceration. We can't begin the healing process until the Church hierarchy begin to acknowledge that there is hurt in the parishes where Father served and until they acknowledge that there is hurt in our family and the many families who are collateral damage. Many of the churches where Father served still hang his photograph on church property. He has yet to go through any canonical court proceedings and still proclaims that he is a "Catholic Priest."

On April 30, 2019, the priest who molested our son was sentenced to ten years of hard labor, three of those years are suspended, and upon release, he will be on supervised probation for another three years. At the time we are writing this chapter, he has filed a motion for a hearing for the judge to reconsider his sentence because he is claiming that it is too harsh for him. He is still a priest with the Diocese of Lafayette, Louisiana, but his status is on leave. We are, again, set back in the healing process as is the community and the Diocese. People are conflicted with the idea that the priest, who consecrated the Eucharist, gave them spiritual direction, administered the Sacraments to their children, heard their confessions, and married them, is now in jail. It is a hard pill to swallow that a man who stands in Persona Christi would be capable of such heinous sexual acts and feel like he needs no punishment for his crimes.

The majority of my brother deacons, along with Diocesan leadership, refuse to acknowledge the situation publicly. This is part of what we feel is the second betrayal. The clergy, priests and deacons, who don't know how to deal with this situation or are too concerned about their positions and what their parishioners will think, say and do nothing. They do nothing, while there are hundreds of victims and thousands of family members who suffer from the effects of clergy abuse. Many of my brother deacons and priests have said, "It's not my problem," or, "I can't get involved." The fact that they won't get involved is why we have a problem. To those members of the clergy who have offered their support, we are so appreciative of their courage and support. They give us hope that all is not lost. They give us hope that we are making the right decision to stay and fight for the Truth, our faith, and, most importantly, for our son and all victims.

In 2001, I chose to become Catholic. This conversion has been the driving force that moved Letitia and I to live a more Christ-centered life. Letitia and I left behind good paying careers and a large house in a great neighborhood, so that we could focus on what meant the most in our life: Christ, our marriage, and our family. We wanted to live the Gospel and be faithful Catholics. We were open to life and family. We downsized our secular lives in order to be good parents to our children.

Today, everything we have done to strive towards "living a good Catholic life" has been used against us in this battle for justice for our son. The perpetrators have taken on the role of victim, while the victims have been chastised for being faithful to the teachings of the Church.

As much as we did not want to be in the public eye, we realize that our story being shared in public has helped others. Our hope is that the hierarchy, as well as priests at the parish level, will realize the full extent of the trauma to the victims, their families, and the communities. I don't believe that the full extent of the abuse can be measured just by knowing the number of victims. With each victim comes a family that has to suffer as well. The victims, their families, and the communities need healing and hope.

Don't Quit Before The Miracle

Valarie Brooks

While I guess I am not a true "Cradle Catholic," I grew up Catholic. The first five years of my life, my family didn't attend any church at all, but once it became time for me to go to school, my mother wanted to send me to a parochial school. She was a fallen-away Catholic, and my father was not religious or Catholic. However, back in the late 1960's and early 1970's, everyone seemed to agree that Catholic schools provided a superior education. Even though we lived way out in the country, my mother would get us both up in time to drive into town so I could get a better education.

I attended Catholic grade school for six years, and all my friends were Catholic. We attended daily Mass before our classes would start. We learned our prayers together, received the Sacraments together, and played together. My friendships led me to enjoy and respect these practices, which moved me to ask my mother to please start going to Sunday Mass with me. She was happy to do so. If her schedule allowed, she also began attending daily Mass when she dropped me off at school. I lived in my little Catholic world and felt very secure there. Even though these were the tumultuous years following Vatican II, when there were so many changes happening in the Church, I received great formation and a solid foundation. Our parish was small and only had one classroom for each grade, but we had everything we needed, including some truly wonderful nuns and priests who deeply cared about us.

I entered public school in seventh grade, because there were no secondary Catholic schools in our tiny little Southeastern New Mexico town. There, I met many people of different beliefs. Nobody seemed to really care what religion someone was or what church they attended. I still went to Mass, but only on Sundays and Holy Days. If someone asked what church I attended, I would proudly tell them I was Catholic. Life was simple and being Catholic didn't complicate it.

Though I had grown proud of my faith in my younger years, I became more interested in what the world offered me during High School. I strayed from all things religious. I found the party scene much more to my liking than sitting and attending church. I started drinking and smoking pot. It was a very small town, and most of the kids I was partying with were kids I had grown up with, although I did meet a few new people, as well. But many of my partying buddies were also Catholic. For several years, I only sporadically found myself sitting in the pews, and my parents never questioned me about it.

I had an English teacher who was interested in the New Age Movement and introduced various religions in class. She inspired me to research all the different religions I could think of, including Wicca. I found them all fascinating but not enough to motivate me to darken the doors of any other churches. Before I graduated High School, I had found a 12-Step Program that helped me to stop drinking and smoking pot. Everyone there talked about "God As You Understand It," meaning that no matter how you interpret God, you need to have one! This was an important component of my recovery. I spent a lot of time really thinking about God and what I believed. I even prayed about it, asking to be led to whatever religion/belief system was the Truth. My prayers led me back to Rome.

Through all of that soul-searching, I came to remember my love for Catholicism. I love the "smells and bells," the liturgical seasons, the Sacraments, the pomp and pageantry, the rosary, and all the saints. Somehow, those nuns and priests had managed to foster in me a deep love of all things sacred, even though I'd tried to ignore it for so long. I started attending Mass again. I went back to Confession and dug out my dusty rosary. I felt so peaceful, so joyful! I had grown up enough to realize that life is pretty messy, and all of those tangible things that the Catholic Church had to offer me gave me a very real sense of security. It was my safe space.

During this time, I experienced my first real opposition to Catholicism. A girl in my geometry class asked me, "Have you been saved?" I very naively replied, "From what?" She was visibly horrified and never spoke to me again. I also had a Protestant boyfriend who felt it was his mission in life to rescue me from the evils of Catholicism. He was convinced that we worshipped the Blessed Virgin Mary and the saints, and no amount of explanation about the untruth of that would convince him otherwise. This was when I realized that being Catholic was more important to me than having a boyfriend!

I eventually began dating my future husband, who was also Protestant, but he didn't have any issues with me being Catholic until we began discussing marriage. When I told him that I would only be willing to marry him if the wedding was done in a Catholic Church by a Catholic priest, he was very angry. I remember him storming out of the room and me sitting there thinking, "Well, this probably won't end well!" After several minutes, he came back and told me that if it was that important to me, then he would go along with it, but he wanted to know why it was so important. What was so special about being Catholic? Why did it matter what church we were married in? What is that rosary thing you keep using?

This was the second time in my life that I really did some soul-searching about my faith, and why it was important to me: so important that I would rather be single than be married outside of the Church. This time, I did my soul-searching with my boyfriend. The more I explained my faith, the more I loved it, and so did he. He began meeting with one of the priests at my parish, and they formed a close friendship. The priest was young, newly ordained, and very enthusiastic about sharing our faith. He was brilliant at explaining difficult theological concepts in a simple and straightforward manner that my boyfriend could understand. We were married by that same Catholic priest, and my husband converted to Catholicism.

After being married for two and a half years, our first child was born. We were living in a new city and didn't have any friends. We wanted to have community with other young couples who had young children. We attended Mass at our local parish, but it was cold and unwelcoming. Most of the parishioners were older and didn't have young children. We tried going to a few gatherings there, but nobody even noticed that we were new! Our neighbors, however, kept inviting us to join them at their Baptist church. We were lonely, so we accepted. We didn't really have any problems with the Catholic Church as a whole. Since we hadn't received much of a welcome at our local parish, we thought we'd accept our neighbors' invitation to start attending services at their church. We jumped ship for the sake of fellowship! We never really considered what we were leaving behind.

About a year later, we moved again, to a small town not far from the one I grew up in. Even though we were now living back in my original Diocese, we continued to attend a Baptist church because we'd grown accustomed to it and loved all of the programs and Bible studies that most Baptist churches offer for all members of the family. But every year, during Lent and Advent, I would start to feel homesick for the traditions and liturgy of the Catholic Church. I would make it a point to attend at least one service during those seasons, just to get my "Catholic Fix", I guess. During one of those pilgrimages, when I was pregnant with our second child, I felt very strongly drawn to return to the Church. My husband was okay with whatever made me happy, so we went back for a while.

This was the first time I realized that maybe not all priests were okay. The parish we were attending had a priest who was suddenly removed from our midst. Nobody seemed to know exactly what had happened, just that he was gone. The whole thing felt awkward and suspicious. We hadn't cared for that priest much, because he was a chain smoker and always had a cigarette in his hand, even when he was participating in activities with the children. He was also sort of brash or rude. We decided to go to a different parish in town, even though that particular parish was almost exclusively Hispanic. The priest there was one of the wonderful priests from my happy childhood at my home parish. While we loved that priest, the cultural differences kept us from really making any friends at our new parish. Again, at the urging of friends, we started attending a Protestant church, once again seeking fellowship and community.

We moved again, this time across the country to North Carolina, which is part of the "Bible Belt." There were not many Catholics in the area, and those who were there tended to be older and done raising children. We had made the decision to homeschool our children, and so finding a social outlet for our kids was very important to us. We joined the local homeschool group, which was very Protestant. At first, we didn't mind. We were still Christian, after all! All of our new homeschooling friends assured us that the Catholic Church was, at best, misdirected, and at worst, the whore of Babylon! While we never fully bought into that lie, their assurances made it easier for us to turn away from our Faith.

We remained out of the Church for about twelve years, with me making my bi-annual pilgrimages to Mass during Lent and Advent. But in 2005, on the Feast of St. Patrick, I had a long conversation with my best friend from childhood about how, in spite of the fact that both of us had left the Church, our worldviews were still, and would always be, Catholic. We talked about how much we had loved growing up Catholic and how grateful we were for that formation. During the conversation, something began to stir deep within my heart. I realized that, no matter where I go or what I do, I am Catholic. It's not just a church or a group of folks to 'fellowship' with, but it is my identity. Every idea, every feeling, every action, is filtered through my Catholic worldview. I began to feel a deep longing for the Church and participation in Her liturgy and form.

On Palm Sunday of that same year, when I announced I was going to attend Mass instead of our regular church service, my two oldest boys said they wanted to go with me. Sure, why not? Even though both of them had been baptized in the Catholic Church, neither of them really remembered anything about Mass. I was stunned afterward, when they came to me and said they wanted to become Catholic. I actually tried to talk them out of it! I told them that becoming Catholic wasn't just a matter of going up for the altar call and making a "decision" for Christ. There would be a lot of work that they would have to do to receive the Sacraments and become members. They didn't care. They were all in.

Next, I talked to my husband, and he confessed that he had been wanting to return as well. He and I discussed how empty we'd been feeling in Protestant services. We knew it was because no other Christian denomination has the Eucharist, the Real Presence. We started really talking about phrases I'd heard as a child but never really thought about, like "Apostolic Succession" and "Fullness of Faith." We took a long hard look at the long, rich history of the Catholic Church, with all of her Sacraments, saints, and mysteries. We knew God was calling us to return. We made an appointment with our pastor and told him that God had called us back to Catholicism. He was surprised, but to his credit, he gave us his blessing (we're still friends).

Our new parish had a great homeschooling community, and we quickly became a part of it. The priest was phenomenal! He asked both boys to become altar servers and taught them all about the Mass, the vestments, and the various sacred items on the altar. They got to serve at Chrism Masses with the Bishop and hold the canopy for him during Eucharistic processions. They attended the annual March for Life in Washington, D.C. My oldest son even met his future wife at one of those marches!

Seeing how much the Church helped my boys to grow and bloom gave me great joy! I admitted to myself that even in all the years we had spent attending other denominations, I still loved Catholicism! For me, the Catholic Church was the one constant in my world. It had stood the test of time, and after 2,000 years, was still there. Steady, faithful, and true. I was home. I felt safe.

We faced quite a bit of resistance from many of our homeschooling friends who very sincerely felt that we'd gone over to the "Dark Side." Some of them even tried to convince us we'd made a horrible decision by aligning our family with a Church that was full of pedophile priests! Of course, I'd heard rumors here and there that that sort of thing had happened, but I chalked them up to isolated cases. I never once believed that there were any more pedophile priests than there were Boy Scout leaders or Sunday School teachers. I believed that the media was making a big deal out of a few priests who were bad, because the Catholic Church had enough money to be worth suing. I assumed it was just about some disgruntled adults who were angry at the Church for any number of reasons and decided to make accusations against the priests, and I put it all out of my mind. I had been raised to trust all priests, to pray for them, and protect them no matter what. They are, after all, the representatives of Jesus on this earth. To malign a member of the clergy was a grave sin!

In recent years, however, there have been more and more reports about not only priests who were abusers, but Bishops and Cardinals! Thanks to social media, I started experiencing a seemingly constant barragement of new reports about priests who'd sexually abused not only minors, but adults in seminaries. I started seeing terms like "Lavender Mafia." News reports about one cover-up after another began to be daily occurrences. By this point, both of my sons were grown and both had left the Church. I am ashamed to admit that my first, very selfish, thought was, "How could these priests do these things? Don't they know that this is the sort of thing that will prevent my sons from ever coming back to the Church?"

But as the reports kept filing in, I started to feel a very different sort of anger. An anger that is birthed from a deep, intimate betrayal of everything I had ever trusted or believed in. I felt angry for the victims and for their families. I felt, at times, a burning rage toward the fact that these priests' selfish, evil actions were not only doing great, often irreparable, harm to their victims, but to others, like myself, who felt betrayed and lost. How many people have left not only the Catholic Church, but Christianity altogether, and now stand in danger of the fires of hell?

I sat at my computer, reading story after story, feeling more and more betrayed. I wanted to leave the Church, too. How could I go to Mass and receive Communion? After Archbishop Vigano's letters, I realized that the corruption was like a late-stage cancer that had infected not only priests here in the United States, but all over the world. It appears that even Pope Francis is complicit in some of the cover-ups!

I began to feel a deep sense of despair. My husband and I had many long conversations about how angry we felt and how deeply we now distrusted the hierarchy of the Church. We realized we could no longer blindly give our trust to all priests. We cannot help but wonder, every time we meet a new priest (or sometimes even one we already know), "Is he one of 'them'?" We very seriously considered leaving. But I kept hearing the words of St. Peter from John 6:68, "Simon Peter answered him, 'Lord, to whom shall we go? You have the words of eternal life.'"

Indeed. To whom shall we go? No other Church has the fullness of faith. No one else has the Body and Blood, Soul and Divinity of Jesus Christ Himself! Quite simply, there is no other Church. Not for us. So, we were faced with a decision of not whether or not to stay, but how to continue being Catholic, in spite of our deep sense of betrayal, and yes, sometimes even rage.

This was not an easy decision. We struggled with it so much! It often seemed like it would be so much easier to just leave. To sleep in on Sunday mornings and bury our heads in the sand. Yet, we knew we had to stay. Faith is a decision, not a feeling. It is our grateful response to the salvific work that Christ completed on the cross. We couldn't just turn our backs on God and throw away our own salvation because of this atrocity committed by His shepherds. We knew that if we left the Church because of the sins of others, no matter how horrific, we would become collateral damage. Many years ago, the priest who married us made a comment that has stuck with both myself and my husband. He said, "If all the good Catholics keep leaving the Church, who will stay to fight for her?" But...how? How do we fight for her? How do we stay and stand against something that seems so all-consuming?

We found our answer in God's Word. St. Paul talks about putting on the Armor of God, which seems more relevant to us now than ever before. It's like he looked into the future, saw the mess that our Church is in today, and knew we'd need encouragement and advice. In

Ephesians 6:10-18, Paul gives us just the instructions we were looking for:

> *"Finally, be strong in the Lord and in the strength of His might. Put on the whole armor of God, that you may be able to stand against the wiles of the devil. For we are not contending against flesh and blood, but against the principalities, against the powers, against the world rulers of this present darkness, against the spiritual hosts of wickedness in the heavenly places. Therefore take the whole armor of God, that you may be able to withstand in the evil day, and having done all, to stand. Stand therefore, having girded your loins with truth, and having put on the breastplate of righteousness, and having shod your feet with the equipment of the gospel of peace; besides all these, taking the shield of faith, with which you can quench all the flaming darts of the evil one. And take the helmet of salvation, and the sword of the Spirit, which is the word of God. Pray at all times in the Spirit, with all prayer and supplication. To that end keep alert with all perseverance, making supplication for all the saints."*

We have our marching orders, if you will. St. Paul reminded us of the source of the abuse: principalities, powers, world rulers of this present darkness, and spiritual hosts of wickedness in the heavenly places. It is, in short, demonic. The abusers, along with those who have protected and hidden them, are in very real danger of the fires of hell, as are the many victims who have turned completely away from God and His Church because of what was done to them by those they thought they could trust. They all need our prayers! And not just our prayers. They need our presence. Someone has to be there to care for them and to gently nourish them back to spiritual health. When looking at the situation from this point of view, how could we possibly leave? Like our priest had said all those years ago, someone has to stay and fight!

In many ways, this scandal has strengthened us in our Catholic Faith. It has caused us to, yet again, examine our beliefs very closely and to remember we cannot depend on any man, but only upon God. We have committed, once again, to become more involved in our parish, more fervent in prayer, and more mindful of why we go to Mass and what we're doing there. We are making a conscious effort to receive the Sacraments more frequently and to spend more time in Adoration.

We firmly believe all the Truths that the Holy Catholic Church teaches. We understand that priests are still human, and therefore, like all of us, still sinful. We all need the grace that is offered to us through the Sacraments. And in spite of how widespread and rampant the clerical abuse may be, we still believe that there are many, many more good and holy priests who need our support and prayers. They need us to stand and fight alongside them. Together, with the Holy Spirit, we can and we will win this battle!

First Steps to Healing

Elizabeth Terrill, LPCC

"United with the broken Body of Christ, we die like the grain of wheat. By the power of Christ's Passion, we share in His Resurrection and are transformed into bread for the world."[1] Dr. Theresa Burke

In my practice as a mental health counselor, I often hear people say, "What doesn't kill you makes you stronger." While I agree with the overall sentiment behind this frequently used phrase, it brushes past that many of us, who have been abused, betrayed, wounded, discarded, and generally injured by others, often do experience a death of a part of ourselves or of who we were before the trauma. Those who come out the other side of abuse are survivors, and their journey to surviving is an ongoing, painful process that often can feel worse than not surviving at all. In this chapter, we will discuss the warning signs of a potentially abusive situation or person, the typical short and long term effects of sexual abuse, how we can begin to heal from abuse, and what we as individuals, the Church, and our communities can do to protect children and prevent sexual abuse.

It is good to begin with a definition of sexual abuse.

*According to the American Psychological Association: "**Sexual abuse** is unwanted sexual activity, with perpetrators using force, making threats or taking advantage of victims not able to give consent."[2]*

Everyone's experience of abuse is unique and can vary in the level of sexual activity that occurred. We know that, no matter the extent of unwanted sexual activity, all forms have long lasting effects on the survivors of the abuse. Oftentimes, when people suffer through trauma, they find themselves comparing their experience to others and weighing whether they have the "right" to be traumatized by their experience if it was not as "bad" as someone else's. I think Viktor

Frankl, a psychiatrist who was a Holocaust survivor whose entire family almost died in the concentration camps, understood the varying ways we experience suffering the best. Frankl wrote in his book, "Man's Search for Meaning":

> *"To draw an analogy: a man's suffering is*
> *similar to the behavior of a gas. If a certain quantity*
> *of gas is pumped into an empty chamber, it will fill*
> *the chamber completely and evenly, no matter how*
> *big the chamber. Thus, suffering completely fills the*
> *human soul and conscious mind, no matter whether*
> *the suffering is great or little. Therefore the "size"*
> *of human suffering is absolutely relative."[3]*

Rates of reporting child sexual abuse have increased over the past two decades. A study from 1999 showed that only 12% of child sexual abuse cases were reported in the United States to the authorities, whereas a study from 2010 shows that now 38% of child sexual abuse cases are reported to authorities[4]. The increase is likely due to mandatory reporting requirements and a better understanding of child sexual abuse and survivors. As more institutional abuse scandals were revealed and reported, the public at large has become more and more aware of the risk of sexual abuse to our children. In order to continue to protect children from perpetrators, we need to continue to educate parents, educators, clergy, parish staff, and really everyone on the warning signs of sexual abuse and the red flags that can help identify a potential perpetrator.

Since the 2002 USCCB Dallas Charter, the Catholic Church has also increased its protective steps to keeping children safe and to ensuring that sexual abuse is reported to the authorities. The program we use in the Diocese of Gallup and in many other dioceses is VIRTUS.

> *VIRTUS is the brand name that identifies*
> *best practices and programs designed to help*
> *prevent wrongdoing and promote "right doing"*
> *within religious organizations. The VIRTUS*

programs empower organizations and people
to better control risk and improve the lives of
all those who interact with the Church. [6]

VIRTUS concretely identifies the most typical warning signs of a potential abuser as well as the overall grooming process that takes place in sexual abuse cases. They identify three basic elements of the grooming process:

- Physical grooming—This can begin with a simple pat on the back, but over time it becomes more intimate.
- Psychological grooming—Psychological grooming takes many forms, all of which are designed to drive a wedge between the child and the parent or guardian and to pull the child under the control of the perpetrator. Psychological techniques include a wide variety of activities from telling a child that the sexual contact is "an act of love sanctioned by God" to threatening harm to someone the child loves if he or she tells anyone about the abuse.
- Community grooming—While the physical and psychological grooming are progressing with the child, the perpetrator is grooming the parents, guardians, and the rest of the community. The purpose is to convince us that this is someone who really cares about kids and is committed to their well-being so that we will not notice the warning signs or will disregard them because we can't believe the perpetrator would commit such a crime.

It is important to remember that grooming can happen very quickly or over a longer period of time. The people who are most trusted by children and parents can often be the most likely to sexually abuse children. Child sexual abusers are highly manipulative, and they understand how to conceal their true intentions from everyone around them. In my practice, I work with many children who have been recently abused, and I often have to reassure parents that even **the most protective and attentive parents can fall victim to the manipulation of these abusers.**

There are many warning signs of a potential child sexual abuser, and this list is not exhaustive. Rather, this list is to highlight the common signs so that everyone can be aware of how to keep children safe.

Warning Signs of an Abuser:

VIRTUS[56]

1. Always wants to be alone with children in areas where no one can monitor the interaction.
2. Allows children to do things their parents would not permit.
3. Thinks the "rules" don't apply to him or her.
4. Is always more excited to be with children than with adults.
5. Discourages others from participating in activities involving kids.
6. Goes overboard in physical touching.
7. Uses sexual language, tells sexual jokes, and shows pornography to children.
8. Gives gifts without permission and demands secrecy about those gifts.

Department of Education

9. Isolating students from others.
10. Gifts and other positive things are given.
11. Traps children or young people in areas or situations that can't be monitored.
12. Goes overboard touching children.
13. Targets vulnerable or marginal students who are hungry for attention.

Children often do not report sexual abuse after the first sexual contact. Often the abuse will continue for years or happen multiple times before a child discloses the abuse. There are other warning signs that a child may be sexually abused that we can look to, especially in cases where a child is too afraid or embarrassed to disclose the abuse

directly. According to the Mayo Clinic[7], children who are being abused
(sexually or physically) may exhibit the following behaviors:

- Withdrawal from friends or usual activities
- Changes in behavior — such as aggression, anger, hostility
  or hyperactivity — or changes in school performance
- Depression, anxiety or unusual fears, or a sudden loss of self-
  confidence
- An apparent lack of supervision
- Frequent absences from school
- Reluctance to leave school activities, as if he or she doesn't
  want to go home
- Attempts at running away
- Rebellious or defiant behavior
- Self-harm or attempts at suicide

Specific signs of sexual abuse also include:

- Sexual behavior or knowledge that's inappropriate for the
  child's age
- Pregnancy or a sexually transmitted infection
- Blood in the child's underwear
- Statements that he or she was sexually abused
- Inappropriate sexual contact with other children

It is not uncommon to see an abused child begin to regress, which
means to act younger or move backward in developmental milestones.
The most common example of this is a child who has been reliably
potty trained and then begins to have bedwetting or daytime accidents.

In the short-term, children who have suffered through sexual
abuse struggle with feelings of confusion, guilt, anxiety, aggression,
sexually acting out, and low self-esteem. We know that several factors
encourage a more complete and rapid healing in children when the
abuse is reported, and the healing process begins early on. For adult
survivors, we often see the same feelings of confusion, guilt, anxiety,
depression, and low self-esteem. These feelings are magnified in adult
survivors, especially when they have not yet processed through their
trauma. We also see failed romantic relationships/marriages, sexual

promiscuity, debilitating trust issues, and self-medicating through drugs and/or alcohol. It is often common to have to first address a substance abuse addiction with a survivor before being able to focus on the abuse itself.[8]

The process of healing is different for every person, and we often refer to this as a personal journey. The long-term effects of child sexual abuse on survivors leads to many complications in their lives and is not easily reversed. One of the first steps in this process is an acknowledgement of the abuse, pain, and overall suffering that the survivor has had to endure. Often, they have isolated themselves from others, and even close family members or friends may not know about the abuse. We know that it is hugely beneficial for adult survivors to have a family member or friend who can help support them through the healing process. This support largely consists of listening and understanding the effects of abuse on the survivor. This is especially important inside of marriage and can be immensely healing to involve the spouse in counseling to ensure an understanding of the survivors' experience.

There are many ways to receive help as a survivor of sexual abuse. If a person is abused by a member of the clergy in a specific Diocese, they should first report the abuse to law enforcement, then reach out to that Diocese's Victim's Assistance Coordinator. The contact information for coordinators is typically found on the website for parishes and Dioceses. Policies for providing counseling vary from Diocese to Diocese. Dr. Theresa Burke also offers support through her retreats *From Grief to Grace*:

> *"Recognizing the critical importance of providing an integrated psychological and spiritual healing program for the aftermath of abuse, Dr. Burke set out to create Grief to Grace. This program focuses specifically on healing the wounds of abuse and offers new Living Scripture exercises in a retreat format to help survivors unite their suffering with the agony, betrayals, abandonment, and suffering of Christ.* [1]*"*

If you are having difficulty reaching out directly to the Diocese, there are secular supports that are also available. Online and over the phone resources are available through RAINN (Rape, Abuse & Incest National Network) which operates the National Sexual Assault Hotline (Contact information provided at the end of the chapter).[9]

When choosing a counselor, it is important to know the differences between a counselor/therapist, a psychologist, and a psychiatrist. A counselor/therapist are typically persons who have a master's degree in counseling and who practice talk therapy with clients. A psychologist is typically a person who has a Doctorate degree in Psychology, and they also practice talk therapy as well as more in-depth evaluations of mental health and functioning. A psychiatrist is a medical doctor, who may practice talk therapy, and typically focuses on evaluations and prescriptions for medication. If one-on-one counseling is uncomfortable or intimidating, which it can be for people initially, there are also survivor support groups. These groups exist online and in person and vary from location to location.

Survivors all experience their abuse and recovery in different ways. Typically, there is a process by which a person experiences trauma in the following steps:

1. Shock/Denial – A person who has been abused will often not be able to process the trauma initially. They may deny it happened, loose pieces of memory of the event(s), emotionally shut down, or believe they are to blame for the abuse.
2. Anger – As the reality of the trauma sets in, it is common to experience deep feelings of anger/rage at the abuser and even at yourself. When there is no closure, such as prosecution or arrest of the abuser, the anger will often be misdirected at the people you interact with most frequently and with whom you feel the safest.
3. Grief – As the anger ebbs and flows, the grief sets in. Often this grief is associated with losing who you were before the abuse or who you could have been without this trauma. It is typical to grieve the loss of the abusive relationship itself because of how

the grooming process will make survivors feel loved by their abusers.

4. Depression/Anxiety – These feelings often go hand in hand in a cycle unique to each person. Some individuals may have more of a tendency towards depression and others towards anxiety. Most typically fluctuate between the two. This stage of recovery is often the longest and can take years and a variety of interventions to treat successfully.

5. Release/Forgiveness – We know that forgiveness is beneficial to the healing process of any person. Forgiveness is not always directed at the abuser, but rather at the survivor themselves or maybe a parent/family member who they feel failed to keep them safe. Forgiveness is not for the people that hurt you, it is for you to take back control of your life, memories, and feelings. The abuser does not get to define who you are and who you will become.

6. Healing – To heal from something physical is often straightforward. Emotional and spiritual healing tend to be more complex and do not take place in a straight line. The entire process of healing is more like a circle, where you experience every step of healing multiple times. As time goes on, the circle widens and the experiences are spaced further and further apart. Different events in your life or society at large can trigger feelings that were thought to be processed through.

7. Growth – In counseling many professionals are moving away from the term posttraumatic stress disorder in favor of posttraumatic growth[10]. This terminology focuses on the positive impact suffering a trauma can have on a person's life. It is not dismissive of the horrific nature of many experiences of trauma, but rather, it focuses on trauma as a catalyst to growth. It is similar to a common counseling technique called reframing, wherein we take a thought or experience and frame it in a more helpful way. For example, a survivor may have a recurring thought of "Why did this have to happen to me?!" and we would work with them to reframe the thought to, "I was strong enough to survive this". It is not so much about

answering the many questions that survivors struggle with as it is about focusing on the strengths with which they survived.

TRAUMA CIRCLE

The Church has been continuously developing policies and procedures since The Charter for the Protection of Children and Young People which "is a comprehensive set of procedures originally established by the USCCB in June 2002 for addressing allegations of sexual abuse of minors by Catholic clergy.[11]" These polices have been implemented and are consistently audited by the USCCB. As we have seen in recent months, we still have much work to do as a Church to keep children and adults safe from abuse. **The number one preventive measure is to bring these problems to the surface and shine the light on them.** We need to know what we are fighting, before we can truly fight it. Each member of every community has an obligation to educate themselves on the dangers of abuse and to be vigilant in protecting people from abusive situations. There are many who have been deeply abused by the Church, and we all share in their suffering. We all can stand with them, listen to them, and validate their experiences. This is a painful time for our Church and for our people. It is not a time without hope, and the true healing that we will find will be in the support we give to each other.

Endnotes

1   http://grief-to-grace-lsi.squarespace.com/retreat-overview

2   https://www.apa.org/topics/sexual-abuse/

3   Frankl, Viktor Emil. Man's Search for Meaning. Boston: Beacon Press, 2006.

4   Hanson, R. F., Resnick, H. S., Saunders, B. E., Kilpatrick, D. G., & Best, C. (1999). Factors related to the reporting of childhood rape. Child Abuse and Neglect, 23(6), 559–569.

5   National Catholic Services, LLC. (2003). Practical Advice for Parents on Preventing Child Sexual Abuse. Retrieved from https://www.virtusonline.org/virtus/ParentHandbook.pdf

6   Womack Doty, S., J.D., M.H.R. (2005, September 26). Are the Protecting God's Children Principles Practical in the Real World? Retrieved from https://www.virtusonline.org/virtus/PrintArticle.cfm?a=352&theme=0

7   Mayo Clinic Staff. (n.d.). Child Abuse. Retrieved from https://www.mayoclinic.org/diseases-conditions/child-abuse/symptoms-causes/syc-20370864

8   Darkness to Light. (n.d.). Child Sexual Abuse Statistics. Retrieved from https://www.d2l.org/wp-content/uploads/2017/01/all_statistics_20150619.pdf

9   https://www.rainn.org/ 1-800-656-HOPE (4673)

10   (Tedeshi, R.G., & Calhoun, L.G., 2004)

11   http://www.usccb.org/issues-and-action/child-and-youth-protection/charter.cfm

Healing the Brokenhearted

Dr. Deborah Rodriguez

The Face of Trauma

"I just want to feel better."

"Cathy" was a teenage patient I recently met. She was very anxious, fidgety, and unpredictable. Sometimes she would just sit and shake. Other times, she cried or even screamed. She didn't trust the office staff and told them so. She spoke to her mother in harsh words in a raised voice. "What's wrong with her?" someone in the office asked.

As a physician, I am trained to diagnose an illness, a disease, or condition of health and then offer a treatment. Most of the time it is straight forward: an ear infection or a broken arm. This was not the case with Cathy. Hers was an inner wound, and this wound made every part of her body cry out in pain. Her wound could not be fixed with an antibiotic or a cast. Her wound came through child abuse. It happened several years before I met her, but her mind and her body reacted as if it was happening now. She was reliving a horror that seemed all too real, even though she was safe in my office. After she left, I explained to my staff, "That is what trauma looks like."

I sat in the back of the church. Hopefully no one would see me—not likely as the church was small and not many were there that morning for daily Mass. It's not that I didn't want to be recognized; I just didn't want anyone to see me hold my clenched hands near my face and take deep breaths, trying not to fall into another panic attack. This was supposed to be a safe place—a beautiful church with a great pastor. Maybe it would be different this time. Maybe I could make it through all of Mass without wanting to run out, nauseous and light headed. "She always leaves Mass so quickly. She never talks to anyone." "She seems so uncomfortable." "What's wrong with her?"

This is what trauma looks like. And this is part of my story.

Cathy's story and my story are two among many. We are survivors of abuse. Our stories of abuse are different, and our journeys of healing are different. Yet, there are similarities among all survivors. Each survivor story (I call them "sacred stories") comes from a beautiful child of God. I have the great privilege of ministering to survivors of abuse through support groups and survivor ministries. Every survivor that I have met, whether in my practice or in ministry, is a sign of hope and strength. Each story of hurt and abuse is also God's story. Every patient I see and every survivor I meet is a blessing to me and is a window into God's heart.

This chapter is meant to help us understand abuse, trauma, and survivors. I also hope to share ideas of how to make our churches places of welcome and refuge for survivors. If we want to help the brokenhearted, we must learn to see survivors as God sees them. We must come to see their stories as ways to encounter God and His story of salvation. I hope to help us answer the following:

- What is the connection between abuse and trauma?
- What does trauma look like and how does this knowledge affect the Church?
- How common is abuse?
- What are the immediate and long-term effects of trauma?
- What is trauma-informed ministry?
- What does healing look like for survivors of abuse and trauma?
- How can Trauma-Informed Ministry help pastors, lay ministers, parents, families, friends, and even strangers welcome and support survivors of abuse?
- How can we set up our church communities and families to prevent further abuse and trauma?

"Therefore if anyone is in Christ, he is
a new creature; the old things passed away,
behold, new things have come." 2 Cor 5:17

Dr. Deborah Rodriguez   Healing the Brokenhearted

What's in a Name?

I use the term "survivor" more often than "victim", because that is the term I personally prefer. There are those who prefer other terms, or none. Our Church seems to prefer the term victim (there are Victim Advocates, Victim Assistance Coordinators, etc.), so I will use both terms. In Spanish the word for Survivor is *sobreviviente*. It is really two words, "above" or "over", *sobre*, and "alive" or "living", *viviente*. When I identify myself as a survivor of clergy abuse, I am stating that I not only survived the crime of child abuse, but that I have come to know a new life, a life **above** and **beyond** my abuse.

My journey has not been easy. I not only survived child abuse, but I also survived reporting my abuse to Church authorities. Over 60% of survivors of child sexual abuse will never report their abuse [1,2,3,4]; clergy sex abuse survivors are no different [5,6]. It's not hard to discover why. Church authorities are severely under educated in how to compassionately listen to the stories of abuse survivors and support the healing process. It is critical for all supporters, especially Church leaders, to understand the physical and psychological effects of abuse so as not to repel those most in need of healing.

Given that 1 in 3 women and 1 in 6 [21] men have reported some form of sexual abuse or assault before age 18 [1,7,8], we can estimate that on any given Sunday, every other person in the pew is either a survivor of trauma or knows a survivor well. Our Church must be better prepared to minister to the many people living with these hidden wounds. If we are to help survivors of abuse, we must first learn about abuse and trauma. All abuse causes trauma, but not all trauma comes from abuse. An auto accident causes physical trauma, such as broken bones or lacerations. A soldier who returns from combat with bodily wounds and with PTSD has both physical and emotional trauma.

Abuse in all its forms causes psychological or emotional trauma. Unlike physical trauma, psychological trauma often has no obvious wound, such as with my patient Cathy. The evidence of psychological trauma may manifest in difficult behaviors, addictions, or mental health conditions. Trauma can also increase the risk of chronic medical conditions, such as heart disease or cancer. [9]

Current best practices for working with survivors of abuse and trauma involves a trauma-informed approach. Trauma-Informed Care (TIC) is based on an understanding of the prevalence of trauma and the impact of trauma on a person's physical, emotional, and psychological well-being. [10]

I have worked to incorporate the principles of Trauma-Informed Care (TIC) with a Christ-centered view to form Trauma-Informed Ministry (TIM). Specifically, I've tried to incorporate Scripture, Catholic teaching, and Tradition that speaks to trauma, suffering, and healing into a science-based approach grounded in medical practice. This model can be utilized by anyone who works with survivors or as I say, "anyone who knows or loves a survivor." It can be used by clergy or lay persons, families or friends. It can be used by any health care professional when they encounter a person with a history of abuse or trauma who wishes to incorporate faith practices into their healing.

What is trauma?

How does this affect the Church?

The Substance Abuse and Mental Health Services Administration (SAMHSA) describes psychological trauma as "an event, series of events, or set of circumstances that is experienced by an individual as physically or emotionally harmful or life threatening and that has lasting adverse effects on the individual's functioning and mental, physical, social, emotional, or spiritual well-being" [10]. My own definition of trauma is an event or series of events that causes physical or emotional harm and overwhelms a person's ability to cope with the event.

This inability to cope with the abusive or traumatic event comes from feelings of powerlessness and betrayal. The victim is often unable to change the circumstances, to stop the abuse, or to ultimately end the pain in the soul that results from the abuse. The abuser also betrays the victim.

Surviving a disaster such as war or a hurricane causes trauma and feelings of powerlessness. You can't be betrayed by a cyclone or earthquake. You can, however, be betrayed by a parent, a spouse, or a priest. These two-fold feelings of powerlessness and betrayal are what makes clergy sexual abuse (as well as other forms of sexual abuse) so much more damaging to the survivor. We trust our parent, spouse, or priest and don't expect them to abuse us.

This betrayal destroys the relationship, and it breeds doubt, despair and hopelessness. This can cause confusion and shame in the victim-survivor. Even self-hatred can often result from this combination. Survivors sometimes repeat to themselves, "How could I have been so weak?" or "Why didn't I say anything?" or "I must have deserved it."

The Church tells us that the human person is both body and soul, created in the image of God. (1 Cor 15:44). In sexual abuse, the abuser destroys not just the body, as it was created by God, but also destroys the holy union of body and soul. Some survivors will adopt this fragmented self as their own new identity. Because of the abuse, especially at the hands of clergy, the survivor may live a "spiritual deadness" or soul-less life.

> "So God created man in his own image,
> in the image of God he created him; male
> and female he created them." Gen 1:27

In the Garden, man and woman walked in the company of God in this Paradise (Gen 3:8). Satan, too, was present in the Garden and from the beginning sought to destroy what God created. (Gen 3:1-6). Satan destroys through lies and deception. As the "Father of Lies", Satan feeds lies to victims of abuse with repeated words of shame and accusation. Abuse victims will talk of hearing and believing that we are "worthless" and "sinful". We hear that the abuse was "our fault", and that "we asked for it." The words of accusation continue as adults: "just get over it" (as if it is like a sprained ankle) or "why didn't you say something earlier?" (putting the blame again on us) or "that was in the past." (telling us it is somehow wrong that the damage lasts a lifetime).

Satan also works by showing survivors all the sin that was involved in our abuse. Images of the abuser's sin get replayed in our memories, and over time, we start to believe it is our sin. Satan's script of lies and accusations plays over and over in our heads. We now have a new self-image—not the one God intended for us, but the false one Satan presents for us. Some of us then turn to other persons or behaviors that will confirm these lies. Survivors often have trouble having healthy relationships or fall into addictions. It is not unusual for survivors to have abusive relationships as adults, and Satan's influence continues. Those of us who minister to survivors need to **understand this influence of Satan, and therefore be prepared and armed for the spiritual battle.**

"Come to me, all you who labor and are burdened, and I will give you rest." Mt 11:28

A Safe Refuge

The Church can be a safe refuge for abuse and trauma survivors. We can each play a part in creating this safe refuge. This can occur by incorporating the principles of trauma-informed ministry into larger efforts to bring awareness and healing to anyone who has a story of wound or trauma.

There are generally accepted principles for trauma-informed organizations, which I describe in a later section. There are also key assumptions in creating a trauma-informed understanding and approach to care and ministry. Some call these assumptions the 4 "Rs" of trauma-informed care. [10] They are:

- **REALIZE** the prevalence and widespread impact of trauma and understand potential paths for recovery

- **RECOGNIZE** the signs and symptoms of trauma in clients, families, staff, and others involved with the system

- **RESPOND** to persons with trauma in a sensitive way

- Avoid **RE-traumatization** as the organization ministers to those with trauma

REALIZE

The first part of TIM is to realize that abuse is common, abuse causes trauma, and there are predictable patterns to trauma and its healing. As Christians, we should also realize that abuse and trauma are described in Scripture. God's story of salvation reveals how God intervenes particularly in stories of abuse and woundedness. When God intervenes in these dark moments, there is greater glory and, ultimately, redemption.

Abuse is very common. The Centers for Disease Control and Prevention (CDC) showed in a landmark study (The Adverse Childhood Experiences, "ACE" Study), that 1 in 5 Americans was sexually molested as a child; 1 in 4 was beaten by a parent to the point of leaving a mark on their body; 1 in 4 have alcoholic relatives, 1 in 8 witnessed their mothers being abused physically, and 1 in 3 couples engages in physical violence. [9]

If abuse is so common, why don't we hear more about it in our churches except when a pastor or leader gets caught? Scripture admonishes us that we cannot be in denial, and we must confront abuse and other types of evil (1 Sam 3:13, 1 Tim 5:20).

> *For I have told him that I am about to punish his house forever, for the iniquity that he knew, because his sons were blaspheming God, and he did not restrain them. 1 Sam 3:13*

We may remain silent about abuse and its effects, but God does not remain silent. Scripture is replete with stories of abuse. There is temptation (Gen 3:1-6), "wickedness" in every heart (Gen 6:5-8); rape (Gen 34:1-2); infanticide (Ex 1:15-22), incest/rape (2 Sam 13:1-19), rape and murder (2 Samuel 11), and genocide (Mt 2:16-18). And there is the greatest abuse in history, the torturing and killing of God's own son, Jesus. God is fully aware of abuse committed by and to His children. God is deeply moved by human suffering (Ex 2:23-25, Hos 11:8, Mt 9:36, Jn 11:35), and God did not abandon us in our abuse and suffering. Jesus took on flesh and experienced all the abuse and suffering we would inflict and endure. Jesus defeated all sin, suffering, and death at complete cost to himself (Rom 5:8) bringing about redemption for all. In this way, our abuse is also defeated and redeemable.

RECOGNIZE

The second part of trauma-informed ministry is to recognize the nature and effects of trauma in survivors and in those who may be secondarily affected. Trauma affects not only survivors but affects families, communities, and those who work with and minister to abuse survivors. I will discuss the signs and symptoms of trauma in more detail in another section.

Being able to name the type of abuse endured can be a help for both survivor and those working with survivors. I help facilitate a survivor support group called Maria Goretti Network (www.mgoretti.org). We begin our meetings with a simple introduction such as "My name is Deborah. I am a survivor of child sexual abuse and spiritual abuse." Others then have the freedom to name their abuse: sexual, physical, neglect, verbal, and/or spiritual. There is never a requirement to name the abuse. But once a new survivor names this out loud, they know they are not alone. We often kept our abuse secret, hidden by shame or because of threats against us. Even today, abuse still carries a stigma in some circles. As described in another section of this chapter, most survivors will not disclose their abuse for many reasons.

Steven Tracy, Christian pastor and counselor not only classifies the different types of abuse, but also shows how each type is the result of Satan perverting the image of God and the image of who we are before God. This characterization of abuse adds a unique and deeper understanding of the root cause of abuse and its full impact on victims.

The types of abuse and how each perverts the nature of God as classified in *Mending the Soul* by Steven Tracy [11]:

- Sexual, the perversion of "one flesh" (Gen 2:24)
- Physical, the perversion of "let them rule" (Gen 1:26)
- Neglect, the perversion of "cultivate the ground" (Gen 2:5)
- Spiritual, the perversion of "image" (Gen 1:26)
- Verbal, the perversion of "be fruitful" (Gen 1:28)

Long after the abuse has ended, the effects are still felt by many survivors. It is as if the abuse is happening in the present. Even if the memories fade or are suppressed, the body may still remember and show the effects of trauma for years. The "ACE Study" identified an association between the amount of childhood trauma and adult disease, lower quality of life, and early death. These early traumas can have lasting effects on health, behaviors, and life potential.[9] Some survivors can integrate and recover from the traumatic experience. Others, however, experience ongoing intrusions of memories or reenactments of the abuse. Some may have lifelong emotional and psychological disability from the abuse.

Why do some recover from past traumatic events with apparent ease and others go on to develop serious medical conditions such as Post-Traumatic Stress Disorder (PTSD)? I have met survivors who simply shrug off past abuse, no matter the severity. Others re-live the trauma in agonizing uncontrollable episodes and are never able to fully integrate the trauma. Still others deal with vast arrays of chronic medical conditions and cannot begin to address the possible role of trauma in their past. No two responses to trauma are alike just as no two persons are alike. However, the psychological, sociological, and medical fields have been able to help identify reproducible patterns of response to trauma and therefore have begun to offer treatments for survivor's healing. There are several factors which help determine how a survivor will respond to and integrate the traumatic experience. These factors include: the type, severity, and duration of trauma; the biological and genetic vulnerabilities or circumstances of the person enduring the trauma; the health of the relationships of the survivor and whether they are supportive or detrimental to the survivor's healing; and the broader cultural, social, and political context in which trauma occurs. [12] The Church can have the greatest impact on the last two factors. Abuse happens in relationships; healing will also happen in relationships.

RESPOND

"Oh, that happened in the past. We have fixed the seminaries."

This was the response I received in 2014 by a bishop upon hearing my abuse story. I shared my story with him looking for a word of understanding and support. Instead, he told me to get over the way I was feeling, after all, the problem of abuse was over. Taken as statements of fact, these are certainly true. My abuse did happen in the past. But as we come to understand more about the long- and short-term effects of abuse, we see that very often past trauma is still very real in the present situations of many survivors.

With mandatory training for Church staff, including clergy and lay ministers, more people are aware of what to do to protect minors and vulnerable adults. But, I didn't want to hear statistics at that moment. I needed someone to hear me and my story. I also needed the fullness of my faith to walk my road to healing.

The initial response to the survivor who comes forward is one of the most critical parts in the survivor's healing journey. The most important way you may be called to respond to a survivor is to hear their story. Anyone can minister to a survivor. The following are techniques I have found helpful in receiving a trauma story. I utilize four basic steps with a mnemonic tool to help. The mnemonic I use is **"VEEL": Validate, Empower, Explain,** and **Leave** the door open.

Validate— "I have heard you"

The first step in receiving a survivor's story is validation of the survivor and the story. It takes tremendous courage to gather strength and inner resources to finally disclose a story of abuse to anyone. We survivors sometimes carry enormous amounts of shame, self-blame, doubt, and fear. We may have trouble trusting others. Survivors must be able to share their stories in safety if they feel so called. And the response should be a message of having heard the survivor and to realize how precious this story is. Some validating statements are:

"Thank you for sharing your story with me," "You are not alone," "I am sorry this happened to you," "It was not your fault," or "You are not to blame for this." These simple statements can be strong words to help combat the self-blame that so many of us carry.

The Trauma Narrative

The survivor's story or narrative is not usually a coherent tale that is ordered and understandable. As I explain in the section on what trauma looks like, the memories of trauma are stored under extreme stress, much like a frantic file clerk who just must get the files put away and sealed. According to Bissel Vander Kolk MD, survivors remember trauma memories "not as a story, a narrative with a beginning, middle, and end, but as isolated sensory imprints: images, sounds, and physical sensations that are accompanied by intense emotions, usually terror and helplessness." [12]. Judith Herman describes these memories as leaving an "indelible image, a 'death imprint.'" [13]

One of the first steps toward healing is understanding that we survivors have a story. The story may be filled with horror, evil, and pain, but ours is also a story of resilience, strength, and hope. Once we take our trauma and put it into words, it has less power over us. Discovering this story can be painful, can take many years, and because of the effects of the trauma, are not always neat and simple. I call the trauma stories or narratives "sacred stories", and each time I receive the gift of a story, I know I am being allowed into someone's story of pain and vulnerability. But this is also the place where I know Jesus is so present.

If a survivor wishes to share their story, the next step is deciding how to share this story. The Church can help with this part of the healing process. Tools outlined here in this chapter or in other resources can be vital to not causing further trauma to the survivor. Studies show that survivors who felt their stories were compassionately listened to were 2 to 3 times more likely to report partial to complete healing. In other words, healing can begin just by having compassionate and informed people to listen to survivors.[14]

Some survivors may have already disclosed to others, in their relationships or with health care professionals. For many who have already disclosed, some survivors turn to members of their church communities, wanting a healing that medication or therapy do not provide. Many survivors long for a relationship with Jesus and long to do this in a faith community. Many of us know that only Jesus Christ can provide real and lasting comfort and healing.

Disclosure is a gift. It is a gift to the survivor and can be a gift to the receiver. Listening to a survivor's story can also be a lifesaving moment for survivors. Reverend Lewis Fiorelli and Teresa Pitt Green have ministered to abuse survivors for over two decades and have heard many trauma stories. In their book, *Veronica's Veil: Spiritual Companionship for Survivors of Abuse*, they write about the essential need for people to be available to hear trauma stories, "Again and again, I listen as survivors describe a startling turning point in their darkness occasioned by a religious or lay person who was able simply to listen with kindness and without judgment. Like angels with the Easter message, these unnamed helpers have given many survivors safe home in the Church and with God.[15]"

Why Don't Survivors Disclose?

There is overwhelming evidence that most child victims delay or never disclose child sexual abuse to friends, family, or the authorities.[14]

It takes tremendous courage for a survivor to just remember their abuse. It can take even greater courage to share the memories with another. By sharing with another, the survivor is speaking the trauma aloud, and through their own words, they are sharing the stories they have often kept hidden under layers of shame, confusion, and pain. Some of the reasons that survivors delay or never disclose abuse are:

- Fear of not being believed
- Shame and self-blame
- Concern for self/others
- Fear of upsetting parent/family/spouse
- Fear of consequences (retribution, family discord and disruption, fear of being punished)
- Threats (told not to tell)
- Lack of opportunity (didn't know how or who to tell, who is safe, were they safe before? Can they be trusted)
- Didn't know it was wrong (particularly for some children)
- Thought abuser was a friend
- They are traumatized; they have incapacitating feelings (fear, denial, avoidance, disgust, shame) [18]

There are factors which have shown to create circumstances where survivors are more likely to disclose. Some of these factors are hearing or seeing something from another person that reminds them of their own story. There are more disclosures when news stories report on survivors who have told their stories. Sometimes it is a safe opportunity to disclose such as when a close friend or family shares their own story of abuse or if a doctor or other health care professional asks. Supportive communities such as support groups and ministries that focus on survivors provide safe places for disclosure. Other times, survivors are more compelled to share their stories. These include when someone is rescued from an abusive situation, or there are witnesses who report abuse. Other situations are when the physical, psychological, or behavioral symptoms of trauma become too much for the survivor to bear, as with PTSD, depression, or anxiety. And there are times when the survivor believes it is the right thing to do or to protect others. [19]

Empower

Abuse makes the victim powerless. If a survivor has chosen to disclose a story of abuse, words of empowerment can give the survivor his or her power back. Survival of abuse, determination to continue with life, and choosing to disclose are all events that we survivors don't necessarily see as the right thing to do. Reminding us that what we have endured is significant and disclosing it is courageous often gives us strength to continue the healing journey. Examples of words of empowerment are "You have tremendous courage" or "It took a lot of courage to share your story." Just as important as words of empowerment is giving the survivor choice in his or her next steps. Using words such as "It's your choice," "Whatever you prefer," and "What part of your healing do you want to work on?" can give renewed strength for the survivor to continue to pursue healing.

Explain

*Then Jesus said to the Jews who had believed
in Him, "If you continue in my word, you are truly
my disciples; and you will know the truth, and
the truth will make you free." John 8:31-2*

Survivors have been betrayed and lied to not only by their abusers, but sometimes by the very systems these abusers come from. I am a survivor of clergy abuse and I am a survivor of reporting my abuse to the Church. The original abuse was already devastating. To then wade through a confusing, hurtful, and humiliating Church process of reporting and investigating was like being abused all over again. Trauma-Informed Care is survivor focused and is becoming standard in many health care settings. It should be standard in our Church. This should extend not just to clergy sex abuse survivors, but all persons who have ever been abused or suffered trauma and who seek healing from our churches.

Phrases to consider when explaining the next steps for survivors are "These are the services we offer", or "These are the services we do not offer, but here is someone who can." This is also a time to share any knowledge you have about trauma and what it does to a person, with statements such as "This is what I know about trauma and abuse." One truth I do share with survivors is that, "You won't always feel this way"—there is hope. Early in their healing, survivors may not believe this, but we are people of hope, and hope is one truth I want all survivors to hear.

Leave the Door Open

Disclosure is a process not an event. Healing also is a process, unique to each survivor. After having found the courage to disclose a story of abuse, a survivor may need time and space to heal from this very act. Sometimes a survivor may feel overwhelmed with emotions and refuse or reject offers of help. Again, give the survivor the power and freedom to step back for a while but impart them with the reassurance that you have not abandoned them. Expressions such as, "As your situation changes, I can help you by providing information and support", "You are welcome here anytime", "I will pray for you", and "You have my support either way" can help leave the healing door open.

AVOID RETRAUMATIZATION

The fourth aspect of trauma-informed ministry is to avoid re-traumatization and to work to prevent future trauma and abuse. Often in our best efforts to minister to survivors, we will unintentionally remind them of past abuse or trigger an emotional reaction. If this happens, we should take accountability, apologize, and collaborate to find better methods for interaction. We should not ignore, minimize, or criticize survivors' responses.

THE TRAUMA INFORMED CHURCH

There are six guiding principles in setting up a trauma-informed community or organization:

- **Safety**—This may be the most critical role a church community can establish—make church a safe place for survivors to start to heal. It is about more than physical safety. It assures psychological and relational safety. Is there structure in place that allows survivors to feel included and protected in the faith community? Are staff and clergy trained in trauma-informed ministry? Are staff and resources that address trauma and behavioral health available or easily accessible? What are the mechanisms by which a survivor can disclose? Is there a hotline? Is the hotline staffed by someone who will respond quickly and provide the appropriate resources that a survivor needs? Does the staff know what a survivor may need in all phases of healing? Do they know how to get this training and these resources?

- **Trustworthiness and transparency**—Aside from fostering honesty and integrity, we should be unafraid of admitting that we are all broken and wounded and that we all experience trauma in some way. By speaking more openly about abuse and trauma, the stigma and isolation that survivors feel can be lifted. How is this demonstrated to the parish? Are there homilies, Masses, or prayer services dedicated to addressing the issues of abuse and trauma? Are there listening sessions to discuss abuse and trauma? Who do staff, clergy, and the faithful trust? The most important part of providing Trauma-Informed Ministry in our churches is to trust Jesus. Which personnel in church leadership are trustworthy?

- **Peer support**—Are there structures for survivors to walk alongside others who are also in recovery and healing? Groups such as the Maria Goretti Network, Hopeful Hearts Ministry, and Celebrate Recovery are excellent peer support ministries. These groups create a safe environment for a survivor to tell their story, not feel judged, and feel accepted and supported by other survivors who understand what it is like to be a survivor. It is through sharing our stories that we can promote healing for ourselves and others.

- **Collaboration and mutuality**—Everyone can play a role in the healing of survivors under the trauma-informed model. Have we allowed survivors to share their gifts with the Church? Survivors have a unique perspective on faith. Have we asked if they would be willing to share their gifts or their testimonies with others?

- **Empowerment, voice and choice**—The strengths and experiences of each individual are identified and built upon in the Church. Do survivors feel they are fully integrated into the church community? Do survivors have a voice that is equal to other voices in the Church?

- **Cultural, historical, gender issues**—Are we aware of how abuse is treated in different cultures? How has our parish changed historically in how it talks about abuse and trauma? Does our parish have a history of abuse and trauma? Have we adequately addressed previous or current stories of trauma? [20]

Trauma isolates survivors, and it divides families and communities. Dr. Judith Herman, psychiatrist, author, and researcher of child abuse and recovery from trauma notes: "All the perpetrator asks is that the community do nothing. He (sic) appeals to the universal desire to see, hear, and speak no evil. The victim, on the contrary, asks the community to share the burden of the pain. The victim demands action, engagement, and remembering." [13] The Church can be the place of connection and belonging that the survivor lost at the hands of the abuser. The Church can be the place where we finally can engage with one another, with survivors, to acknowledge not just the abuse but to acknowledge that we are together, in Christ, sharing the burden, and bringing healing to the brokenhearted.

Endnotes

1   Townsend, C., & Rheingold, A.A., (2013). Estimating a child sexual abuse prevalence rate for practitioners: studies. Charleston, S.C., Darkness to Light. Retrieved from www.D2L.org.

2   Broman-Fulks, J. J., Ruggiero, K. J., Hanson, R. F., Smith, D. W., Resnick, H. S., Kilpatrick, D. G., & Saunders, B. E. (2007). Sexual assault disclosure in relation to adolescent mental health: Results from the National Survey of Adolescents. Journal of Clinical Child and Adolescent Psychology, 36, 260 – 266.

3   Smith, D. W., Letourneau, E. J., Saunders, B. E., Kilpatrick, D. G., Resnick, H. S., & Best, C. L. (2000). Delay in disclosure of childhood rape: Results from a national survey. Child Abuse & Neglect, 24, 273 – 287.

4   https://www.nsvrc.org/sites/default/files/publications_nsvrc_factsheet_media-packet_statistics-about-sexual-violence_0.pdf

5   Consequences of abuse by religious authorities: A review. By McGraw, Danielle M.,Ebadi, Marjan,Dalenberg, Constance,Wu, Vanessa,Naish, Brandi,Nunez, Lisa. Traumatology, Feb 07 , 2019, No Pagination Specified

6   https://www.independent.co.uk/news/uk/home-news/child-sex-abuse-survivors-truth-inquiry-independent-inquiry-religion-church-a8936476.html

7   https://www.bjs.gov/content/pub/pdf/cv14.pdf

8   https://www.rainn.org/statistics/scope-problem

9   Felitti, Vincent J et al. Relationship of Childhood Abuse and Household Dysfunction to Many of the Leading Causes of Death in Adults. American Journal of Preventive Medicine, Volume 14, Issue 4, 245 – 258

10   U.S. Department of Health and Human Services, Substance Abuse and Mental Health Services, Administration Center for Substance Abuse Treatment (2015) Trauma-Informed Care in Behavioral Health Services, Retrieved from https://store.samhsa.gov/system/files/sma15-4420.pdf

11   Tracy, Steven. Mending the Soul: Understanding and Healing Abuse.

12   Kolk MD, Bessel Van der. The Body Keeps the Score: Brain, Mind, and Body in the Healing of Trauma.

13   Herman, Judith. 2015. Trauma and Recovery: The Aftermath of Violence--From Domestic Abuse to Political Terror.

14   Gillespie, R J. 2019. "Two Generation Approach to Trauma." presented at The Trauma Informed Pediatric Provider Conference, San Antonio, TX, March.

15   Pitt-Green, Teresa. Veronica's Veil: Spiritual Companionship for Survivors of Abuse: A Guide for Integrated Faith with Recovery. 2013.

16   Tener, Dafna, and Sharon B. Murphy. 2015. "Adult Disclosure of Child Sexual Abuse: A Literature Review." Trauma, Violence & Abuse 16 (4): 391–400. https://doi.org/10.1177/1524838014537906 .

17   London, Kamala, Maggie Bruck, Daniel B. Wright, and Stephen J. Ceci. 2008. "Review of the Contemporary Literature on How Children Report Sexual Abuse to Others: Findings, Methodological Issues, and Implications for Forensic Interviewers." Memory (Hove, England) 16 (1): 29–47. https://doi.org/10.1080/09658210701725732 .

18   Bottoms, et al., 2007; London, et al., 2005: London, et. al, 2008, Darkness to Light www.D2L.org http://www.d2l.org/wp-content/uploads/2017/01/all_statistics_20150619.pdf

19   Kellogg, Nancy. 2019. "Why didn't you tell? Understanding sexual abuse disclosures." presented at The Trauma Informed Pediatric Provider Conference, San Antonio, TX, March.

20   adapted from "Intermountain Ministry" http://www.intermountainministry.org/wp-content/uploads/2016/04/What-does-it-mean-for-a-ministry-to-be-trauma-informed.pdf

21   https://www.cdc.gov/features/sexualviolence/index.html

Signs and Symptoms

Dr. Deborah Rodriguez MD

*"The Spirit of the Lord is upon me ,because he
has anointed me to bring glad tidings to the poor
He has sent me to proclaim liberty to captives and
recovery of sight to the blind, to let the oppressed go
free, and to proclaim a year acceptable to the Lord."*

Lk 4:18-19

Our Savior Jesus Christ came to set all captives free from all forms
of darkness and to bind up the brokenhearted (Lk 4:18). In order to
heal, we must know what the wound is. As a doctor, I can treat pain or
infection, but it would help to know what caused the pain or infection.
From what we know about abuse and trauma, trauma affects bodies,
minds, memories, and behaviors. We could and should treat these
effects of the trauma. But until we go to the source of the problem,
we may not be offering true healing.

Signs and Symptoms of Trauma

In another chapter, I gave basic definitions of abuse, trauma, and
trauma-informed ministry. In this chapter, I hope to describe what
trauma does to the human body, mind, and spirit. The trauma I refer to
is not physical trauma, but psychological or emotional trauma. Abuse
causes trauma, but not all trauma comes from abuse. Trauma can result
from any experience or event that overwhelms a person's ability to
cope with and integrate the event. Although psychological trauma is
not the same as physical trauma, the effects of psychological trauma
impact the body in very real ways. By understanding what trauma does
to a person, not only can we as a Church better minister to survivors
of abuse, but we can also help bring healing to any person who has
experienced any form of trauma. Because the effects of trauma are

often the same, the remedy too can be the same. Our Church can be the refuge to not just clergy abuse survivors, but to all trauma survivors.

> *"The trauma carves a painful dividing line*
> *in the survivor's personal narrative, a line that*
> *splices his life in two: there's the person he was*
> *before, and the person he's become since."[1]*

Abuse affects how we survivors view and relate to ourselves, others, and God. Our lives are changed after the abuse, and this change can last a lifetime. After the abuse, no matter how long it lasted, or when it started or ended, the world suddenly became a different place. The rest of the world never really changed, only our world did.

If we were abused as children, our minds could not comprehend the enormity of the events. Our protective mechanisms reflexively activated, and we wanted to protect ourselves in any way we could. Our brains meanwhile tried to put the horrible events into some context. Unfortunately, little children are not yet able to process such conflicting events. If we cannot escape the abuse, or if the abuser is someone we depend on for sustenance and protection like a parent, then our brains must try to help our bodies cope with the need to fight back or escape. If the abuser is a trusted adult, such as a priest, the same process occurs. The result is a dissonance of perception. What we perceived as good is harming us. What we perceived as reality is too traumatic. Our minds and bodies want to escape this reality, but too often the circumstances created by the abuser and the abuse prevent us.

This inability to escape causes our minds and bodies to self-protect in other ways. Trauma isolates and traps a survivor. Survivors become trapped not by physical chains, but by threats, lies, and confusion. The stress of abuse, and especially the unpredictability or confusion about the abuser, causes a cascade of stress responses that affect every organ system and can last a lifetime.

To better understand the effects of abuse and trauma, it is helpful to understand the body's normal stress response. The following is a very basic model for understanding how the brain and body respond to stress and trauma. For me and many survivors, understanding that the responses and reactions of my body and mind to the trauma were not "all in my head" or signs that I was "crazy" was a turning point. Unfortunately, many survivors are told to "get over it" when our bodies and minds are still incapable of processing the abuse. A basic understanding of normal biologic responses can help both survivor and those that minister to them. We can stop asking survivors, "What's wrong with you?" and start asking "What happened?".

The Brain Under Stress

The "primitive" or instinctive brain, located in the brainstem, is responsible for basic self-protection. This part of the brain initiates the "fight or flight" response. It is also where the basic human instincts to feed and procreate originate. Newborn babies are born with a functioning primitive brain to signal that they are experiencing cold, heat, pain, discomfort, hunger, or fear.

The "feeling" or emotional brain includes the limbic system, which includes the amygdala and the hippocampus. Here is where both basic emotions and learning originate. This part of the brain functions best in trusting and supportive relationships. Think of the pets in our lives. My dog, whose brain is mostly the emotional and primitive brain, responds well when his basic needs of hunger and safety are met. He learns when there is consistency and a sense of order. He is forever loyal to those who provide this consistent, loving environment. Human beings have this response too. Think about the young child who sees his parent after a long absence or the joyous reunions when a soldier reunites with family members after deployment. This part of the brain is also where the response to fear and danger starts.

The "fear center" of the brain is comprised of parts of the instinctive or primitive brain and the emotion regulation center of the limbic system (amygdala and hippocampus). This part of the brain further helps us to respond to perceived danger or threat with instinct and emotion. We need to recognize danger and react quickly (and sometimes with great feeling) in order to protect ourselves.

These areas of the brain also help store memories of these events. We want to remember where we experienced danger and try to avoid it in the future. However, memories associated with trauma are not always stored in an orderly fashion. Because these memories are usually generated during times of great stress and emotion, the brain cannot always separate stimulus from emotion from reaction. These memories are what are responsible for the emotional and physical responses to previous trauma: the "trauma triggers" or "trauma reminders." Memories of persons, places, objects, and sensations, such as smell, sights, and sounds, will be stored quickly with no context. Later, a similar smell or a piece of clothing may elicit a traumatic memory of an abuser or an abusive situation. Some of the triggering experiences can be intrusive, severe, and prolonged, such as what can occur in PTSD.

Post-traumatic Stress Disorder (PTSD) is a serious condition that can occur in some survivors of abuse. After a traumatic event, such serious injury or sexual or physical violence, some survivors may re-experience the traumatic event through intrusive memories, flashbacks, and emotional and physical responses. These responses can be so disturbing and disruptive that survivors will try to avoid any situation which can remind them of the trauma. Over time, the survivor may experience symptoms of hyper-arousal, hypervigilance, and hyperreactivity which will impair their normal everyday functioning[2]. Post-traumatic Stress Disorder (PTSD) is diagnosed and best treated by professional behavioral health care specialists.

Many adult survivors of child abuse have learned to manage their trauma reminders and become quite good at avoiding triggering situations. These protective behaviors may lead others to assume the survivor is unfriendly, aloof, or "different", when all they are doing is protecting themselves from ongoing stress responses. This was my own situation for many years every time I spent time in a Catholic

Church. I would get in and out as quickly as possible. While it might have seemed like I was avoiding friendly conversation, what I was really trying to do was avoid triggering memories. Again, it is helpful not to ask or think, "What is wrong with that person?" but instead ask, "What might have happened to that person?"

The "thinking brain" consists primarily of the prefrontal cortex and may not fully develop until the late 20s. This part is responsible for sensory perception, reasoning, conscious thought, and long-term memory. It is also critical for the "executive functions" of impulse control, working memory, and mental flexibility. A child does not have a fully developed "thinking brain" and is therefore not fully capable of understanding that the abuse will ever end. To a child, the terror of abuse is forever, and there is no escape. Adults, however, can have a concept of a future without pain and abuse. Regardless of who the survivor is, instilling a sense of hope and future without pain and abuse is essential to healing.

The Stress Response

In the body, there are organs that respond to the stress signals sent from the brain. The brain sends messages in the face of danger or threat, and the body responds to these signals. There is an immediate response and a chronic response. While both involve similar brain and body actions, the long-term effects can be very different. Adrenaline is the primary hormone involved in the immediate stress response; cortisol is involved in the chronic stress response. Both hormones will set off a cascade of physical responses. Putting it all together is the brain-body stress response.

The immediate stress response begins with the amygdala which is like the body's alarm system. The amygdala sends a signal to the adrenal glands, which produce adrenaline and cortisol. Adrenaline generates the normal responses to stress: dilated pupils, increased heart rate, and accelerated and shortened breathing. Because we are preparing to respond to the stress, blood gets shunted to the arms, legs, heart, and lungs and gets shunted away from the gut and other systems non-essential to the stress response. Some of these "non-essential" systems are the immune system and the reproductive system. We are not too concerned with having a great meal or reproducing when we think our lives are in imminent danger.

This response is solely to put all effort and energy in preserving one's life. It is to allow the body to run away from danger or fight the danger. In some situations, this same cascade of responses will cause the person to freeze in place ("deer in the headlights" phenomenon).

It is critical to note that these responses are reflexive, normal, and universal. It is helpful for survivors to know that their bodies did what they could to protect them as much as possible during the abuse. Human beings, like any other mammal, are programmed for self-preservation. Even young children will understand these reactions. In my office, I use the example of imagining a bear suddenly crashing through your house. We would all experience the same responses: pupils dilating, heart and breathing racing, and feeling frightened. We wouldn't want to sit down to a meal at that time, and even if we tried, we'd probably feel nauseous. Though our bodies' responses would be the same, our reactions may not. Some of us would scream, some would run away, and some of us would grab whatever weapon we saw to try to fight off the bear. Some of us would freeze in place. These responses and reactions are normal, are not under conscious control, and survivors need to know this. We survivors have been asked too often, "Why didn't you just run away?", "Why didn't you scream?". Given what we know of the brain-body stress response, we know that some survivors were responding in the way their own brains and bodies naturally reacted. There is no fault in our biology. The fault is solely with the abuser.

Now, what happens when the bear who just crashed into your house and caused this stress response lives in the house? A child who lives with the abuser or endures repeated abuse will have the same immediate stress response, but this happens repeatedly. The child never knows if the abuser will provide love and support or will hurt and abuse. The child's stress response is always "on." The amygdala is always alarming and sending signals that cause the fear response in the body. It is as if the child's system is constantly "bathed" in cortisol (the hormone produced in this state of chronic stress). This constant state of fight or flight can produce immediate and even lifelong illnesses. These lifelong illnesses are due to cortisol affecting every system of the body, from the brain to the heart to the immune system. A study[3] of adults who had history of various forms of trauma showed that the greater the number of traumatic events as children, or "adverse childhood experiences", the greater the chance of having adult illnesses, including: heart disease, cancer, and depression. Thankfully, this is not inevitable, and there are ways to mitigate the impact of the trauma.[4]

Another parallel response to chronic stress is meant to mediate the stimulating effects of cortisol. This other response involves the hormone oxytocin, which is involved in the bonding between persons, such as what occurs between mother and her infant or between husband and wife. This hormone will lower heart rate, breathing, and many of the heightened responses generated by cortisol.[4,5] Unfortunately, oxytocin can't tell whether the person we are bonding with is truly supportive or merely nearby. Therefore, oxytocin may also cause a victim to bond, or affiliate, with their abuser. This may be what makes it so difficult for victims to leave or criticize their abusers.

What happens after the stressful or traumatic experience is just as important to long term health as the initial protective responses. Survivors need to integrate, or make sense of, the event. Integration requires safety and support. Let's go back to the scene with the bear. Once the bear has departed, our bodies will hopefully have returned to normal. The adrenaline and cortisol response would end. We might still feel a bit agitated, but over time, our heart rate and breathing would return to normal.

In time, we would probably need to talk about the event and learn from it. The fear center, having done its job, helps us recall the events but they will likely be imperfect, fragmented scenes. The other part of the fear center involves the hippocampus, which is an important part of the memory storage center of the brain. I call this the filing cabinet of the brain. Here all our memories are stored for our thinking brain to later make sense of and learn from. If a survivor does not have opportunity to talk about and process these traumatic experiences with a compassionate and supportive guide, those memories can remain forever imperfect, fragmented scenes.

This faulty memory storage is as if the file cabinet is full of unorganized memories, which a survivor carries for the rest of their life. Sometimes we survivors try to retrieve a memory as simple as grandmother's apple pie recipe, which brings back the sights and sounds of childhood, and instead we pull out a crime scene, images which elicit the same responses we had when we first endured a traumatic event.

If we suffer a traumatic event and then process it with supportive people and in safety, we can heal from even the most traumatic experiences. For example, a young, sick, or injured child who must undergo a complicated medical procedure, such as surgery, will no doubt experience a very stressful event. This child's normal fear responses activate. The amygdala sends the alarm and the adrenal glands produce adrenaline and cortisol. If that child has supportive and compassionate persons to help process the events, the child will respond in a healthy way and later integrate the traumatic experiences back into the context of love and support. The child learns that while the adults around them may not be able to prevent the painful experience, these support persons can help calm the child (thus diffusing the stress response) and finally bring closure to the event with love and support. The same is true for adult survivors of trauma. In both cases, a supportive environment makes it possible for the survivor to integrate the trauma experiences with their memories and bring healing. This is part of trauma-informed ministry.

There are several factors that determine how traumatic events will be integrated into a person's life:

- **The type of trauma.**
  A one-time medical procedure, such as a root canal, versus ongoing traumas, such as a soldier on the battlefield or the child who is repeatedly abused by a trusted adult, each elicit different long-term responses in the body.

- **The age of the person who endures the trauma.**
  Children who suffer abuse have both higher risk for long term adverse health consequences, and at the same time, they have a high capacity for resiliency and healing. Trauma will affect children differently, not just based on the age of the child, but is also dependent on the "developmental age", the temperament, and the circumstances of the abuse.

- **Individual Resiliency**
  There is also variation of response to trauma. Some children will rebound quickly no matter the adversity; others will require greater time and care to recover. Even children in the same family, who endure similar traumatic events, can each perceive and integrate the events differently. Any person or community can help foster resiliency and recovery in any survivor.

- **The support a survivor receives after the trauma.**
  Some survivors never find a safe place to begin to process past trauma. The greatest chance for healing from trauma is finding a compassionate and available support person or community.

Biblical Models of Healing

If we look at all the documented healing miracles of Jesus in Scripture, we will find:

- No healings are the same. Jesus used different words or actions for each healing (Mt 20:29-34; Mk 10:46-52; Lk 18:35-43)
- Those who are healed are also very different. Some were devout Jews (Jn 11:1-45) and others were outcasts (Mt 15:21-28).
- Sometimes it was a family or household member who asked for healing for someone else, as with the Centurion's servant (Mt 8:4ff) or the friends of the paralytic (Mt 9:1-8).
- Sometimes healings were very public ,such as healing the paralyzed man (Lk 5:18) or casting out demons (Mk 1:21ff); other times, it was more private, such as with Jairus's daughter (Mk 5:21ff).
- Sometimes those wishing to be healed were persistent and vocal, such as the blind man (Jn 9:1ff), or sometimes the cry for help was in silence, as with the woman with hemorrhage (Mk 5:21ff).
- Sometimes we don't understand Jesus' timing in the healing, as with Lazarus (Jn 11:1-45).
- Sometimes Jesus heals so that a person can return to a life of community, as with the healing of the lepers (Lk 11:17-19).

Just as each survivor is unique, no two healing journeys are alike. Sometimes the healing doesn't always look like we expected. We who support survivors can also learn from Jesus that healing may happen quickly because of our efforts, or it may take years and only through the work of many.

One Model for Healing and Restoration

At the heart of every traumatic experience is disempowerment and betrayal. This leads to isolation and disconnection from self, from community, and from God. Healing begins with empowerment and choice, which leads to re-connection with others and with God.

There is a predictable nature to the responses of persons who have experienced abuse and trauma, as well as healing. Dr. Judith Herman is a psychiatrist, researcher, and author who has focused on the understanding and treatment of child sexual abuse, traumatic stress, and community response to trauma. In her book, *Trauma and Recovery*, Dr. Herman describes three stages of recovery from trauma. While there is great variation to how each survivor heals, these stages have been a useful framework from which to guide survivors. The three stages are: 1) Safety and Stabilization, 2) Remembrance and Mourning, and 3) Reconnection and Integration.[5] Inviting Jesus into this framework of healing gives a destination, a companion, and a meaning to the abuse and to the healing.

1. **Establishment of safety**
   The first stage in healing is to establish safety for the survivor. Because of the effects of trauma, survivors may feel unsafe in their own bodies, their emotions, their memories, and their relationships. This first stage is the longest stage. Survivors have been betrayed by their abusers and by those who were supposed to protect them. It may take survivors years to feel safe enough in a relationship to disclose their abuse. The survivor must feel they can trust their support system. As the Church, we can set up a safe environment in our churches and communities for survivors to disclose their stories and to begin healing. I've described this in the section on "setting up a trauma-informed church."

2. **Remembrance and mourning**
   This second stage involves remembering, not just the trauma story, but remembering who we are in God's eyes.

As the survivor tells their story, it begins to hold less power over them. The trauma story is often scattered images of the past. Dr. Herman describes them as "scenes without words, akin to a silent movie"[6]. More importantly, they are scenes without a context. The work of reconstruction, which transforms the traumatic memories into a meaningful story, can be extraordinarily difficult. This is where trauma trained counselors and advocates can help.

Trauma brings loss. The survivor must grieve what has been lost or taken. Survivors often pass through the stages of grief[7] as they remember the past and start to contemplate the future. Survivors talk of their life before and after their abuse. Losing the old self involves grief. There is loss of self-image, integrity, and relationships. There is also loss of faith, hope, and love. Healing must acknowledge this loss.

3. **Reconnection with ordinary life**
   The final stage is reconnection. The survivor will take what has happened in the past and create a future[8]. They have mourned the old self that the trauma destroyed; now they can develop a new self. Dr. Bob Schuchts, a psychologist, therapist, author, retreat leader, and founder of the John Paul II Healing Center, writes about healing. In his retreat, called *Restoring the Glory,* he notes that before healing, "when we look at our story (of trauma), we see either shame or despair. When we look back at our story, we see shame. When we look forward, we see despair."[9] This is the lie that Satan feeds to survivors. Because abuse and trauma are so isolating, survivors often live the lie of being abandoned and rejected. Healing changes this script. Dr. Schuchts, in his book, *Be Healed*, describes some of the signs of healing from a deep wound are feeling connected, understood, accepted, and valued.[10]

Healing doesn't necessarily re-write our story, but God can edit out the errors that Satan has imposed. Through salvation history, each time Satan works to destroy God's people, God intervenes. In Jesus, the intervention is perfect and eternal. Some of the survivors I have journeyed with see easily how Satan has been intervening in their lives, but they have trouble seeing how God has been intervening. Trauma-informed ministry helps a survivor look back at the past and see how God has been present in their own story of abuse. If the survivor can see where God has been in the past, the survivor is more likely to see how God is intervening in their present and can be a part of their future.

It is in this final stage, which can come years after the initial disclosure, that the survivor can begin to integrate the trauma story into their future story. This is also where reconnecting with self, with others, and with God occurs. Some survivors may use this reconnection and reintegration to develop a new mission, perhaps advocating or supporting other survivors. Survivors who have reached this stage, in some form, are often some of the most powerful witnesses to God's healing presence and mercy. This is the time to allow survivors to create, and if they wish share, their testimonies of healing.

It is important to remember that this healing process is not linear in progression. Survivors may oscillate between the stages, sometimes making swift progression only to return to earlier stages. Survivors must not be forced into any stage.

Secondary trauma

> *"If one member suffers, all suffer together with it;*
> *if one member is honored, all rejoice together with it."*
> *(1 Cor 12:26)*

Just as abuse and trauma can affect individuals, trauma can also affect communities. In *Trauma and Recovery*, Dr. Herman also notes what happens on an individual level can happen on a wider societal level, and what affects the individual also affects the wider society.[11] Just as a survivor will utilize denial, repression, and dissociation to deal with the symptoms of trauma, an organization or a society can also engage in the same coping mechanisms.

Secondary trauma is the adverse emotional effect a person experiences as a result of hearing the firsthand trauma experiences of another. This type of trauma can occur suddenly as when one hears about a tragic event, such as the personal accounts of war or natural disaster. There can also be cumulative effects for counselors, first responders, and pastors who hear and see stories of abuse and trauma frequently.

Another recent experience has been in our Catholic parishes and communities, who have been hearing the many accounts of abuse in our Church. Sometimes those faithful Catholics, who suddenly leave the faith or those who respond in anger, may be those suffering from secondary trauma. If this trauma is not recognized, it can cause the same symptoms as someone who has suffered primary trauma.

One of the most insidious aspects of secondary trauma is that it is often seen in those who are closest to the abused. Repeated exposure to stories of abuse and its repercussions can lead to reactions from spouses and family that are very similar to PTSD. This can place unique strains on relationships, and it is one reason that trauma victims also suffer higher rates of separation and divorce. The frustration and confusion caused by secondary trauma may in turn negatively affect the original victim, creating a vicious cycle. We must be aware of these risks and make an effort to support those who are supporting survivors.

Part of trauma-informed ministry is to be aware of secondary trauma on the individual basis and on the larger community as well. As we intervene and foster healing for individuals, we must also help with the healing of the larger group as well.

A Word About Shame.

"O my God, I am too ashamed and embarrassed
to lift my face to you, my God, for our iniquities

> *have risen higher than our heads, and our*
> *guilt has mounted up to the heavens."*
>
> *Ezra 9:6*

Every survivor, at some point, will face shame. Shame is one of the most destructive parts of abuse. But not all shame belongs to the survivor. According to Dr. Steven Tracy, pastor, author, and counselor, it is helpful to look at two forms of shame.[12] Healthy shame, which is what we should have in response to our own sin, should draw us closer to God. A healthy conscience responds to willful sin by creating a sense of guilt before God and others. With this type of shame, we should want to confess our sins and make amends to God and to others. This helps us grow in holiness.

Toxic shame, on the other hand, is the shame that belongs to our abusers. It comes from their sins and should stay with them. Our abusers are the ones who sinned and committed evil. Because of our protective reflexes and desperate need to make sense of the horror of abuse, we sometimes turn the blame to ourselves.

Dan Allender, a therapist and author, who has studied the effects of abuse and trauma recovery, calls this toxic shame a "silent killer, much the way that high blood pressure is a quiet, symptom-free destroyer….Shame has the power to take our breath away and replace it with the stale air of condemnation and disgust."[13] He goes on to say, "The shame label is one of Satan's most powerful and effective tools." Shame blinds us to God's love, presence, and mercy. Shame can be so toxic that it becomes difficult, if not impossible, for survivors to see God and God's mercy. "It's difficult to pray to someone whom you believe is judging you a failure."[14]

"I did not feel worthy to be in church," one survivor once told me. This survivor always sat in the back of the church, if she came into the sanctuary at all. She felt everyone could see her shame. And she never once thought God could ever overlook this shame and just see her. In fact, the thought that God might see her, was too terrifying. She told me that, "If they knew the truth about me, they would want nothing to do with me."

One of the most liberating truths is knowing God loves me as I am, right now, no matter what. I can't disappoint God. There are occasions where I will willfully disobey or reject God, but I can't ever lose God's love. Toxic shame, the shame inflicted on us by the abuse and by the abuser, keeps us from seeing ourselves as God see us. We can't imagine why God would want or love us. It helps survivors to hear, "It was not your fault," or "You are not to blame." God does not blame us for the abuse. But sometimes, we survivors believe we are responsible for what has happened to us. The Church can never remind us enough that God loves us. One exercise I give to survivors is to meditate on the scene of the Baptism of Jesus Christ (Mt 3:12; Mk 1:9, Lk 3:20). I tell them to imagine hearing the heavens open and a voice say, "This is my beloved, in whom I am well pleased." Too often, survivors think that God could never be pleased with them. We as the Church need to be delivering this message more often.

Forgiveness

For survivors of abuse and trauma, forgiveness can be one of the most difficult acts to do, and it can be one of the most healing. In my work with survivors of trauma, especially from abuse, I remind them of the difference between forgiveness and reconciliation. No one should ever ask us to forget or excuse what has happened to us. We should, however, be reminded of how freeing and healing it can be to explore forgiveness. There are many resources which address forgiveness. June Hunt, Christian counselor and author, provides one such resource to distinguish forgiveness and reconciliation.

FORGIVENESS

- Can take place with only one person
- Is directed one way
- Is a decision to release the offender
- Is a change in thinking about the offender
- Is a free gift to the one who has broken trust
- Is extended even if it is never earned
- Is unconditional, regardless of repentance

RECONCILIATION

- Requires at least two persons
- Is reciprocal, occurring two ways
- Is the effort to rejoin the offender
- Is a change in behavior by the offender
- Is a relationship based on restored trust
- Is offered because it has been earned
- Is conditional, based on repentance

From *Choosing Forgiveness* by June Hunt[15]

Trauma-Informed Ministry can help a survivor to consider the potential for healing that can come with forgiveness, but it should not confuse and pressure a survivor toward reconciliation.

Conclusion

We are a wounded Church made up of wounded people. We must let survivors know that we, as the Church, can be their trusted companion on their journey of healing. We must provide safety from future harm. We must allow survivors a chance to mourn their loss and reassure them that they were not to blame. We can help them find a way to reconnect to a life where they remember their past without shame and contemplate their future without despair.

My prayer is that every survivor of abuse and every person who has experienced trauma will know the loving presence of Jesus Christ. I pray that this loving presence can come through the Church and through family and friends. I pray that the Church be a leader in trauma-informed ministry to be a place of welcome and refuge for the wounded.

Endnotes

1   Naparstek, Belleruth. 2004. Invisible Heroes: Survivors of trauma and How They Heal.

2   American Psychiatric Association. (2013) Diagnostic and statistical manual of mental disorders, (5th ed.). Washington, DC

3   Felitti, Vincent J et al. Relationship of Childhood Abuse and Household Dysfunction to Many of the Leading Causes of Death in Adults. American Journal of Preventive Medicine, Volume 14, Issue 4, 245-258.

4   Kolk MD, Bessel Van der. The Body Keeps the score: Brain, Mind, and Body in the Healing of Trauma.

5   Herman, Judith. 2015. Trauma and Recovery: The Aftermath of Violence--From Domestic Abuse to Political Terror.

6   Herman, J. p 175

7   https://en.wikipedia.org/wiki/Kübler-Ross_model

8   Herman, J. p. 196

9   Schuchts, Bob. John Paul II Healing Center. https://jpiihealingcenter.org/

10   Schuchts, Bob. 2011. Be Healed.

11   Herman, J. p. 212.

12   Tracy, Steven. Mending the Soul: Understanding and Healing Abuse. 2008.

13   Allender, Dan. The Wounded Heart: Hope for Adult Victims of Childhood Sexual Abuse. p 59

14   Allender, p. 14

15   Hunt, June Hunt. Choosing Forgiveness.

The Suffering Church

Michael Vanderburgh

Christ promised for us a suffering church. I think that is a very important thing to remember, not only for our individual faith journeys, but also for a sense of community and accompaniment of one another as members of the same body. Jesus did not give us an invincible Church; he instead gave us a vulnerable Church. And that should be no surprise to anyone who is familiar with Jesus's life among us in the flesh. At every turn, He modeled for us a humble, purposeful vulnerability, not a barricaded, bunkered invincibility. He knew that we would suffer, because He knew all too well the grip of sin in our lives, a grip that would spare no one, not even his apostles and priests whom he sent to lead us.

In the Gospel of John, chapter 21, Jesus tells Peter that he will suffer at the hands of others. In Matthew, chapter 10, Jesus tells us that He is sending us like sheep in the midst of wolves. And in Matthew, chapter 24, Jesus tells us, "You will be hated by all nations because of my name. And then many will be led into sin; they will betray and hate one another. Many false prophets will arise and deceive many; and because of the increase of evildoing, the love of many will grow cold." Christ promised for us a suffering Church.

The silver lining of suffering – or perhaps more accurately its constant companion – is love itself. Because the deeper we experience suffering, the deeper we can experience love. St. Catherine of Siena noted that as love grows, suffering grows with it.[1]

But never a suffering so great or a love so strong that we could surpass the suffering or love of God Himself, which we witness as He pours Himself out completely on the cross and, in full knowledge of our sins, offers us eternal life with Him. The whole idea that suffering can also be redeeming when we look to God in the midst of our suffering, especially when we accompany others as they suffer, transforms us from hapless objects of desires to humble witnesses of the triumph of the Cross and eternal life through Jesus.

This was a life-saving realization for me as a 12-year-old, who suffered greatly at home from a severely alcoholic and emotionally abusive father and who suffered also at church from a priest who couldn't control his compulsions to sexually engage with men and boys. Even as a 12-year-old, I knew that my own horrible situation was not the crucifixion I saw as I gazed upon God on the Cross.

But as great as Jesus's passion and resurrection instructs us, perhaps it is easier for us to see the relationship between love and suffering with a common example. Imagine two friends observing a new mother holding her infant child. One friend says to the other, "Oh, looook – the baby looooves his mama!" The other replies, "No. That baby knows nothing about love. The baby is warm. The baby is comfortable. The baby is fed. The baby is happy. But he knows nothing of love." His mother, though, through embracing her vulnerability in pregnancy, from the day she knew she was pregnant onward, she has suffered for him. Suffering of every sort: physical, mental, and spiritual. She knows that her love has grown in the same measure of that suffering, and she seeks to continue growing that love through all the uncertainties of his life. The infant boy, over time, as he grows into a toddler, a schoolboy, a teen, and an adult, will gradually learn love through his witnessing of others and his own experiences with vulnerability, affection, sacrifice, and suffering for others.

The redemptive aspect of our suffering is greatly affected by the tenderness of each other's mercy. So let us remember the power of the tenderness of our own mercy toward one another, as we experience suffering and accompany suffering. That is key to our healing as the Church, as we attempt to emerge from the abuse crisis.

For nearly eleven years, I spent most of my time working quite closely with hundreds of priests, a few dozen deacons, and about a half dozen bishops. It was my job, and I was completely committed to it. The majority of those relationships were, and are, solid sources of grace and encouragement for me, but many of them have been particularly draining and challenging to my faith. My proximity to them in my work exposed me to certain evils in their lives: alcohol addiction, cocaine addiction, adulterous affairs, attempted suicide, theft in office, abusiveness to staff and parishioners, or just plain contempt for any authority but their own.

I have learned much about suffering over the years, through my own experiences, through my accompaniment of others, and through my observations of others. Suffering from each of these sources has greatly deepened my experience of love; within the Church's current suffering from the abuse crisis are seeds of faith leading us into deeper communion with Our Lord Jesus Christ. We should not waste our suffering! Let's not run from it. Let's learn from our suffering. Let's build authentic love alongside our suffering, with the humility and vulnerability that Christ modeled for us.

We are all very accustomed to individual suffering, but now I call your attention to the suffering of the Church, and the redemption that can accompany that suffering.

I would like to remind you of a story. It's a story that each of us knows, at least in part. It is a story that we know holds great truth, though there is no definitive version of it. In fact, the story has been in human memory for so long that apparently none of the Scripture writers or Church fathers saw fit to reduce it into writing, except by oblique reference in various places like Ezekiel and Isaiah. I believe that this absence of clarity in Scripture provides a particular blessing for each of us, because the uncertainty of "what actually happened" compels us to continually examine how this story plays out time and time again in our own lives.

Before God created Man, one of the seraphim angels, purportedly so smart and beautiful that he was named "Morning Star" or "Light Bringer" or, in Latin, Lucifer, became so consumed by his own vanity that he burst with pride at his awesomeness. He was convinced that he was omnipotent like God, and he recruited other angels to join him in choosing a path for themselves, a path apart from what God planned for them. A much lesser angel, whose original name must have been so insignificant that it did not appear in the story, was armed only with his sense of God's will for him and his complete trust in God. We now know him by the Hebrew words for the rhetorical taunt that he asked: "Mich-a-el (Who is God)?!" Michael led the other loyal angels in casting Lucifer and his allies forever out of God's presence in heaven.

Have you ever pondered why God left all of this to his angels? For me, it brings to mind the spiritual work of mercy we call fraternal correction, which is perhaps the trickiest work of mercy because of its susceptibility to pride. But nevertheless, God called on lesser angels to deal with evil, just as He calls on you and me to fully participate as members of the Church. We are part of the Body of Christ, each of us with roles as priest, prophet, and king. Each of us has a role in turning evil away and building the Kingdom.

Among the seven capital sins in our catechism, pride is chief among them. In my own reflections, I assert pride as the beginning point for every sin and humility to accept grace as the antidote for every sinful inclination.

Ponder with me the role of pride and its particularly insidious nature in church structure. Consider this advice from Archbishop Fulton Sheen:

"Satan always tempts the pure — the others are already his. Satan stations more devils on monastery walls than in dens of iniquity, for the latter offer no resistance. Do not say it is absurd that Satan should appear to our Lord, for Satan must always come close to the godly and the strong — the others succumb from a distance."[2]

Consider this enshrinement of individualism in this statement in a Supreme Court opinion from nearly thirty years ago:

"At the heart of liberty is the right to define one's own concept of existence, of meaning, of the universe, and of the mystery of human life."[3]

You might be saying to yourself, what does this have to do with pride and the Church?

Remember that this is the ecosystem, the backdrop and the cultural air that we breathe, as we seek to go and make disciples of all nations, baptizing them in the name of the Father, the Son, and the Holy Spirit. We bring it into the institutional Church with us. It hardens our hearts and makes us defensive about our attitudes and choices, and sometimes offensive about our attitudes and choices!

I mentioned the reality of our post-Christian society, a radically individualist ecosystem in which we must witness the Gospel and minister to all of God's people. But we have also created our own institutional Church ecosystem, which over the centuries has enshrined a clerical structure that glorifies and rewards rank and ambition. Until a few years ago, daily Vatican press updates that officially announced new Archbishops routinely referred to "so-and-so, elevated to the dignity of Archbishop." It's also in our liturgies! Various forms of the Ordination rite refer to "deserving of being promoted to a higher honor in the Church" or "rank of presbyter or rank of Bishop." This provides a convenient trap that the Evil One sets for us. It's a trap that weaponizes our celebration of faith.

How do you treat a deacon, priest, or bishop? Is each a successively higher rung on the ladder to heaven – an achievement? Do you treat them in such a way that feeds their human tendency for pride, or your own pride at being their friend or relative? This is not a question to be asked once and answered once with finality. It is a question that you should revisit regularly, because you and I create the culture of our Church by our attitudes and actions. In my experience, our attitudes toward clergy are common origins of pride that creates a path of self-righteousness with great power to inflict suffering. Fulton Sheen once remarked that "Satan stations more devils on monastery walls than in dens of iniquity."[1]

There is much to explore about pride in general, applicable to laypeople and clergy alike. For our purposes here, I will focus on the effects of pride on our priests and bishops, and how we might rebuild trust in the Church by helping them avoid pride and practice humility.

About twelve years ago, I became familiar with a seminarian who really stood out from his peers. He was athletic, strong, and youthful, and he had a few years of work experience before entering the seminary. He always had an appearance of strong purpose about him, paying close attention to every detail for beautifully and emphatically celebrated liturgies. As a seminarian, he was jovial and approachable, but that immediately changed upon his ordination to the priesthood. At once, he became distant and aloof; only much later I discovered that he detested the fact that I still called him by his first name. He then received his first pastor assignment in a very rural area, and I didn't hear of him for several years. Recently, he was assigned as pastor of a large suburban parish, which included a very fine young priest as parochial vicar. This priest I had also known through his seminary years. His academic prowess, congeniality, and humility made him a favorite of his peers and formators in the seminary, and his aura of joyfulness was palpable. Overarching all of this, though, was a great humility and tenderness that exuded holiness. In short, he was very popular, and his new boss was not. The pastor began cutting his vicar out of meetings and decisions and made increasing demands on him for liturgies and sacramental preparation. The situation was made worse by parishioners flocking to the vicar's Masses, which resulted in last-minute changes to celebrant assignments and restriction of parish communications. Over a beer recently, the young vicar told me that as a seminarian he couldn't comprehend why young priests were leaving the priesthood, but now he could clearly see why that might happen.

Of course, we know that day to day comfort is not a worthy goal for a Christian, and any true relationship requires tension and friction, but how do we know when God is leading us and not our own pride? We know that humility is the antidote for pride, but where and how do we find it?

Jesus Christ himself gave us very direct answers on this subject. No fewer than three times did He squarely address humility as the antidote for pride. See Matthew 23:12, Luke 14:11, and Luke 18:14.

In my many years of service to my Archbishop (there were two
of them over that period), my primary work relationships were with
about 180 pastors. As I stated earlier, most of those relationships were
solid sources of grace and encouragement for me, but many of them
have been particularly draining and challenging to my faith. As I look
back, by the numbers, I would say that it was about twenty priests,
so perhaps a bit more than ten percent. But those twenty men took up
about fifty percent of my time, and to this day, I wish that each of them
would've had Matthew 23:12 tattooed to their mind's eye!

How we treat our priests and bishops matters. If you are enamored
by the prestige of priesthood, that is not helpful. If you put them on a
pedestal, they will have difficulty staying grounded. The Greek root of
humility is humous – literally "dirt"! On the other hand, treating our
priests and bishops with great respect also matters very much, just as it
matters that we treat every person with great respect.

Bishop Vincent Long Van Nguyen is the Bishop of Parramatta in
New South Wales, Australia. He recently spoke about suffering abuse
from clergy as an adult many years ago when he came to Australia
from Vietnam.

He said, ". . . it is my conviction that the priesthood 'pedestalized'
is the priesthood dehumanized. It is bound to lead us into the illusion
of a messiah complex and an inability to claim our wounded humanity
and to minister in partnership."

> *'The church, he said, needs to dismantle the pyramid*
> *model of church which "promotes the superiority of*
> *the ordained and the excessive emphasis on the role*
> *of the clergy at the expense of nonordained ..."* [4]

There are two sources of suffering for the church community:
external and internal. Our external sources of suffering are political,
legal, and cultural. These are things like a broken immigration system,
Roe v. Wade, and rampant individualism and relativism, and in some
parts of the world, outright persecution and murder of Christians.
Though each of us has a part in participating in our civil structures that

can affect these outcomes, the Church, acting on its own, can do little to prevent them.

Interestingly, our internal sources of suffering are also political, legal, and cultural. I spent a decade as an assistant to several bishops, and I can attest that the fear of scandal was a constant primary consideration in managing any crisis or potential crisis. "How will this look?" and "What will they think?" are internal political sources of suffering in the Church when the fear of scandal itself becomes a scandal. In this way, the Church, in minding its image before other considerations, suffers the same pride that is the origin of all sin.

Over many centuries, the Church has developed instincts to heavily draw upon rules and structures to drive decisions, often leading with a formulaic response to a crisis instead of a pastoral response. That is an internal, legal source of suffering. Though some can persuasively argue that such legal expression is a necessity for safeguarding theological truths and discipline in the Sacraments, nevertheless we must recognize that the primacy of legal proceedings – in civil and canon law – has often yielded years-long suffering in the Church, for victims and non victims alike.

That leads to our primary cultural source of internal suffering in the Church, which is clericalism. Our emphasis on describing clergy as "set apart" from laity has led to an exclusive and hierarchical system that has created double standards in law and in practice. I don't think that I need to convince anyone that if you are a lay employee of your Diocese, the consequences for your misbehavior are much more likely to be swift and severe than for a similarly situated clergyman or religious. Even with all the progress we have made by applying zero tolerance since the Dallas Charter, we still have instances when bishops have struggled to take decisive actions that never would have been delayed in the case of a layperson. I do not offer this observation as an indictment, but I offer it as a reminder that our individual brokenness provides a constant source of suffering, and that none of us is immune from inflicting suffering on ourselves and others.

So what is redemptive suffering? It's when we see Christ with us in our suffering. When we say that we are in excruciating pain, we are actually saying "pain from the cross", ex cruce is Latin for "from the cross", though that's likely not foremost on my mind whenever I'm in great pain. If we are able to see Christ in our suffering, then we are able to gaze upon Love itself and feel God's embrace in the midst of our agony. Just as a child, of any age, looks to his mother when in crisis or pain and his mother tenderly responds however she is able, we can do the same with Our Lord, but with perfect confidence of His eternal love and embrace.

As an adult, my first real experience of this was with the tragic death of my brother Rob, who many years ago took his own life at age twenty-two. He was the eighth child in our family, and I was the ninth. We fought a lot, the way young brothers do when they spend a lot of time together. His death blew a big hole in my life, which brought my attention to God-sized holes in my life, and God's infinite ability to fill any hole, address any pain, and endure any suffering right alongside me. Over time, I grew to appreciate Jesus's numerous examples of personal vulnerability throughout His active ministry, leading up to the Way of the Cross. It was then that I realized that He first promised for us a suffering Church before His promise of eternal life.

Like many victims of child sexual abuse, my spiritual and emotional suffering was latent, hidden from view, for twenty years. And also like many victims, the priest in my story was not the only bad actor in my life, for in fact I had already been greatly wounded for several years when he came along. To be sure, if he had never come along there still would be plenty of childhood trauma haunting me to this day. That reality makes our response to suffering continually important as we accompany one another.

Also like many other child victims, as an adult my outer life is very high functioning. I have a good job, a stable and growing family, and an active faith life. My inner life is quite another story. The truth is that I struggle in my vocation as a husband and a father, and I am not a good steward of myself. But in those struggles, I realize that my weakness is my strength. My vulnerability to others is the key to receiving and delivering God's mercy in my life. When I am "closed in", when I have a bunker mentality, I can no longer see Jesus in the eyes of others. But when I challenge myself to be present and open to others, that is the place where God's grace and mercy pour out among us. I must be willing to accompany others and to be affected by the friction between and among us. Without friction, there is no relationship. With no relationship, there is no community. With no community, there is no opportunity to share the Gospel, mercy, or forgiveness. With true community, there is openness to vulnerability and an embrace of individual weakness. It is there, the community that is the Body of Christ, that our weakness is our strength.

Today I work for the Society of St. Vincent de Paul, which keeps me surrounded by mercy and accompaniment every day. One thing Vincentians practice very well – in the face of all sorts of suffering – is mercy. Mercy is the love that binds the wounds of sin and suffering, poured out from the Holy Spirit and into the hearts and hands of His collaborators. Mercy provides the unconditional love we need to accompany the poor and marginalized, many of whom hurt themselves and others through their actions and inactions.

Mercy flooded over me in 2004 when I first told my priest abuse story to the caring chancellor of my Diocese. He was my field hospital, and he got me on a path to continuing healing. I also encountered the grace of a humble and apologetic Bishop – the same Bishop who supervised the offending priest so many years before. And I was freely offered a lifetime of accompaniment and professional assistance, which have been abundant mercies continually poured out for me.

The Church's wounds to itself and its individual members are more visible and more prominent than wounds that people outside the Church inflict. Because of the Church's unique place at the forefront of our earthly Christian story, which is vulnerability, tenderness, mercy, and love pointing to the transcendent immortal embrace of God, it firstly and prominently displays its wounds; this is similar to how our Lord firstly takes our wounds to Himself, prominently displayed for all on the Cross. But of course, we, as spotted members of the spotless bride of Christ, bring these wounds upon ourselves, and our bishops sometimes wound the Church through their failings of leadership and responsibility.

In these nearly twenty years since the Dallas Charter, there have been many graces poured out from the Holy Spirit. A great amount of courage was required by our bishops to take the leap of "zero tolerance" and begin a unified approach to protecting our children, the most vulnerable sheep in the flock. But our journey down this path has not been without additional suffering and failure.

So what can you do? Help your priest. Help him be a good shepherd. Help him be *the* Good Shepherd, in imitation of Our Lord Jesus Christ. The Good Shepherd is not a practical shepherd. A practical shepherd cares for the overall health of his flock. The good of the many outweighs the good of the one. If a stray lamb or two were lost, he could still have a successful season. For a priest or bishop who seeks to be a practical shepherd, this line of thinking might be borne from a fear of scandal or a fear of financial loss for the Church. The Good Shepherd tenderly cares for each lamb, even through great struggles and personal risk. This is inefficient and expensive, and hardly a model for a successful business venture. Sometimes, we see a priest or bishop act as the Good Shepherd to other priests and a practical shepherd to others. One receives abundant mercy while the other is left unattended. It's a real challenge to be the Good Shepherd! So please help your priest and bishop be the Good Shepherd.

But, of course, the truth is that each of us struggles with weakness. Some realize it and try to hide it. Others realize it and embrace the opportunity to be vulnerable and receive God's mercy through our Christian community. The Church must learn to embrace its weaknesses and practice vulnerability. I think this is what Pope Francis means when he says he wants a poor Church for the poor. Our weakness is our strength. Our suffering invites mercy to flood over us and redeems love; a love we are called to share with abandon.

Help your priest or bishop be weak. Help him be vulnerable. Help him be the Good Shepherd to care for each lamb and not just the good of the flock. If he shows a bunker mentality, help him out of it. If he stands apart from the flock, help him engage and embrace his sheep!

The best way to encourage vulnerability is to practice it. Can you be vulnerable to others as you witness your faith? One of my inner struggles is that structured prayers and devotions are very difficult for me. Many times in my life the experience of deep meditation has been too intense for me, with overwhelming emotions of sadness and joy in equal measure. Other times, I have felt a draining spiritual dryness where I cannot feel God's embrace.

As I shared with you earlier, the young priest had been a model of humility and universally attracted parishioners and non parishioners with his effective witness to the Gospel. But over that beer, he confessed to me that in the few months serving under his new pastor, he had become angry when celebrating Mass, Confession, and Anointing. He now understood why a young priest would leave the priesthood. When he shared this with me, I could plainly see how the anger he mentioned had completely drained him. It was a Holy Spirit moment for me. I said, "You are at a juncture. You need to decide whether you are going to be a wounded warrior or a wounded healer. The path of the wounded warrior is not going to take you where you want to go."

My advice for him came from my own experience of anger, humiliation, and humility. By the way, isn't it interesting how humiliation and humility are related? As I mentioned, the root of both of them is "humous" which means "dirt" or "grounded," as in "close to reality." The literal difference is between "being put to the ground" in the case of humiliation and keeping yourself on the ground in the case of humility, but both certainly have a grounding effect!

You have probably heard the saying, "Christ came to comfort the afflicted and to afflict the comfortable."

Pope Francis received a lot of grief for taking his Curia to the woodshed for Christmas 2017. The negative attention overshadowed much wisdom within.

He said,

> *"A faith that does not put us in crisis is a faith in crisis; a faith that does not make us grow is a faith that must grow; a faith that does not question us is a faith on which we must ask ourselves; a faith that does not animate us is a faith that must be animated; a faith that does not upset us is a faith that must be upset. In reality, a merely intellectual or lukewarm faith is only a proposal of faith, which could be realized when it comes to involve the heart, the soul, the spirit and our whole being, when God is allowed to be born and reborn in the manger of the heart, when we allow the star of Bethlehem to guide us to the place where the Son of God lies, not among kings and luxury, but among the poor and the humble."[5]*

One phenomenon that I have come to recognize in my life is that humility is never firm in its foundation unless the ground it rests upon is vulnerability. Think of God in the flesh, a completely vulnerable infant in a feeding trough in the backwater of backwaters of the Roman Empire. That is the ground of vulnerability to which God's humility cleaves to our memory. Think again of the vulnerability of Jesus when his parents lost Him before he was found in the temple. Think of his adult ministry. He never modeled for us a trust in any thing or any one other than the Father. But he did model for us vulnerability. At first, it seemed slight and simple. Turn the other cheek. And then it became radical vulnerability – all the way to the Cross.

Recently, I visited a priest friend at a retreat center, and he asked me, "Why do you trust Father So-and-So?" It was a fair question, since up to that point, he had heard of several of my bad experiences with priests and bishops. Without hesitation, I blurted out, "I don't trust anybody. I try to think of things in terms of vulnerability. Humans will always fail me at some point, so I am vulnerable in various degrees to them. I am more vulnerable to Father So-and-So than I am to other priests, because I have come to know him fairly well. But even he will fail me at some point. God will never fail me, so I save my trust for Him."

On that same visit, I shared with him that part of my lived experience of redemptive suffering is learning how to cry. I don't know about you, but when I grew up, I came to associate crying with shame. The minute tears would well up, I felt like Adam in the Garden, hiding in shame. As an adult, when my childhood terrors finally caught up with me, and I was crying far more than I ever remember as a child, I wanted to figure out how to embrace the sadness and tears in a redemptive sort of way. Then, one day it hit me: What if I could experience my tears as God's physical presence washing away my suffering? What if its uncontrollable nature was because my own likeness of God was welling up inside of me and overflowing to remind me that God is in me and I am in Him?

I have learned that we also have a compulsion to skip over uncomfortable "little sufferings" in our lives. It's easy to infer that our general unwillingness to be uncomfortable, which is much the same as an unwillingness to be vulnerable and humble, puts us on a path for big trouble with our pride, just as little sins lead to big sins.

For the last several years, my youngest son, George, has been infamous for watching the same cartoons over and over again, with the Netflix remote in hand, rewinding his favorite parts of each episode and fast forwarding over boring or scary parts. It was very aggravating, to say the least, if anyone attempted to sit and watch any of his shows with him. But just a few weeks ago, I discovered that he was also doing this with episodes he had never seen before. He would anticipate moments that he thought would be boring or scary or uncomfortably mooshy for an 11-year-old and fast-forward until he could tell that scene was over. He didn't seem to mind that he was missing details in the middle, because of course, everything worked out well for the good guys in the end anyway. The minute I realized this, I had one of those moments that every father has – the feeling that I was the stupidest, worst father in the world. Almost as bad as when I dropped his big brother on his head at four weeks old. How could I not notice that my son has been conditioning himself for avoidance for years now?!

Pope Benedict, as Cardinal Ratzinger, wrote about the humility lacking in many members of the Church, a phenomenon which he called "Pelagianism of the Pious." He said,

> *"They do not want any forgiveness from God, nor indeed any gift at all from him. They want to be okay themselves, wanting not forgiveness but their just reward. They want security, not hope. By means of a tough and rigorous system of religious practices, by means of prayers and actions, they want to create for themselves a right to blessedness. What they lack is the humility essential to any love— the humility to be able to receive what we are given over and above what we have deserved and achieved. The denial of hope in favor of security that we are faced with here rests on the inability to bear the tension of waiting for what is to come and to abandon oneself to God's goodness. This kind of Pelagianism is thus an apostasy from love and from hope but also at the profoundest level from faith too. Man hardens his heart against himself, against others and ultimately against God: man needs God's divinity but no longer his love. He puts himself in the right, and a God that does not cooperate becomes his enemy. The Pharisees of the New Testament are an eternally valid representation of this deformation of religion. The core of this Pelagianism is a religion without love that in this way degenerates into a sad and miserable caricature of religion."*[6]

Faith itself is a gift. I think that is very important to remember. My agnostic, alcoholic father finally managed to give up drinking. I was never quite sure how he did it, since he didn't believe in a higher power so the 12-step programs were no good for him. As time went by, he became an atheist, and in the last years of his life, a militant atheist. I spent more time with him than anyone except my mom. I held his hand as he lay dying in a hospital bed. It's an intense experience to accompany an atheist on his deathbed. He didn't have the gift of faith, or perhaps he did as he was slipping away. But he's Dad. I love him, so I wanted to be with him at the end, and I pray for him every day. I'm not his judge or anyone else's judge. I'm made for love and for mercy. Graces overflow my life, and I am grateful for my suffering in faith to recognize them.

Several years ago I was meditating on my own brokenness in Adoration of the Blessed Sacrament, and these words flooded my mind:

Stay with me.
See the beauty in my brokenness.
Touch the wounds in my side, my hands, my feet.
Feel the tenderness of my mercy.
And there. THERE. Know the love of your God.

Endnotes

1   https://www.catholiccompany.com/getfed/catherine-of-siena-on-suffering-6049
2   http://www.ewtn.com/library/ANSWERS/ISADEVIL.htm
3   *Planned Parenthood v. Casey 1992*
4   https://www.ncronline.org/news/people/australian-bishop-urges-end-clericalism -
     "Australian bishop urges end to clericalism" Peter Feuerherd- *National Catholic
     Reporter 12-13-2017*
5   Christmas Greetings to the Roman Curia, Pope Francis December 21, 2017 http://
     w2.vatican.va/content/francesco/en/speeches/2017/december/documents/papa-
     francesco_20171221_curia-romana.html
6   The Yes of Jesus Christ: Exercises in Faith, Hope and Love, Pope Benedict XVI,
     Crossroad Publishing Company 2005 pp. 81-82 https://books.google.com/books/about/
     The_Yes_of_Jesus_Christ.html?id=0W2OAAAAMAAJ

I Wish to See

Chapter introduction by Allen Hebert

Around the time when I recognized my relationship with Fr. Andy as sexual abuse, I also began to delve deeply into learning and living out my Catholic faith and making Jesus the Lord of all aspects of my life. My abuser, perhaps as part of his method of grooming, told me everything I had learned about the Church's teachings on sexual morality, from my parents, my Catholic school, and the Church, were outdated, prudish, and ultimately would not bring me happiness. He taught me that I needed to explore my sexuality, and there was absolutely nothing wrong with having sex before marriage; such exploration was in fact good and healthy. My view of human sexuality was severely distorted and in much need of repair due to his influence and instruction. This distorted view of the human body and sexuality led me to years of living in anxiety and fear. While I experienced fleeting pleasures, I had little joy.

After reading a Catholic novel, I had a conversion of heart. I desired to live according to God's plan instead of my own, and so, I accepted the Church's teachings even though I didn't fully understand them. In the winter of 2000, I encountered Pope Saint John Paul II's *Theology of the Body,* and over the course of several years, this good news would help uproot the lies that deprived me of peace and union with God for so many years. I couldn't imagine writing a book seeking to provide healing to victims and the Church without including at least an introduction to this great gift that St. John Paul II gave to the world.

Sexual abuse indeed has a devastating effect on the family, whether it is perpetrated by a family member or someone outside the family. This type of abuse affects far more people than solely the person who suffered the physical abuse, since they are part of a family and may one day have their own family. Sexual abuse of a child forms them in a twisted view of human sexuality and robs them of their innocence. Since many sexual abuse survivors go on to lead a promiscuous lifestyle, in a sense, they share their abuse with their peers, cause their parents suffering due to their departure from the true teaching of the faith in the area of sexual morality, and, if they marry, they carry a lot of baggage into that union. Victims have a right to reclaim their original dignity and to receive the blessings that God desires to bestow on them, in this life and the next.

Come and Become One Who Sees:

Sexual Chaos, Theology of the Body, and the Triumph of the Immaculate Heart

Christopher West

For most of human history, a total eclipse of the sun was an ominous event. Before astronomers understood the phenomenon, inexplicable blackness in the middle of the day spelled the end of the world, until, of course, after a few minutes of sheer terror, the sun reappeared.

In our post-sexual revolution world, we are experiencing a total eclipse of the body. The umbra has cast its darkness over our humanity, and we simply can no longer see the fundamental significance of the human body to human identity. Governments, in fact, are now demanding in law that we identify every-body without identifying any-body. But when we identify some-body without reference to his or her body, we identify, quite literally, no-body. In turn, a fork in the relationship of the human body and human identity creates a fork in the tongue.[1] This is why words like male/female, man/woman, father/mother, gender, sex, marriage, and family are being warped today beyond recognition; their true meaning totally eclipsed.

What has passed in front of the sun blocking the body's meaning? Are there any "astronomers" out there who can explain this phenomenon, who can help us understand why this has happened and if, when, and how the darkness will pass? In this essay, I will point to three: Our Lady of Fatima, St. Paul VI, St. Pope John Paul II.

In Part I, I will demonstrate that "the beautiful woman from heaven" who appeared in Fatima, Portugal in 1917 actually warned of the eclipse of the body that was coming upon the world. Then, I will demonstrate how, building on the wisdom of the ages, St. Paul VI's encyclical, *Humanae Vitae,* properly recognized the modern embrace of contraception as the cause of the eclipse. In Part II, I will demonstrate how St. John Paul II's Theology of the Body provides a solid basis for hope that we won't remain in the umbra indefinitely; the eclipse of the body will pass when, as Mary promised, her Immaculate Heart triumphs.

PART I:

They Look But Do Not See

Our Lady of Fatima and the Errors of Russia

As most Catholics know, between May 13 and October 13, 1917, Mary appeared to three peasant children in Fatima, Portugal delivering a three-part message: the "three secrets" of Fatima, as they've come to be known. The first secret presented a horrifying vision of hell. The second involved a prophecy of World War II and the warning that "Russia would spread her errors throughout the world." However, Mary assured the children, that "in the end" her Immaculate Heart would triumph and an "era of peace" would be granted to the world.

Mary also told the children that "the Holy Father will have much to suffer." This brings us to the "third secret" of Fatima, which was not publicly revealed until the year 2000. We will revisit this at the end of the essay. For now, I'd like to speak about the "errors of Russia."

When we hear of the errors of Russia, we rightly think of the spread of communism, the atheistic ideology based on Marxist economic theory. As most of us learned in school, Karl Marx considered class struggle to be the defining factor of history. But digging deeper, Marx also believed that the fundamental "class struggle" was found in monogamous marriage and, indeed, in the sexual difference itself. "The first division of labor," Marx co-wrote with Frederick Engels, "is that between man and woman for the propagation of children." In turn, Engels affirmed that Marxist theory "demands the abolition of the monogamous family as the economic unit of society."[2]

It seems the deeper revolution, and the deeper "error of Russia", is the one aimed at destroying marriage and the family. In fact, much later in her life, Sister Lucia (the only of the three visionaries of Fatima to live beyond childhood; she died in 2005) wrote that "a time will come when the decisive battle between the kingdom of Christ and Satan will be over marriage and the family."[3] The modern agenda to deconstruct gender, marriage, and family life often draws straight from Marx. As feminist author Shulamith Firestone wrote in her 1970 manifesto *The Dialectic of Sex*: "[J]ust as the end goal of socialist revolution was ... the elimination of the ... economic class distinction itself, so the end goal of feminist revolution must be ... the elimination of ... the sex distinction itself [so that] genital differences between human beings would no longer matter culturally."

But what kind of revolution would be needed to render the sex distinction meaningless? To answer that question, we first need to understand the natural meaning and purpose of the sex distinction, more specifically, the meaning of genital difference.

The Facts of Life?

Imagine, if you will, that an alien being from a genderless galaxy landed on earth to study the human being. Coming from such a world, the male-female difference would likely be the first thing to catch its attention. "What is this difference for?" it would ask. Upon study, this alien would readily observe that each member of the human species is amazingly self-sufficient in his or her functions as an organism. The heart, the lungs, the kidney, the pancreas, the stomach, the bladder, the rectum, etc. all work together to carry out their functions. And both male and female have all the same organs ... except ... except what we fittingly call the genital organs.

There is one function this alien has discovered, and a critical function indeed, that simply cannot be carried out without cooperation from another member of the species. And that other member of the species must be of the opposite gender (that is, must have different, complementary genital organs) or said function doesn't function. This is the light that illuminates for the alien the most basic purpose of the gender difference. The genital organs of male and female actually work together in a stunning, harmonious inter-dependency to generate new members of the species. It's where we get the word gender, which, based on its Greek root, means "the manner in which one generates." We see the same root in words like genesis, generous, genitals, progeny, genes, and genealogy.

Furthermore, since the child born to them cannot survive on its own, the alien rightly realizes that the man and the woman who cooperated in generating this new life, if they are to be responsible, must commit themselves to rearing their child. Precisely this commitment (the commitment to responsible genital intercourse as the foundation of future generations) is called marriage.

It used to be obvious to everyone: genitals are meant to generate. We called it "the facts of life." But today, those facts are entirely up for grabs, and the fundamental link between gender, genitals, and generating has all but vanished from the way we understand ourselves and our genital relationships. As a culture, we are desperately in need of recovering what should be an obvious and celebrated truth: sex leads to babies. Tragically, as I will demonstrate, when we fail to respect the fact that genitals are meant to generate, we begin to degenerate.

The Crack in the Dam

How did we as a culture come to forget – or, rather, dismiss – the fact that genitals are meant to generate? Since the beginning of history men and women have sought ways, usually crude and ineffective, of thwarting the generative power of their genitals. However, only with the vulcanization of rubber in the mid-1800s and, all the more so, with the invention of the Pill a century later, did we have consistently reliable ways of doing so.

Still, if a true contraceptive revolution was to occur, it needed not only new technologies, but new mentalities. As difficult as it may be for us to imagine today, contraception in much of the western world was not only frowned upon at the turn of the 20th century as immoral, it was also illegal. Those who campaigned for its acceptance knew they would make little progress without the "blessing" of Christian leaders. Few today realize that, until 1930, all Christian denominations were unanimous in their firm opposition to any attempt to separate genitals from generating. That year, the Anglican Church succumbed to pressure and opened the door to contraception at its Lambeth Conference. In doing so, it was the first Christian body to break with the continuous teaching of the early Church, the saints throughout the ages, and all the Reformers from Luther to Calvin and beyond.

Within a matter of weeks, Pope Pius XI responded as follows:

> *Since, therefore, openly departing from the uninterrupted Christian tradition some recently have judged it possible solemnly to declare another doctrine regarding this question, the Catholic Church ... raises her voice in token of her divine ambassadorship and ... proclaims anew: any use whatsoever of matrimony exercised in such a way that the act is deliberately frustrated in its natural power to generate life is an offense against the law of God and of nature.*[4]

In the years that followed, every major Protestant denomination shifted from condemning contraception to not only to accepting it, but advocating it. Unimaginable global pressure was now being put on the Catholic Church to follow suit and it seemed to many that it was having its desired effect. In the early 1960s, the Fathers of the Second Vatican Council stated that they reserved judgment on certain "questions which need further and more careful investigation." These "have been handed over ... to a commission for the study of population, family, and births, in order that, after it fulfills its function, the Supreme Pontiff may pass judgment."[5]

The point in question was the birth control pill, a new technology at the time, that seemed to some not to qualify under the traditional teaching against contraception. The Council's tacit admission of uncertainty on this point gave people the impression that a papal blessing on the Pill was forthcoming. In fact, the majority of the papal commission studying the question advised Pope Paul VI not only to accept the Pill, but to follow the lead of other Christian communities and change Church teaching on contraception all together. When the "Majority Report" was leaked to the press in early May of 1967, there was a sense of certainty that a change in teaching was imminent. One week later, Pope Paul VI visited Fatima. He came on her feast day (May 13) and prayed specifically against "new ideologies" that were threatening the Church by introducing a "profane mentality" and "worldly morals."[6]

A little over a year later, on July 25, 1968, Paul VI shocked the world when he issued his encyclical letter *Of Human Life* (*Humanae Vitae*) reaffirming the traditional Christian teaching against contraception, including the Pill. Although he was mocked and scorned globally, both from outside and, sadly, from within the Church, his words were prescient. He warned that a contracepting world becomes a world of rampant infidelity; a world where women and childbearing are degraded; a world in which governments trample on the rights and needs of the family; and a world in which human beings believe they can manipulate their bodies at will.[7] In other words, Pope Paul VI showed himself to be an "astronomer" who understood the power of contraception to eclipse the meaning of the body, casting a dark shadow over the meaning of the gender difference itself and, hence, the meaning of marriage and the family.

Wise men and women throughout history have always understood that fertility was the light that illuminated the sexual relationship, and that rendering it sterile would cast a long shadow over civilization. In fact, when Margaret Sanger first started her global campaigns for contraception in the early 1900s, there was no shortage of predictions that embracing contraception would lead to the societal chaos in which we're now immersed. You might be just as surprised as I was to read what the following prominent thinkers of the early 20th century had to say about contraception and what they predicted would happen if we embraced it.

Sigmund Freud, for example, while he was clearly no friend of religion, understood that the "abandonment of the reproductive function is the common feature of all perversions. We actually describe a sexual activity as perverse," he said, "if it has given up the aim of reproduction and pursues the attainment of pleasure as an aim independent of it."[8]

Theodore Roosevelt condemned contraception as a serious threat against the welfare of the nation, describing it as "the one sin for which the penalty is national death, race death; a sin for which there is no atonement." The "men and women guilty thereof," he believed, exhibited a "dreadful" lack of character.[9]

Gandhi insisted that contraceptive methods are "like putting a premium on vice. They make men and women reckless." He predicted that nature "will have full revenge for any such violation of her laws. Moral results can only be produced by moral restraints." Hence, if contraceptive methods "become the order of the day, nothing but moral degradation can be the result. ...As it is, man has sufficiently degraded woman for his lust, and [contraception], no matter how well meaning the advocates may be, will still further degrade her."[10]

When a committee of the Federal Council of Churches in America issued a report suggesting it follow the Anglican acceptance of contraception, The Washington Post published a stinging editorial with the following prophetic statement: "Carried to its logical conclusions, the committee's report if carried into effect would sound the death knell of marriage as a holy institution by establishing degrading practices which would encourage indiscriminate immorality. The suggestion that the use of legalized contraceptives would be 'careful and restrained' is preposterous."[11]

Also in response to the Anglican break with Christian moral teaching, T.S. Elliot insisted that the church "is trying the experiment of attempting to form a civilized but non-Christian, mentality. The experiment will fail; but we must be very patient in waiting its collapse; meanwhile redeeming the time so that the Faith may be preserved alive through the dark ages before us; to renew and rebuild civilization and save the world from suicide."[12]

Perversity? National death? Moral Degradation? The death of marriage as a holy institution? World suicide? Isn't that a bit much to pin on contraception? It would certainly seem so, if it weren't for the fact that much of what these forecasters predicted has, indeed, come to pass. What did they understand that we have forgotten?

Untying the Tight-Knot-Nexus

Civil law used to understand, defend, and protect the fact that marriage, sex, and babies belong together … and in that order. In the age-old Christian understanding, God, in his loving design, has united these three realities in a tight knot to reveal in our flesh the truth of His own eternal covenant love and Fatherhood. Contraception not only loosens the knot of this fundamental and society-ordering nexus, it cuts the ties.

Separate sex from babies and you also separate sex from marriage both in principle and in practice. So long as the natural connection between sex and babies is retained, we realize intuitively that sexual intercourse is the domain of those who have committed themselves to raising children: that commitment, as our alien friend realized earlier, is called marriage. Insert contraception into the tight-knot-nexus of marriage-sex-babies and everything will start to unravel as follows.

The temptation to commit adultery is certainly nothing new. However, one of the main deterrents, throughout history, from succumbing to the temptation has been the fear of an unwanted pregnancy. That's the tight-knot-nexus of marriage-sex-babies doing its job. What would happen to rates of adultery in a given population if we untied that knot with contraception? Incidents of infidelity would be sure to rise. What happens when incidents of infidelity rise? Rates of marital breakdown and divorce rise.

It gets worse. The temptation to engage in sex before marriage is nothing new. However, one of the main deterrents, throughout history, from succumbing to the temptation has been the fear of unwanted pregnancy. Once again, that's the tight-knot-nexus doing its job. What would happen to rates of premarital sex in a given population if we untied that knot with contraception? They would certainly rise.

It gets worse. Since no method of contraception is 100 percent effective, an increase in adultery and premarital sex in a given population will inevitably lead to an increase in unwanted pregnancies. What happens when large numbers of women find themselves pregnant and didn't want to be? Demand for a legal "right" to abortion logically follows, as a way of solving this problem.

The common wisdom is that better access to contraception decreases rates of abortion. But even a cursory look at the data shows that in every nation that has embraced contraception, abortions have multiplied, not diminished. Once we've severed the knot uniting marriage, sex, and babies, we don't like it when nature's nexus reasserts itself. The initial impulse to indulge libido without commitment and without consequence now morphs into a demand to be "free" to do so, even at the cost of extinguishing an innocent human life. While there's an initial logic to the idea that contraception curbs abortion, when we take a deeper look we realize that trying to solve the latter with the former is like throwing gasoline on a fire to try to put it out. In the final analysis, there is only one reason we have abortion: people have rejected the God-given purpose of sex. They've sought to separate genitals from generating. Contraception doesn't solve that problem; it fosters it.

It gets worse. Not everyone will resort to abortion of course. Thanks be to God for that. Some will offer their children up for adoption, a heroic decision. Most mothers, however, will raise these children on their own. This, too, can be heroic, but now the number of children who grow up without a father, which has already been increased by the rise in divorce (brought on by the rise in adultery, brought on by the acceptance of contraception), will be compounded.

Certainly God's grace can supply what is lacking and those raised without a father can lead healthy, holy lives. Still, as numerous studies (and common sense) indicate, the chances dramatically increase that "fatherless" children will: grow up in poverty; have emotional, psychological, and behavioral problems; suffer poor health; drop out of school; engage in pre-marital sex; obtain abortions; do drugs; commit violent crimes; and end up in jail. All of these social ills compound exponentially from generation to generation since "fatherless" children are also much more likely to have out-of-wedlock births and, if they marry at all, divorce.

Redefining Marriage, Sex, and Babies

As history clearly shows, when we begin untying the tight-knot-nexus of marriage, sex, and babies, we end up redefining all three. Babies become mere "clumps of cells." Sex becomes mere uncommitted pleasure-exchange between consenting partners (gender being irrelevant and malleable). And marriage becomes a demanded societal and governmental "stamp of approval" on one's preferred method of sexual pleasure-exchange.

And this is why embracing contraception has lead, as a matter of course, to the normalization of homosexual behavior. Pardon the frankness, but as a plain-talking professor of mine once put it: "As soon as you sever orgasm from procreation, any hole will do." It's hard to argue with that logic. Deliberately sterilizing sexual intercourse effectively nullifies the natural and essential meaning of the sexual difference. When we recognize this, we come to see the hard truth that Christians themselves unwittingly began to "homo-sexualize" marriage when they began to embrace contraception.

In truth, it's impossible to raise what two men or two women might do with their genitals to the level of what God invites a man and a woman to do with their genitals in marriage: generate the next generation. But it is possible to reduce what men and women do with their genitals in marriage to what same-sex couples do with theirs: engage in the pursuit of sterile pleasure. That's what contraception has done to marriage: it has reduced it to the same thing pursued in same-sex unions. Hence, when married couples claim a "right" to sterilize their union, it's only a matter of time before those inclined to inherently sterile unions (i.e., same-sex unions) claim a "right" to marry on the basis of "equality." When the essential meaning of the genital difference is eclipsed by a contraceptive mentality, the genital activities of opposite-sex couples and same-sex couples do, indeed, become "the same thing," as those who have successfully campaigned for "marriage equality" have insisted.

Seventy-two years after the 1930 Anglican decision, Archbishop of Canterbury Rowan Williams observed that "the absolute condemnation of same-sex relations" has nothing substantial to rely upon in "a church that accepts the legitimacy of contraception."[13] He was correct. But rather than question the legitimacy of contraception, he took that as a given and justified homosexual behavior. If we're being logically consistent, it has to be one or the other.

In a 1984 interview, the future Pope Benedict XVI predicted that we will atone in our day for "the consequences of a sexuality which is no longer linked to ... procreation. It logically follows from this that every form of [genital activity] is equivalent. ...No longer having an objective reason to justify it, sex seeks the subjective reason in the gratification of the desire, in the most 'satisfying' answer for the individual." In turn, he observed that everyone becomes "free to give to his personal libido the content considered suitable for himself. Hence, it naturally follows that all forms of sexual gratification are transformed into the 'rights' of the individual." From there, he concluded that people end up demanding the right of "escaping from the 'slavery of nature,' demanding the right to be male or female at one's will or pleasure."[14]

Who can deny that this is the world we live in today?

PART II:

Come and Become One Who Sees

We Need a "Total Vision of Man"

Theology of the body (hereafter: TOB) is the working title that St. John Paul II gave to the first major teaching project of his pontificate. Delivered over the course of 129[15] Wednesday Audiences between September 5, 1979 and November 28, 1984, these catechetical addresses present an in-depth biblical reflection on the meaning of human embodiment, particularly as it concerns our creation as male and female and the call of the two to become "one flesh."

St. John Paul II was inspired by something St. Paul VI said in Humanae Vitae: he observed that, in order to understand Christian teaching on sex and procreation, we must look "beyond partial perspectives" to a "total vision of man and of his vocation."[16] This is what John Paul II set out to do in his TOB—provide the "total vision of man" that would enable us to understand and live joyfully the Church's teaching on the meaning and purpose of human life (humanae vitae).

The operative term here is vision. John Paul II understood that, while the people of the modern world were obsessed with looking at the human body, "They look but do not see" (Mt 13:13). His TOB was an invitation to every human being to "Come, and become one who sees" (Jn 1:39).[17]

Inadequate, legalistic formulations of moral theology coupled with disparaging treatments of sexual matters by some previous churchmen had led countless people to turn a deaf ear to the Church whenever she spoke on sexual matters. John Paul II was confident, however, that he had something to say that could make a difference. He believed he could demonstrate that *Humanae Vitae* was not against man but unstintingly for him; that *Humanae Vitae* was not opposed to erotic love and sexual pleasure, but called men and women to the most spiritually intense experiences of them. To get there, however, questions surrounding sexual morality needed to be reframed. Instead of asking: "How far can I go before I break the law?" we need to ask: "What does it mean to be human?" "What is a person?" "What does it mean to love?" "Why did God make me male or female?" "Why did God create sex in the first place?"

In short, John Paul II's long-studied answer to that final question is this: human sexuality is a sign – in fact, a sacramental sign – that's meant to proclaim, reveal, and enable human beings to participate in the "great mystery" hidden in God from all eternity.

John Paul II's Thesis

Sacramental signs refer to the making visible of the invisible. We cannot see God. As pure Spirit, he is invisible. And yet, the invisible God has made himself visible. How so? This brings us to the thesis statement of John Paul II's TOB, the brush with which he paints his entire vision:

> *The body, in fact, and only the body, is capable*
> *of making visible what is invisible: the spiritual and*
> *divine. It has been created to transfer into the visible*
> *reality of the world the mystery hidden from eternity*
> *in God, and thus to be a sign of it. (TOB 19:4)*

Let's begin unpacking this dense statement. Think of your own experiences as a human being: Your body is not just a shell in which you dwell. Your body is not just a body. Your body is not just any body. Your body is somebody—you! Through the profound unity of your body and your soul, your body reveals or makes visible the invisible reality of your spiritual soul. The "you" you are is not just a soul "in" a body. Your body is not something you have or own alongside yourself. Your body is you. Which is why if someone broke your jaw in a fit of rage, you wouldn't take him to court for property damage but for personal assault. What we do with our bodies, and what is done to our bodies, we do or have done to ourselves.

Once again, our bodies make visible what is invisible— the spiritual and the divine. It's from this perspective that John Paul II studies the human body—not merely as a biological organism, but as a theology, as a "study of God."

The body is not divine, of course. But it is the most powerful sign of the divine mystery in all creation. A sign is something that points us to a reality beyond itself and, in some way, makes that transcendent reality present to us. The divine mystery always remains infinitely "beyond"; it cannot be reduced to its sign. Yet the sign is indispensable in making visible the invisible mystery. As the Catechism says, "Man needs signs and symbols to communicate... The same holds true for his relationship with God" (CCC 1146).

Tragically, because of sin, the "body loses its character as a sign" (TOB 40:4)—not objectively, but rather subjectively. In other words, in itself, the body retains its character as a sign of the spiritual and divine, but we've been blinded to it. We "look but do not see" (Mt 13:13). As a result, we tend to consider the human body merely as a physical "thing" entirely separated from the spiritual and the divine. And this is why the very expression "theology of the body" seems so odd to people today, even to Christians. It shouldn't, if we believe in the Incarnation. As John Paul II put it, "Through the fact that the Word of God became flesh, the body entered theology ... through the main door" (TOB 23:4).

Everything in Christianity hinges on the Incarnation. God's mystery has been revealed in human flesh rendering the human body a study of God, a theology. "Theology of the body," therefore, is not merely the title of a series of papal talks on sex and marriage; theology of the body is the very logic of Christianity. For in "the body of Jesus 'we see our God made visible and so are caught up in love of the God we cannot see'" (CCC 477).

The Divine Mystery

Several times already we have spoken of the divine mystery or the "mystery hidden in God from all eternity" (see Eph 3:9). "Mystery" refers to the innermost "secret" of God and to His eternal plan for humanity. As the Catechism says, "God has revealed His innermost secret: God Himself is an eternal exchange of love, Father, Son, and Holy Spirit, and He has destined us to share in that exchange" (CCC 221). God is not a tyrant; God is not a slave driver; God is not merely a legislator or lawgiver; and He's certainly not an old man with a white beard waiting to strike us down whenever we fail. God is an "eternal exchange of love." He's an infinite Communion of Persons experiencing eternal love-bliss. And He created us for one reason: to share that eternal love and bliss with us.

This is what makes the Gospel good news: there is a banquet of love that corresponds to the hungry cry of our hearts, and it is God's free gift to us! We needn't climb some high mountain to find it. We needn't cross the sea. The "great mystery" of God's love is very close to us, intimately part of us. Indeed, God inscribed an image of this "great mystery" in the very form of our bodies by making us male and female and calling the two to become one flesh.

The Spousal Analogy

Scripture uses many images to help us understand God's love. Each has its own valuable place. But, as John Paul II wrote, the gift of Christ's body on the cross gives "definitive prominence to the spousal meaning of God's love."[18] In fact, from beginning to end, in the mysteries of our creation, fall, and redemption, the Bible tells a nuptial or marital story.

It begins in Genesis with the marriage of the first man and woman, and it ends in Revelation with the marriage of Christ and the Church. Right in the middle of the Bible, we find the erotic poetry of the Song of Songs. These bookends and this centerpiece provide the key for reading the whole biblical story. Indeed, we can summarize all of Sacred Scripture with five simple, yet astounding words: God wants to marry us: "For as a young man marries a virgin, so shall your Maker marry you" (Isa 62:5).

In the midst of unfolding the biblical analogy of spousal love, it's very important to understand the bounds within which we're using such language and imagery. "It is obvious," writes John Paul II, "that the analogy of ... human spousal love, cannot offer an adequate and complete understanding of ... the divine mystery." God's "mystery remains transcendent with respect to this analogy as with respect to any other analogy." At the same time, however, John Paul II maintains that the spousal analogy allows a certain "penetration" into the very essence of the mystery (see TOB 95b:1). And no biblical author reaches more deeply into this essence than St. Paul in his letter to the Ephesians.

Quoting directly from Genesis, Paul states: "For this reason a man shall leave his father and mother and be joined to his wife, and the two shall become one flesh." Then, linking the original marriage with the ultimate marriage, he adds: "This is a great mystery, and I mean in reference to Christ and the Church" (Eph 5:31–32).

We can hardly overstate the importance of this passage for John Paul II and the whole theological tradition of the Church. He calls it the "summa" of Christian teaching about who God is and who we are.[19] He says this passage contains the "crowning" of all the themes in Sacred Scripture and expresses the "central reality" of the whole of divine revelation (see TOB 87:3). The mystery spoken of in this passage "is 'great' indeed," he says. "It is what God ... wishes above all to transmit to mankind in his Word." Thus, "one can say that [this] passage ... 'reveals—in a particular way—man to man himself and makes his supreme vocation clear'" (TOB 87:6; 93:2).

So, what is this "supreme vocation" we have as human beings that Ephesians 5 makes clear? Stammering for words to describe the ineffable, the mystics call it "nuptial union" ... with the Infinite.[20] Christ is the new Adam who left his Father in heaven. He also left the home of his mother on earth. Why? To mount "the marriage bed of the cross," as St. Augustine had it, unite himself with the Church, and consummate the union forever. "On the Cross, God's eros for us is made manifest," proclaims Pope Benedict XVI. "Eros is indeed … that force which 'does not allow the lover to remain in himself but moves him to become one with the beloved.' Is there more 'mad eros' … than that which led the Son of God to make himself one with us even to the point of suffering as his own the consequences of our offences?" he asks.[21]

The more we allow the brilliant rays of Christ's "mad eros" to illuminate our vision, the more we come to understand, as the Catechism observes, how the "entire Christian life bears the mark of the spousal love of Christ and the Church. Already Baptism, the entry into the People of God, is a nuptial mystery; it is so to speak the nuptial bath which precedes the wedding feast, the Eucharist" (CCC 1617). In the Eucharist, "Christ is united with his 'body' as the bridegroom with the bride," John Paul II tells us.[22] And this is why only a man can be ordained to the sacramental priesthood. Priesthood is not a career choice; it's the call to spiritual fatherhood. A woman cannot be ordained a priest because she is not ordained by God to be a father; she is ordained by God to be a mother. This is where the sexual difference matters—in the call to holy communion and generation. If a woman were to attempt to confer the Eucharist, the relationship would be bride to bride. There would be no possibility of Holy Communion and no possibility of generating new life.

This is all readily apparent … unless … unless we have eclipsed the meaning of gender with a contraceptive mentality. Rob the genitals of their ability to generate and the natural purpose of the gender distinction is lost. In turn, since grace builds on nature, when we're confused about the natural reality, we're also confused about the supernatural reality: "If I have told you earthly things and you do not believe," asks Jesus, "how can you believe if I tell you heavenly things?" (John 3:12).

Ethics of the Sign

We can argue against contraception without any appeal to faith or the Bible. But John Paul II's project was to show the deepest theological reason for the immorality of contraception. Here it is: rendering the one-flesh union sterile falsifies the sacramental sign of married love. It violates what John Paul II calls "the ethics of the sign."

As a sacrament, marriage not only signifies God's life and love, it really participates in God's life and love—or, at least, it's meant to do so. For sacraments to convey grace, the sacramental sign must accurately signify the spiritual mystery. For example, as a physical sign of cleansing, the waters of baptism really and truly bring about a spiritual cleansing from sin. But if you were to baptize someone with tar, no spiritual cleansing would take place because the physical sign no longer conveys the spiritual reality.

All of married life is a sacrament. All of married life is meant to be a sign of God's life and love. But this sacrament has a consummate expression. Sexual intercourse is the full-bodied sign language of God's love. Here, like no other moment in married life, spouses are invited to participate in the "great mystery" of God's creative and redemptive love. But this will only happen if their sexual union accurately signifies God's love. Therefore, as John Paul II concludes, we can speak of moral good and evil in the sexual relationship based on whether the couple gives to their union "the character of a truthful sign" (TOB 37:6).

As John Paul II's TOB so brilliantly illuminates, the human body has a language written by God into the mystery of the sexual difference: it is meant to proclaim the truth of divine love and enable men and women to participate in it. Hence, John Paul II insists that the language of the body is "prophetic." However, we must be careful to distinguish true and false prophets. For if we can speak the truth with the body, we can also speak lies. Insert contraception into the language of the body and (knowingly or unknowingly) the couple engages in a counter-sign of the "great mystery." Rather than proclaiming, "God is life-giving love," the language of contracepted intercourse says, "God is not life-giving love." In this way spouses (knowingly or unknowingly) become "false prophets." They blaspheme. Their bodies are still proclaiming a theology, but it's a theology that falsifies divine love.

Incarnating Divine Love

"Love one another as I have loved you" (John 15:12). This "new commandment" of Jesus summarizes the very meaning of life. It's a commandment that God inscribed right from the beginning not in stone tablets, but in the very mystery of our bodies, in the very mysteries of sex, gender, and marriage.

How did Christ love us? First, he gives himself freely ("No one takes my life from me, I lay it down of my own accord"—John 10:18). Second, he gives himself totally: without reservation, condition, or selfish calculation ("He loved them to the last"—John 13:1). Third, he gives himself faithfully ("I am with you always"—Matt 28:20). And fourth, he gives himself fruitfully ("I came that they may have life"—John 10:10). Another name for this kind of love is marriage. This, in fact, is precisely what a bride and groom commit to at the altar. The priest or deacon asks them: "Have you come here freely and whole heartedly to give yourselves to each other in marriage? Do you promise to be faithful all the days of your lives? Do you promise to receive children lovingly from God?"

When the bride and groom each say "yes," that word expresses the language of their hearts. In turn, spouses are meant to express that same "yes" with the language of their bodies whenever they become one flesh. "In fact, the words themselves, 'I take you as my wife/as my husband,'" John Paul II says, "can only be fulfilled by conjugal intercourse" (TOB 103:2). In other words, sexual intercourse is where the words of the wedding vows become flesh.

If spouses say "yes" to being open to children at the altar, but then contradict that yes by rendering their union sterile, they are being unfaithful to their wedding vows.* Someone might retort, "Come on! I can commit to being 'open to children' at the altar, but this doesn't mean that each and every act of intercourse needs to be open to children." But that makes as much sense as saying, "Come on! I can commit to fidelity at the altar, but this doesn't mean that each and every act of intercourse needs to be with my spouse." If you can recognize the inconsistency of a commitment to fidelity, but not always, then you can recognize the inconsistency of a commitment to being open to children, but not always.

Natural Family Planning

Assuming a couple has a serious reason to avoid a child (this could be financial, physical, or psychological, among other reasons), what could they do that would not violate the consummate expression of their sacrament? In other words, what could they do to avoid conceiving a child that would not render them unfaithful to their wedding vows? I'll bet you're doing it right now. They could abstain from sex. If we understand the dignity of the human being and the astounding meaning of becoming one flesh, we will logically conclude, as the Church always has, that the only method of "birth control" in keeping with human dignity is self-control.

A further question arises: Would a couple be doing anything to falsify their sexual union if they embraced during a time of natural infertility? Take, for example, a couple past childbearing years. They know their union will not result in a child. Are they violating the sacramental sign of their marriage if they engage in intercourse with this knowledge? Are they contracepting? No. Contraception, by

---

* This, in turn, becomes the standard for assessing the morality of any sexual act: Does an act of masturbation image God's free, total, faithful, fruitful love or does it miss the mark? Does an act of fornication (sex between two unmarried people) image God's free, total, faithful, fruitful love or does it miss the mark? What about an act of adultery? What about homosexual behavior? What about lusting after pornographic images?

definition, is the choice to engage in an act of intercourse, but then do something else to render it sterile. This can be done by using various devices, hormones, surgical procedures, and the age-old method of withdrawal (coitus interruptus).

Couples who use natural family planning (NFP) when they have a just reason to avoid pregnancy never render their sexual acts sterile; they never contracept. They track their fertility, abstain when they are fertile and, if they so desire, embrace when they are naturally infertile. Readers unfamiliar with modern NFP methods should note that they are 98–99 percent effective at avoiding pregnancy when used properly. Furthermore, any woman, regardless of the regularity of her cycles, can use NFP successfully. This is not the outdated and much less precise "rhythm method."

To some people this seems like splitting hairs. "What's the big difference," they ask, "between rendering the union sterile yourself and just waiting until it's naturally infertile? The end result is the same thing: both couples avoid children." To which I respond, "What's the big difference between killing Grandma and just waiting until she dies naturally? The end result is the same thing: dead Grandma." Yes, the end result is the same thing, but one case involves a serious sin called murder, while in the other case, Grandma dies, but there's no sin involved whatsoever. Give it some thought: those who can understand the difference between euthanasia and natural death, can understand the difference between contraception and natural family planning.

Most couples who use contraception simply have no idea what they are doing or saying with their bodies. They haven't ever heard or understood the "great mystery" of their sexuality. Hence, the conclusions we're drawing here about the objective seriousness of contraception is not a matter of assigning culpability: "Father, forgive them; for they know not what they do" (Luke 23:34). The good news is that Christ came into the world not to condemn but to save (see John 3:17). It doesn't matter how "dyslexic" or even "illiterate" a person has been in reading the divine language of the body. As John Paul II boldly proclaims, through the gift of God's mercy "there is always the possibility of passing from 'error' to the 'truth'" (TOB 107:3).

CONCLUSION

The Third Secret of Fatima

The "third secret" of Fatima was shrouded in mystery for 83 years. In the year 2000, at the beatification ceremony of two of the young visionaries to whom Mary appeared (Francesco and Jacinta), John Paul II finally unveiled it. In 1917, the three children had seen a vision of bullets and arrows fired at "a bishop dressed in white."

Sixty-four years later, while driving through the crowd in Saint Peter's Square, a "bishop dressed in white" was indeed gunned down by Turkish assassin Ali Agca ... on the memorial of Our Lady of Fatima: May 13, 1981. Thankfully, while the bishop in the vision fell dead, John Paul II miraculously survived. Many years later the Pope himself reflected: "Agca knew how to shoot, and he certainly shot to kill. Yet it was as if someone was guiding and deflecting that bullet." That "someone," John Paul believed, was the Woman of Fatima. "Could I forget that the event in Saint Peter's Square took place on the day and at the hour when the first appearance of the Mother of Christ ... has been remembered ... at Fatima in Portugal? For in everything that happened to me on that very day, I felt that extraordinary motherly protection and care, which turned out to be stronger than the deadly bullet."[23]

The fact that John Paul II was shot on the memorial of Fatima is well known. What few people realize is that the Pope was planning to announce the establishment of his Institute for Studies on Marriage and Family on that fateful afternoon. This was to be his main arm for disseminating his Theology of the Body around the globe. Could it be that there were forces at work that didn't want John Paul II's teaching to spread around the world? (In fact, by May 13, 1981, John Paul II was only about half way through delivering the 129 addresses of his

TOB. Had he died, obviously, the full teaching never would have been presented.) And could it be that, by saving his life, the Woman of Fatima was pointing to the importance of his teaching reaching the world?

It would be over a year later that John Paul II officially established his Institute (of which I'm a proud graduate). On that day, October 7, 1982 – not coincidentally the Feast of Our Lady of the Rosary – John Paul II entrusted the Pontifical Institute for Studies on Marriage and Family to the care and protection of Our Lady of Fatima. By doing so, he himself was drawing a connection between his miraculous survival and the importance of the Theology of the Body. "Precisely because the family is threatened, the family is being attacked, so the Pope must be attacked," he would write some years later. "The Pope must suffer, so that the world may see that there is a higher gospel, as it were, the gospel of suffering, by which the future is prepared, the third millennium of families."[24]

If the third millennium is to be the "millennium of families," it's an understatement to say we're not off to a very good start. It was Father Carlo Caffarra, in his role as President of the John Paul II Institute for Studies on Marriage and Family, to whom Sister Lucia had written in the early 1980s, saying: "Father, a time will come when the decisive battle between the kingdom of Christ and Satan will be over marriage and the family." She added, however, that there was no need to be afraid "because Our Lady has already crushed his head."[25] In May of 2017, just a few months before his own death, Caffarra stated: "What Sister Lucia wrote to me is being fulfilled today."[26]

The Triumph of Purity of Heart

At the start of this chapter, we learned that the errors of Russia go deeper than communism: at the heart of the Marxist worldview is a calculated attempt to eliminate the purpose of gender, that of generating children, so that the male-female distinction itself becomes culturally irrelevant, thus destroying the anthropological basis of marriage and the family. There is no doubt that this error has taken hold of much of the world and continues to spread today at rampant speed. But here's the good news: just as John Paul II's vision of the human person inaugurated a revolution that led to the fall of communism, that same vision has the potential to topple today's sexual ideology (or, shall we say a-sexual ideology) as well. It's called the *Theology of the Body* and it has already started a growing movement that is spreading from heart to heart around the world.

In a 2005 interview, Lech Walenza, who led the movement in Poland against communism, reflected on the revolution of conscience that John Paul II ignited: "For twenty years I could only find ten people who wanted to fight [the communist regime], from a nation of forty million. Nobody, I repeat, nobody thought that communism would end. Then, this incredible thing happened – a Pole became ... the Pope. And within a year after his visit to Poland [in June of 1979] – in one year – it went from ten people to a movement of ten million."[27]

The political philosopher Zbigniew Strawrowski reflects on the experience of the Polish people after John Paul II's historic visit to his homeland as follows:

"When we are talking about a revolution of conscience, we are talking about people who suddenly asked themselves: 'Who am I? What am I doing here? What is the purpose of my life?' We lived within something that was permeated by the feeling of nonsense. We fully realized that it was false, that it was a lie, one huge lie. However, you were trapped in it. And suddenly someone arrives who says, 'No! There's no need to lie any longer.'"[28]

In the same way, today's gender ideology (more aptly, gender-less ideology) is based on a lie. And lies eventually collapse on themselves, doomed from the start by their own falsity. We are now in the umbra of the eclipse of the body, but the light of truth will emerge, perhaps sooner than we think. In the book of Revelation, the sexual distortion of the nations – symbolized by the "whore of Babylon," that mysterious feminine figure who mocks the Bride of the Lamb and seduces the world with her harlotry – is brought to ruin in "one hour" (see Rev 18:10-17). And then comes the triumph of the New Jerusalem, the Bride who has "made herself ready" for her Bridegroom. She is dressed in "fine linen, bright and immaculate" (Rev 19:7-8). She is "clothed with the sun" (Rev 12:1).

This radiant Bride, in other words, magnifies the light of the sun rather than eclipsing it. And, let us not overlook this illuminating detail: the Bride in the book of Revelation is pregnant… (see Rev 12:2). John Paul II pointed out the difference between the Bride and "the hostile and furious presence" of Babylon as follows: the woman clothed with the sun "is endowed with an inner fruitfulness by which she constantly brings forth children of God." In contrast, Babylon embodies "death and inner barrenness."[29] In fact, this feminine figure prefers barrenness. She chooses it and seduces the nations with the promise of sexual pleasure without sacrifice (which is to say, without divine love).

The pregnant Bride in the Book of Revelation, of course, is personified in Mary, the same woman who promised the children of Fatima: "In the end, my Immaculate Heart will triumph." What does this mean? In short, it means that purity of heart will triumph. As Cardinal Ratzinger explained in his official commentary on the third secret: "According to Matthew 5:8 ['Blessed are the pure of heart, for they shall see God.'], the 'immaculate heart' is a heart which, with God's grace, has come to perfect interior unity and therefore 'sees God.' To be 'devoted' to the Immaculate Heart of Mary means therefore to embrace this attitude of heart, which makes the fiat – 'your will be done' – the defining center of one's whole life."[30]

Purity is not prudishness or fear of the body and its genital functions. Purity, says John Paul II, "is the glory of the human body before God. It is the glory of God in the human body, through which masculinity and femininity are manifested" (TOB 57:3). Those who are pure of heart are those who have followed Christ's invitation to "Come, and become one who sees" (Jn 1:39). And what they see is the fact that human sexuality "bears in itself the sign of the divine mystery of creation and redemption" (TOB 131:5). What they see is the fact that the body, and only the body, is capable of making visible what is invisible: the spiritual and divine. It has been created to transfer into the visible reality of the world the mystery hidden from eternity in God, and thus to be a sign of it. (TOB 19:4)

The Era of Peace Will Come through the Cross

At the top of page one of the original handwritten manuscript of John Paul II's TOB is the dedication: tota pulchra es Maria (Mary, you are all beautiful) and below that is the date he started writing it: December 8, 1974. Is it merely a coincidence that John Paul II began writing his TOB on the feast of the Immaculate Conception? Right from the start, it seems, John Paul II's TOB is mysteriously connected with the triumph of Mary's Immaculate Heart.

Of course, we know not the day nor the hour of the fulfillment of these prophecies, be they biblical or the Church-approved prophecies of Fatima. But John Paul II himself wrote already in 1994 that the latter "seem to be close to their fulfillment."[31] This much is certain: since the family is the fundamental cell of society, if an "era of peace" is to be granted the world, that peace can only come if there is peace in the marital relationship ... in the womb ... in the family. And this will only happen if we are reconciled to the truth of our own greatness as men and women who bear in our bodies the sacramental sign of the divine plan – a plan that inevitably leads us to the nuptial mystery of the Cross.

As the icon of divine love, marriage has been under attack since the beginning. In fact, as John Paul II observed, "Sin and death have entered into man's history in some way through the very heart of that unity that had from the 'beginning' been formed by man and woman, created and called to become 'one flesh' (Gen 2:24)" (TOB 20:1). But if the enemy entered the sanctuary of married life from the beginning to sow seeds of death and destruction, let us never forget where Christ performed his first miracle: "On the third day, there was a wedding in Cana" (Jn 2:1). And let us also remember that that wedding was a foreshadowing of the "hour" of Christ's death. Unfathomable as it is to human wisdom, this is God's method of victory: the death and resurrection of the Bridegroom is the gift that assures the triumph of the Bride.

We must ponder this anew if we are to understand what is happening in our world today: marriage, it would seem, is going the way of its exemplar. It's already been put on trial, condemned, mocked, rejected, spat upon, scourged, and it's now being crucified. Significantly, on the day of Christ's crucifixion, Luke reports that "darkness came over the whole land ... because of an eclipse of the sun" (Lk 23:45).

Many in the Church today are understandably fearful and anxious because of the darkness that is descending upon us. Three astronomers – Our Lady of Fatima, St. Paul VI, and St. John Paul II – have enabled us to understand what's happening. As with every eclipse, the eclipse of the body is sure to get darker before it gets lighter. The truth proclaimed by Paul VI in *Humanae Vitae* and explained so compellingly by John Paul II in his *Theology of the Body* remains a sign of contradiction fiercely resisted not only by the world at large, but also by strong forces within the Church. A new wave of attacks against this truth may well bring fresh defeats for the Body of Christ and for humanity.

None of this should be surprising. For the Church "must follow her Lord in his death and Resurrection" in order to enter her glory, as the Catechism observes (CCC 677). We know not the day nor the hour of Christ's return, but this we do know: "Before Christ's second coming the Church must pass through a final trial that will shake the faith of many believers. The persecution that accompanies her pilgrimage on earth will unveil the 'mystery of iniquity' in the form of a religious deception offering men an apparent solution to their problems at the price of apostasy from the truth" (CCC 675).

While we can't conclude with any certainty that we are now facing this final trial, it is eerily curious how precisely contraception fits the bill of this "religious deception." With all the forces of darkness arrayed against her teaching, we should not expect "a historic triumph of the Church." Rather, by accepting "the way" of death and resurrection, we will witness "God's victory over the final unleashing of evil, which will cause his Bride to come down from heaven" (CCC 677).

As the eclipse of the body continues to cast its dark shadow over the world, let us take courage: Sun-day is not far off. When "the third day" dawns, there will be a miraculous wedding: the sun will "come forth like a bridegroom from his tent" and "nothing will be concealed from its burning heat" (Ps 19:6-7); and another great sign will appear in the sky, the Immaculate Woman, clothed with the sun, showing the world what it means to open bodily to the divine fire of life-giving love. "Then the glory of the Lord shall be revealed, and all flesh shall see it together" (Is 40:5).

Let it be, Lord, according to your word. Amen.

Suggestions for further study:

- If you have the aptitude, read John Paul II's actual text: *Man and Woman He Created: A Theology of the Body* (Pauline, 2006). If you need help with that, read it in conjunction with my extended commentary *Theology of the Body Explained* or my *Theology of the Body for Beginners*. Visit my ministry's website corproject.com and click on "shop" for a full listing of additional resources.

- Explore what other authors and teachers have written about the TOB. There are so many good resources out there today, each with their own emphases and insights. Google "theology of the body resources" to find them.

- If you would like ongoing formation in the TOB, consider joining a worldwide community of men and women who are learning, living, and sharing this teaching as Members of the TOB Institute Community (visit theologyofthebody.com/community to learn more).

- Consider taking a 5-day "Immersion Course" through the Theology of the Body Institute. Learn more at theologyofthebody.com.

Endnotes

1   My thanks to Daniel Moody for this turn of phrase. See The Flesh Made Word: A New
      Reason to be against Abortion (Amazon, 2016)
2   See The Origin of the Family, Private Property, and the State
3   Sister Lucia wrote these words in a letter to the late Cardinal Carlo Caffarra when he
      served as President of the John Paul II Institute for Studies on Marriage and Family.
      Caffarra has given sworn testimony that these were in fact her words. See https://
      aleteia.org/2017/05/19/exclusive-cardinal-caffarra-what-sr-lucia-wrote-to-me-is-being-
      fulfilled-today/
4   Pope Pius XI, On Chaste Marriage, paragraph 56
5   Gaudium et Spes, section 51, endnote 14
6   See Paul VI homily at Fatima, May 13, 1967
7   See Humanae Vitae 17
8   See Introductory Lectures in Psychoanalysis
9   See State Papers as Governor and President, in Works XVII
10   See India of My Dreams
11   Washington Post, "Forgetting Religion," March 22, 1931
12   See Thoughts After Lambeth
13   "The Body's Grace," Rowan Williams, in Theology and Sexuality: Classic and
      Contemporary Readings (Blackwell, 2002), p. 320
14   The Ratzinger Report (Ignatius Press, 1985), pp. 85, 95
15   John Paul II actually divided his manuscript into 135 talks. However, some of the
      content of his reflections on the Song of Songs was considered too "delicate" for the
      Wednesday audience format, so he condensed 10 talks in that section to four, thus
      delivering only 129. For an extended treatment of the undelivered talks, see my book
      Heaven's Song (Ascension Press, 2008).
16   Humanae Vitae 7
17   John 1:39 is typically rendered "Come and see." As I once learned in my biblical
      studies (from those much more learned than I on such matters), the more accurate
      rendering of Christ's words is "Come, and become one who sees."
18   Mulieris Dignitatem 26
19   See Letter to Families 19
20   See, for example, John Paul II, Novo MIllennio Inuente 33
21   Lenten Message 2007
22   Mulieris Dignitatem 26
23   Memory and Identity pp. 159, 163
24   Angelus Message, May 29, 1994 (my thanks to Jason Evert for pointing this out)
25   See note 3 above
26   Ibid
27   "John Paul II: Ambassador of Peace" (Discovery Channel, 2005)
28   Liberating a Continent: John Paul II and the Fall of Communism, documentary
      directed by David Naglieri (2016)
29   "The Church: a Bride Adorned for Her Husband," General Audience address (February
      7, 2001)
30   http://www.vatican.va/roman_curia/congregations/cfaith/documents/rc_con_cfaith_
      doc_20000626_message-fatima_en.html
31   Crossing the Threshold of Hope, p. 221

Reclaiming Spiritual Fatherhood

Denae and Allen Hébert

*"Cast yourself upon God and have no fear.
He will not shrink away and let you fall. Cast
yourself upon him without fear, for he will
welcome you and cure you of your ills."*

St. Augustine, Confessions

You Are The Man!

In our Church today, a great evil has been identified. Ordained ministers have severely harmed individual members of the faithful, their families, and their communities. Some leaders, perhaps more than anyone could have imagined, protected the abusers and ignored the victims. In other words, many of our leaders abandoned their flocks and sought to hide their sin, just like King David did after having an affair with Bathsheba (See 2 Samuel 11:1-27). In an effort to save his image and hide his sin, he killed a man simply because he had the power to do so. He only admitted his sins when confronted by the prophet Nathan.

> *The LORD sent Nathan to David, and when he came to him, he said: "Tell me how you judge this case: In a certain town there were two men, one rich, the other poor. The rich man had flocks and herds in great numbers. But the poor man had nothing at all except one little ewe lamb that he had bought. He nourished her, and she grew up with him and his children. Of what little he had she ate; from his own cup she drank; in his bosom she slept; she was like a daughter to him. Now, a visitor came to the rich man, but he spared his own flocks and*

*herds to prepare a meal for the traveler who had come
to him: he took the poor man's ewe lamb and prepared
it for the one who had come to him." David grew very
angry with that man and said to Nathan: "As the LORD
lives, the man who has done this deserves death! He
shall make fourfold restitution for the lamb because
he has done this and was unsparing." Then Nathan
said to David: "You are the man!" 2 Samuel 12 1-7*

Through the story of the prophet Nathan, King David saw the injustice and pronounced a just punishment for the unjust rich man in Nathan's parable. Then, Nathan informed the King that the unjust person was him. I am sure this self realization completely changed David's image of himself as well as his immediate plans for his kingdom and his family. But King David trusted in God's mercy and forgiveness.

God is no different today, He is still the just judge that is full of mercy. The Church should not fear God's justice, but should fear His just punishment. The leaders of the Church need to humble themselves before God like King David and not behave like the Pharisees (or Judas) who put the Lord to death on a cross and then refused to repent of their sins after His resurrection. **This is the time when saints are made. We need the leaders of the Church to reclaim spiritual fatherhood.**

Our Family: The Church

The Church is a Dysfunctional Family

A dysfunctional family is a family in which conflict, misbehavior, and often child neglect or abuse on the part of individual parents are regular ongoing behaviors. This leads other members of the family to accommodate such actions. Some characteristics of a dysfunctional family are blaming someone else, failure to take responsibility for personal actions and feelings, and invalidation of other family members' feelings.[1]

I think this description fits the Church pretty well right now. We have conflict, misbehavior, and child abuse. These have been occurring continuously and regularly, and the leaders (Bishops) and some members (Priests) make accommodations which allow the abuse to continue. We have also seen abusive priests fail to take responsibility for their actions; we have seen leaders of the Church who have invalidated victims feelings and also, at times, even accused them of lying.

Child sexual abuse is committed by a sinful man in the Church, but the actions of Church leaders who cover up the abuse, move a priest, and put other children in harm's way is an example of dysfunctional parenting.

> *"I have learned that when there is sexual abuse, similar to someone with an addiction, the problem becomes a family "disease." A certain configuration happens in the family. There are roles everyone starts playing in order not to speak truth about the problem or to cover it up to protect the whole (or the image of the whole). Everyone begins to protect the addict or abuser. Anyone who is evidence of the problem or tries to deal with it in an honest way will be silenced in one way or another. The Church is a family. We are sick with this problem.*
>
> *The Bishops have played their roles and protected the whole (or so they thought) at the expense of the victims and really, in the end, at the expense of the whole."[2]*
>
> *- Shawn Rain Chapman*

The Church as Parent

The Church, in many ways, functions as parent: both Father and Mother. The Church takes on many aspects of fatherhood. It teaches the faithful in the ways of Christ, protects the faithful, and disciplines the wayward. The Church should protect and give the faithful a sense of security. The Church can also be viewed as a mother and in that role it should nurture and bring about healing. The Church has failed victims of clerical sexual abuse in each of these aspects: it fails to consistently teach, protect, discipline, nurture, and heal.

Teach

The Church should always teach the truth. The lack of authentic teaching on sex and marriage has been deafening. This has caused an outpouring of members of the laity to take up this job. Not only do many priests fail to talk about the difficult truths on sexuality, but some even speak falsely and lead people astray. While some priests do boldly speak and uphold the truth, there are many who do not, and I recall many times when I have been in the pews and had to recatechize my own children after Mass. In order to proclaim the Gospel boldly, priests need to believe that God's teaching is truly life giving and not a burden for people to endure.

Protect

The Church has failed to protect the victims and their families. Leaders of the Church, who are called to stand up for injustice, fail to take on the role of fatherhood to protect and do what is right. They have often failed to take priests out of ministry to prevent further cases of abuse. They fail to seek justice for the victim when they do not turn the perpetrators in to the authorities to be prosecuted by the laws of the land. In instances where they do remove abusers from ministry, they do not advocate on behalf of the victim to help them obtain justice through the legal system. The Church actually makes it even more difficult by sealing information instead of bringing information readily forward to the authorities. The effect of this lack of authentic fatherhood has left the flock increasingly insecure and many no longer trust the leaders of the Church, and the faithful continue to leave in droves. A 2019 Gallup poll found that 37% of US Catholics have questioned whether they will remain part of the Church this year; in 2002 only 22% responded in this fashion.[3]

Discipline

The Church must discipline her children. It is not enough to laicize a priest. This is lenient parenting. Perpetrators deserve jail time in hopes that it will help them to understand the gravity of their sin and one day repent from their wrong doings. If we just require an abusive priest to live a life of penance and prayer, we are inadvertently saying, "It was not that bad." Well, the truth is, it is that bad; it is criminal, even if the statute of limitations has expired. All too often, the abusive priest is given a slap on the wrist and is at worst laicized. They still live a relatively comfortable life in retirement, while the victim continues to suffer. We should explore ways in which the Church can advocate on behalf of the victim, who often is unable to stand up for him or her self, to ensure that the abuser is punished to the full extent of both civil and Church law.

The Church should expedite cooperation with the civil authorities in order to fully prosecute the offender prior to the expiration of the statute of limitations. In addition to canonical penalties, such as laicization, the Church should explore the possibility of forfeiture of retirement benefits and/or impose a financial penalty against the abuser to compensate their victims.

When Christ shows compassion for a sinner, it is always accompanied by a sinner's repentance, however, when a sinner is unrepentant, Christ shows righteous anger. He openly condemns the pharisees and Sadducees as well as flips tables[4]. This is what the victims seek: for Bishops to be like Christ, flip a table, and openly condemn the abusers. Too many of the perpetrators are unrepentant, therefore the response should be righteous anger filled with compassion and action.

Nurture and Heal

The Church has failed victims and their families when it has neglected to show true care and concern for their needs. They do not need more empty words, but instead they need to see action. The Church must demonstrate actual assistance towards their healing. Victims need assistance in order to come forward; they need assistance in order to enter into therapy; they need to feel supported and know they will not be walking the road of healing alone. They need an advocate. A strong, loyal, trustworthy advocate who will stand by their side and walk the journey with them--however long and winding it may be.

The Church has an obligation to seek out unknown victims of clerical sexual abuse and do whatever it can to heal the wounds they have suffered. When an abuser has a single victim come forward, it is very likely that there are other unknown victims. In order to provide healing to yet unknown victims, a plan should be carried out to publicize the name and crimes of the abuser in all of the communities where they served. It is not sufficient to publicize in the parish bulletin, because many victims no longer attend Church services. We need to also work with local media outlets to ensure that the message of healing and hope reaches the intended recipient. This will bring about a three-fold aide to open up an opportunity to discover other victims, to aid in the investigation, and to help the community begin to heal.

Do No Harm

Safe Environment workshops present a very difficult topic, the attendees will process the knowledge of the evil of sexual abuse of children in very different ways. If there are any attendees who are also victims of sexual abuse, these sessions can cause much suffering to them. Therapists should be available for those that might need assistance in processing their own wounds during these safe environment workshops. Leaders of the Church should give serious consideration to allowing exemptions for these classes for survivors of sexual abuse.

> *"I resent how I had to stop being a Eucharistic Minister because I can't handle the classes they make us take about sexual abuse in order to serve. This rule is well meaning I know. But.... why do WE have to take those classes?"*[5]

> \- Shawn Rain Chapman

Many survivors have been through a lot of healing, but listening to an instructor describe what happened to them may cause re-traumatization. If we are to be a Church of healing, we need to start acting like one. We need to be prepared to minister to the varied needs of attendees in these classes, especially those traumatized by the content.

Many Church leaders make statements of sorrow without actions toward justice against the abuser as well as actions to implement healing toward other victims and the community. Victims of clerical sexual abuse often perceive statements by leaders of the Church as empty words. Victims need to experience true concern and see the words put into action in order to restore trust. Victims need to see the Church working with them to condemn the actions of the abuser and protect against future harm from the abuser. Victims need to clearly see that the Church has a firm desire to seek out and heal those who were abused. This is necessary in order for the victims to feel that the statements are real.

Without a firm belief that the Church will protect like a father and comfort like a mother, the faithful are left with the question of whether the Church, or even God, really cares for them or if God is even real. How could any Church be the model of God's love and behave in such a grotesque manner as to protect the abuser instead of the victim? It is a grave wound to the body of Christ. To overcome this wound, prayer alone is not enough. The Church must confess her faults and spend much time in reparation to the Sacred Heart. Failure in this area will lead to a catastrophic loss of the lives of many souls. We have seen this in the righteous anger of the victims and their families, many of whom are no longer members of the Church and some even ceasing to believe in God.

Authentic Fatherhood

Another aspect of this problem that is often overlooked is that sexual abuse committed by a priest is far worse, spiritually, emotionally, and psychologically speaking, for the individual victims, as well for the whole community, than sexual abuse committed by other individuals in a victim's life. People know that their friends and family have flaws, some of them very serious, but for far too long, it didn't enter their minds that a priest or Bishop was capable of such atrocities.

The idea that Bishops, Priests, Coaches, and others who hold an office worthy of respect are incapable of doing wrong has caused great harm to many people. We need to respect their office, but also recognize that there are, at times, people in these offices doing very terrible things. We must not condemn the office, but the person who abuses it. Our Heavenly Father is the only perfect Father, and He is to be the icon for all who exercise authority over others.

Many victims have struggled with authority due to their abuse, I am no exception. The aspect of an evil father is extremely wounding for abuse victims, and a purposeful redemption of the rightful fatherhood of priests and Bishops is essential to restore trust and confidence in the Church for victims, their families, and the larger community. Even one case of abuse is horrendous, but a cover-up, or asking a victim to keep it quiet, take a cash payoff, etc., compounds the problem. It makes it worse, because it is a further disfiguring of the role of the father as protector and defender of his family. Forcefully denouncing the acts is the first step, as well as preventing further abuse; the second is to seek justice by criminally prosecuting the abuser. If the crime is past the statute of limitations, then publicly identify the abuser and seek to impose civil penalties. Thirdly, identify and denounce the structures that allowed the abuse to happen. Society needs to see firm leadership in this area, lest it continue to believe that the Church is only worried about protecting its own priests, Bishops, and financial assets.

Love as God loves, seek out one lost sheep, and heal their wounds as a father would seek out his son, seeking to help him restore his lost dignity. Call sin by its name, and be aggressive in rooting it out. Preach the truth in season and out of season. Victims of abuse were formed with lies from very young and impressionable ages by their abusers. They deserve the truth of the Gospel as part of their healing. Victims are hurting, and they may hurt others as they seek to extend healing to them. We must be willing to endure suffering in our efforts to help the victims, like Jesus did for us on the cross. Minister to the victim. Our Church shouldn't let processes and procedures get in the way of compassion towards victims. The rules of men must not prevent the healing love of God from reaching the people of God.

Be Not Afraid

"A good plan, violently executed now, is better than a perfect plan next week" - General George S. Patton

The Church needs to stop asking "what if" questions:
- if we meet with this victim
- if we exempt them from safe environment training
- if we do not have a lawyer present
- if we admit that the diocese or an individual in leadership within the Church personally failed them
- if we share the details about an abuser priest publicly
- if we go against what brother bishops say should be done

Fear of what could happen is preventing the Church from reclaiming spiritual fatherhood. Yes, something bad could happen, and one Bishop may end up being hated by other Bishops, in jail, or losing a lot of the Diocese's money. This fear should not guide the actions of the Church. Did the Church do what was right? Did the Church bring healing and justice to the victim? Then, so be it. It is better to have a clear conscience and the knowledge that the Church acted in a manner that was right and pleasing to God. Be not afraid.

Restore Our Trust

This chapter seeks to help the Pilgrim Church, the Church Militant, on earth to heal from the grievous wound of clerical sexual abuse. The Church is the bride of Christ, a true mother who cares for the faithful. The priests are the visible image of Jesus, Himself, since each priest acts "in persona Christi," in the person of Christ, as he confects and administers the sacraments. Both of these roles have been severely disfigured by priests who have sexually abused children and by Bishops who have protected the abusers. Our Church must be sick for it to have abused our trust, and we need to heal Her in order to restore trust.

Our son, Peter, on his Confirmation day

Our Inheritance

A wealthy landowner had multiple tenants working his land, they were each given a generous amount of land to till and bring forth fruit from the soil. One particular tenant had little regard for his soil, not caring for it well, and instead, he took all the garbage from his household and his friends' home and dumped it onto the land. He polluted the land so much that is was not suitable for growing anything. In some places, he dug up all the good soil and sold it for profit. He did whatever he could to find immediate gain for himself with little regard for his neighbors or those who would be caring for the land after he moved on to a new place or died. When the landowner went out to survey his land, he visited this tenant and found the land in such a very bad state; it was not suitable to grow anything. When he inquired with the tenants who lived nearby, they spoke highly of the dishonorable tenant, for he had given them many gifts from his land and had bragged to them about all the money and riches he had produced from the land. None of them had actually visited his land, they just heard about all the wealth he had amassed, so they were confident that he was a very wise man. Everyone held him in high regard, so no one questioned his methods. In reality, he abused the land, without regard for its future use or concern for the land owner and his property. What should happen to this tenant? How should he be treated? What should be done with the land? How can we ensure this tenant doesn't destroy another piece of land? Who should be held accountable for the damage? What can be done to prevent this from happening again with another parcel of land? What will prevent the other tenants from doing the same thing with their land?

This is the state of our Church today, we have inherited a polluted Church. Forget about what you think you know. Stop listening to what the experts of this world say is the prudent path forward. Remove all concern about Church politics, and return to the Lord, rending your garments, and confessing your sins. Do not place heavy burdens on the backs of the faithful that you yourself are not willing to carry.

A Father After God's Own Heart

The solution to the clergy abuse crisis is so simple that it is left untried. What is this simple solution? Be a father after God's own heart. King David was such a man, and he, like some of our leaders, made some very bad decisions. Then, he spent the rest of his life trying to redeem himself while suffering the effects of his sinful decisions. He never fully cleaned up the mess caused by his sins, but he publicly repented and spent the rest of his life trying to return to a right relationship with God his Father. Every Friday, as the Church prays Lauds, we pray Psalm 51 and thus pray with King David that the Lord will make our hearts clean. His songs of repentance are proclaimed at almost every Mass. His transgressions are well known, but always with the knowledge that he repented and maintained hope in the mercy of God.

With great humility comes great healing. Many leaders of the Church have lost their sense of humility and their sense of being men after God's own heart. The Father loved the world so much that he sacrificed his only Son to save us from our sins, and yet, the Church won't sacrifice even its public image to help victims of clerical sexual abuse to feel loved and find healing. Zacchaeus encountered the Lord, publicly repented, and made reparations to all he had wronged, and yet, our leaders fear losing their prestige, wealth, and power. They insulate themselves with lawyers and judges to deal with victims who come forward looking for the healing love of Christ.

Leaders of the Church are not behaving as if they trust in God's promises anymore and are failing to see that the answer is simple: Love as God loves. The example of many Saints who gave up all earthly comforts to serve others, not counting the cost and seeking to love as God loves, should be our guide. Mother Teresa of Calcutta, my patron, Francis Xavier, Bernadette S., Katharine Drexel, Francisco and

Jacinta Marta (Fatima), and John Vianney all followed God's path for them, which ultimately led to the cross and to Heaven. The action of compassionate love requires that we embrace the cross and suffer with members of our Church who have been abused.

Our History

In the early 1990s, the US Conference of Catholic Bishops adopted "Five Principles" to guide Bishops in their response to allegations of sexual abuse by clergy.

"Five Principles" to Guide the Response of Bishops [6]

1. Respond promptly to all allegations of abuse where there is reasonable belief that abuse has occurred;
2. If such an allegation is supported by sufficient evidence, relieve the alleged offender promptly of his ministerial duties and refer him for appropriate medical evaluation and intervention;
3. Comply with the obligations of civil law regarding reporting of the incident and cooperating with the investigation;
4. Reach out to the victims and their families and communicate sincere commitment to their spiritual and emotional well-being; and
5. Within the confines of respect for privacy of the individuals involved, deal as openly as possible with the members of the community

Yet, despite having these principles in place, many, if not all, were either poorly implemented or not implemented at all. This has been relayed in the witness chapters at the beginning of this book.

At the meeting of the US Conference of Catholic Bishops in 2002 in Dallas, TX, the Bishops produced a plan for the Protection of Children and Young People, officially known as "Promise to Protect, Pledge to Heal"[7]. It provides the essential norms for Dioceses to deal with allegations of sexual abuse of minors by priests or deacons. In 2019, these norms were expanded by the Pope to include Bishops.[8]

The implementation of these norms have varied from Diocese to Diocese but have generally included the creation of a safe environment program to protect youth. These programs usually require training on grooming techniques, learning about the reporting procedures, and background checks for all volunteers who work with youth or vulnerable adults. The other most common action, that has come out of the norms, has been to create an office for providing assistance to victims. The following six principles are recommended to be addressed in each Diocese:[7]

- Creating a safe environment for children and young people;
- Healing and reconciliation of victims and survivors;
- Making prompt and effective response to allegations;
- Cooperating with civil authorities;
- Disciplining offenders;
- Providing for means of accountability for the future to ensure the problem continues to be effectively dealt with through the Secretariat of Child and Youth Protection and the National Review Board.

Again, principles are set in place and, this time, much is done for protection, but little to nothing is done to seek out unknown victims and provide healing.

Speak with the Victim in Mind

We must remember that many victims are triggered by various aspects of the Church depending on how their abuse took place. Some cannot enter a Catholic Church or attend Mass, others have difficulty with the confessional, and some may not even be able to speak to a priest or bishop. We need to recognize that many victims have not attended a Church service since their abuse was recognized. The challenges that victims face should dictate our approach to outreach.

- Seek out Victims in conjunction with the local or community news outlets, not only media designed for current Church attendees

- Provide a town hall meeting away from Church property
- Professional counselors available to provide victim outreach
- Train priests to recognize and effectively minister to victims who they encounter
- Equip family and friends, who are currently practicing Catholics, to help identify potential victims and direct them to resources for healing
- Focus the message on the desire to heal the victim and help them seek justice

The Church is under such intense scrutiny right now; it seems there is always an opportunity for the Church to defend herself or make statements to the press. The news media reports, the Church makes an official response, and concerned members of the laity or society choose sides. It is a vicious cycle, one that often hurts those who are directly affected by clerical sexual abuse. I am sure that everyone is hurting, but often, the public debate about the latest issue needlessly triggers victims. The following "defenses" and attitudes should be acknowledged and changed or removed from the Church's vocabulary all together.

We Have Been Here Before

I have heard a few rebuttals in an effort to defend the Church. One is that the Church has experienced many crises in its two-thousand-plus year history and some are worse than the clerical abuse scandals. It doesn't really help to acknowledge that the Church has experienced times of difficulty in the past, when leaders betrayed their duties and even lived objectively immoral lives. For many of us today, we only knew the Church as a force for good in our society, and this scandal has shattered that image. The Church now needs to be renewed, so we can continue the mission that the Lord gave us to go and share the good news with all nations. Knowing that there have been difficult times in the past and knowing that the Church survived and became stronger because of that challenge is but a small consolation. For victims of clerical sexual abuse, this is salt in the wound and perhaps even comes across as minimizing their very real, ongoing suffering.

Other Organizations Have Abusers Too

There are some who defend the Church by saying that we are being unjustly scrutinized because there are far more cases of sexual abuse by teachers, by troop leaders in the scouts, or in some other organization. While these statistics may be true, they also insult victims and inadvertently make them part of a political battle. For victims and those that love them, the issue of clerical sexual abuse is very personal. It is not part of an attack on the Catholic Church or solely the fault of the liberal or conservative wings of Catholicism. It is the fault of a single priest who chose to sexually abuse a child. It is also the fault of some leaders of the Church that chose to protect the abuser rather than heal and fight for justice for the one who was abused.

These arguments, and others like them, are political battles that further injure the victim and the Church, herself. Let us focus our efforts on healing the victim, the family, and the Church: both the laity and the leaders. Do not defend the undefendable; there can be no defense for the sexual abuse. We must support the victim, advocate for the victim, and prove to them that someone cares about them and desires to protect them. Help them to know the love of God, the good Father, who looks at what happened and is horrified, angry, and offended.

Falsely Accused Priests

One danger in this cleansing of the Church is to worry about false accusations against innocent priests. There have been a few cases recently in which a beloved priest, bishop, or cardinal has been accused of abusing a child in their past. In some of these cases, the laity rally to their side and defend them because they believe they have been unjustly accused. While this may occur, statistics show that fewer than 2% of sexual abuse allegations against clergy in the Catholic Church appear to be false. If an innocent priest is accused, it is an opportunity for him to unite his suffering with the victims and the

Church. Christ was falsely accused, and through the sacrificial offering of Himself, He redeemed the world and called us to do the same.

Seeking the Lost

THE BARQUE OF PETER

The Catholic Church is like a great ship sailing to Heaven that has been infiltrated with double agents who have injured victims and thrown them off the ship. When a passenger falls off a ship, they must first be noticed, and then, the authorities have to be alerted in order to begin the rescue mission. The abuse survivors are treading in the ocean being tossed around by the many waves that the wake of the ship creates. The Catholic Church keeps saying, "Come to me if you need help," but that is equivalent to asking a person drowning in the ocean to swim to a ship. This is absurd and impossible. In order to rescue a person in an ocean, we need to jump into the water with them, bring them the life preserver, and row them back to the ship. It takes a coordinated effort to rescue someone from the ocean. This is the rescue effort that we need the Church to undertake. It is not enough to ask a victim to come forward; it is not enough to pray for their healing. Victims need rescuers who can not only carry them back to the ship, but to also assist in their much needed medical care in order to counteract the effects of the near drowning. There are so many victims drowning in the ocean of their abuse, and instead of sending out rescuers, the Church has forgotten to even look into the ocean to see that they are out there. Those who do notice are usually not adequately equipped to begin the rescue efforts.

Waiting for a victim to come forward is not sufficient, we need to be actively reaching out and extending an offer of healing. Many victims no longer attend Church services and some are slaves to destructive lifestyles that have made it nearly impossible for them to be able to come to the Church for healing. The Church has the ability to teach people how to be rescuers.

So how do we do this? How do we renew the Church in her healing mission? The answer is **hard work**. Just like the victims of sexual abuse have to work very hard to heal from their wounds, so does the Church. It is no longer possible to ignore the problem and hope that people will forget about it with time. Our priests cannot be just good enough and expect to be respected. Our leaders cannot preach the good news and expect that people will accept it because a priest or bishop of the Catholic Church said it. We are, in a sense, starting over. The Catholic Church has lost its place of honor and is often viewed with suspicion, not just by our enemies, but by average people and even many within our own Church who feel betrayed.

It will take Saints to renew the Church, men and women who are not afraid of the truth. Those who are willing to admit that the Church is not perfect and who are prepared to take the difficult steps to prove, through their actions, that the Church cares more about **healing** than it does about its possessions or any good reputation that may be left. We need to do what is right instead of what is easy. When a victim comes forward and the allegation is deemed credible, we need to be decisive in our protection of victims such that their **pain is minimized** and their path to healing is not hindered by the words or actions, or inaction, of a representative of the Church. We should view with horror the abuse that has occurred and, with determination, protect the victim and others from any possibility of further abuse and remove the abuser from our Church. **The abusive priest is the one who harmed the Church, not the victim who reported the crime.** Often the victim who had the courage to come forward to report the abuse is completely worn out by that action. It may have taken years for them to muster up the courage to tell another soul, let alone a representative of the Church. They have watched the news, heard stories from other abuse survivors, and they may justifiably fear that no one in the Church leadership cares about them or desires justice for them. What would Jesus do? He would treat them with compassion and love and weep with them. Then, he would act swiftly and decisively to call the sinner to repentance and seek justice.

To Prevent and To Heal

Prevention and healing are two equally important tasks for the Church today. As much as we have been trying to effectively respond to these two challenges, there is still much to be done.

Preventing Abuse

The Church has done a pretty good job with this task. In 2002, the charter for the protection of youth and vulnerable adults set into place many good procedures to protect and deter further abuse, but it still happens today, as the Peyton family can attest. These protections are mostly good, but many victims feel as though they are paying the price once again for the failings of the Church. When the new guidelines came out, the burden was put on the laity. We were asked to complete background checks, sit in training classes every three years, and be vigilant to help the Church detect abusers who seek to use the Church to gain access to potential victims. While members of the laity have benefitted from increased knowledge of grooming techniques, it is doubtful that most members of the laity would be strong enough to turn in their parish priest and even less probable that they would suspect or report a popular pastor who shows signs of grooming someone. This is, therefore, a false sense of security. A lot of activity was mandated, but in reality, it probably does very little to prevent abuse from happening. The reduction in abuse since 2002 could be due to better formation in seminary and a fear that the abuser may be caught due to the increased attention and suspicion placed on priests[9]. The majority of abuse within the Catholic Church was not perpetrated by lay volunteers, it was by ordained members of the clergy and seminarians.

Child Empowerment Approach

There are also some dioceses who have highly encouraged having children attend safe environment training in middle school or earlier. In 2006, the Catholic Medical Association (CMA) published a book on the appropriate response to preventing clerical abuse of minors and strongly discouraged the use of child empowerment programs. The book even went as far as to describe those programs as forms of grooming, because they expose the children to sexually explicit descriptions of grooming and, in some cases, feature abusers who describe their techniques[10]. Adults have a hard time believing that a respected adult is grooming them or someone else. How can we expect a child to do what most adults cannot? The USCCB has responded to the CMA report claiming that their findings are invalid. The conclusions contained in the "Safe Environment Training" report appears to invalidate its own results.

> *It is clear from the evidence that child sexual abuse prevention programs can be effective in a number of important respects; namely, increasing children's knowledge of sexual abuse, improving their self-protective behaviors, and raising disclosure rates. Although their effectiveness in reducing child sexual abuse is unproven, and is likely to remain so, it would be foolish to discard programs that have such significant and well-proven benefits[11].*

Kavita Desai, Esq. Staff Attorney (CHILDREN AT RISK Institute)
Dawn Lew, Esq. Senior Staff Attorney (CHILDREN AT RISK Institute)
www.childrenatrisk.org

Moral Virtue Approach

Role of Parents

The life of St. Maria Goretti provides a good blueprint for how to avoid abuse: teach what is good and right, equip children with the sword of truth and the breastplate of righteousness, and keep their eyes fixed on the things of heaven. Maria fought against her abuser, and then, before her death, she even forgave him. She desired only heaven for him, and her prayers were effective. Due to his miraculous conversion and repentance, some are advocating opening a cause for sainthood for her murderer, Alessandro Serenelli. In her case, she knew what her attacker wanted was wrong, even at age eleven, and she resisted his continuous attacks. He was much older than her, and her family was subservient to his family. She was truly trapped in a no win situation, but with God, she found a way to win anyway. We will talk more about how parents can protect their children in the next chapter, *the Fortress of the Family*. It is the right and duty of parents to protect their children, not the Church. The Church can and should support the parents in this role.

Role of Bishop - Morally Sound Community of Clergy

There needs to be an increased presence of the bishops in parishes or at diocesan wide events. Confirmations and the occasional visit to the parish to say Mass just do not provide enough opportunity for the people to get to know their bishop and relate to them as spiritual fathers. Monthly, diocesan wide, talks with the bishop could serve as an opportunity to reconnect with His flock and learn the needs of parishioners. Personal relationships come before spiritual ones: learn the smell of your sheep and give them the opportunity to know your smell too. Our leaders need to be known as those who defend the people of God from those who would attempt to pluck them away from the Lord. Right now, the people of God need strong, moral leaders: our moral authority is in question.

Bishops should be vigilant in supervising and mentoring their priests and deacons. They should do whatever is necessary to identify and remove immoral men who have the ability and desire to commit sin or criminal activity. If the spiritual father, the bishop, overlooks unrepentant sin among his ordained ministers, more serious sin will follow. If a priest is known to struggle with alcohol, drug addiction, pornography, masturbation, or lust, he needs to be put on a spiritual improvement plan immediately. He needs a support group to help him overcome these sins before they affect more than himself. Sin loves company, and if sin is allowed to continue, it will only get worse. Unchecked sin causes harm for members of the laity, and it leads to a community that embraces sinful lifestyles and fosters a collective disobedience to the moral law, as in the case of divorce, contraception, sterilization, pre-marital sex, and homosexual behavior. When sin goes unquestioned within the Holy Priesthood, the effects are disastrous because these men are leaders in our communities. Often those engaged in sin will influence other ordained men to be comfortable in their own sin. When ordained members of the Church become slaves to sinful activities, those sins grow beyond the priest himself. This has been the case with sexual sin, growing from harming one to harming other adults and minors.

A child is more likely to let their parents know about an inappropriate request that comes from an adult who is a friend of the family or the parent of one of their friends than they are for a person who is a member of the ordained clergy at their local parish. It takes longer to detect the criminal activities of a priest who has a desire to abuse children, or adults, and the process to remove him from his role within the parish is infinitely more difficult compared to a member of the laity who attempts to perpetrate a similar crime. Thus, it is infinitely more important for each bishop and his leadership team to ensure that priests are not only solidly formed in virtue and holiness, but also monitored with great vigilance. If this seems like micro management, you are correct. Their ability to cause immense harm is vast. The effects of sexual abuse on even a single child, affects numerous people, and the child will suffer the effects of the abuse for the rest of their life.

Legal Implications

Programs provide legal protection, because they can be quantified and documented. We educated this many people and we did this activity to protect children. I can see why the Church prefers this approach. It is almost impossible to gauge the effectiveness of parents teaching their children virtue, but this approach will last a lifetime and apply to more than just one area of harm.

> *Federal agents don't learn to spot counterfeit money by studying the counterfeits. They study genuine bills until they master the look of the real thing. Then when they see the bogus money they recognize it.*

We should be doing the same to combat sexual abuse. We need to teach the truth of sexual morality, so that our children will be able to recognize the true, good, and beautiful and to know what is right or appropriate. This is the first line of defense against abuse. When there is a weakness in understanding God's laws on sexuality, as with the current cultural climate that we are in, it is even more important to shout the truth with conviction. The great confusion in our youth is due to the many conflicting messages they are receiving. The Church needs to improve its efforts to teach what is morally right in the area of sexual morality. In addition, a majority of the adult population is not living in accord with the teachings of the Church and is in desperate need of this good news about God's plan for human sexuality. When people fall into sexual sin, the step into sexual abuse of minors becomes more approachable. When people start to embrace the truth that sexual contact is only appropriate within marriage, between husband and wife, sexual abuse of minors will begin to once again be viewed as the horror it is.

Prevention Doesn't Console a Victim

Healing is the area that has largely been untouched by the leaders of the Catholic Church. The avoidance of ministry focused on healing is to be seen as a source of the anger that is expressed by the laity. It is certainly one of the primary reasons that victims of sexual abuse, both by clerics and by other members of the community, leave the Church and view the official statements by bishops with such disgust. Often victims and other concerned members of the faithful will say that the bishops just do not get it, they do not understand the problem, and they wonder if that will ever change.

> ### TRAUMA CALLS FOR A RESPONSE
>
> A mass murderer has entered the Church. Normally, when a mass murder occurs, a support system is put into place and the counselors are there the next day to help all who have been affected. They remain for an ongoing amount of time to help the people heal. The community rallies behind the families affected and the community comes out to lend their support.
>
> Detrimentally, in the case of this abuse, the Church has yet to sound the alarm. There has been no call to action, no triage station set into place to provide much needed therapy and offer support to the victims, instead there is a denial that anyone was even affected. When will the Church see the hurting families and recognize the aching community? How many more murders must go on before they recognize the collateral damage that has happened? Our communities of faith are bleeding with pain: pain that can and should be healed by the Church.
>
> We, the survivors, are calling 911. We are sounding the alarm to let the Church know that something horrific has happened. It is not over; there is still work to be done; we must clean up after the tragedy. Please come to our aid and be the healer Christ calls you to be.

If the Church is only focused on prevention, those who are still hurting will never feel relief. Every time another news story about abuse in the Church appears, the wound is once again opened up. The Church will never begin to heal unless we seek to heal those who are hurting because of clerical sexual abuse. And if we heal those we have hurt, we will also be able to extend healing to those who have been sexually abused by others outside of the Church. It is estimated, and this estimate is probably low since many victims never report, that 33% of females and 17% of men will be a victim of sexual abuse within their lifetime[12]. So when you look out at your congregation of 1000 at a Sunday mass, there are at least 330 women and 170 men who have suffered abuse. That is a lot of hurting people, who are looking for help to allow healing. The teachings of the Catholic Church provide a potent medicine to aid in the healing. However, if we continue to focus only on prevention, we ignore and alienate all those who have already been abused and those who love and care for them.

Virtue

Virtue is the first line of defense. It is the one thing that has been used throughout the ages to prevent grave sin, even sexual sin, and we, the Church, are blessed with the fullness of Her teaching. We must remember to proclaim it through word and deed in order to be believed. **The Church's role in protecting children is to ensure that all of her priests, staff, and volunteers are morally virtuous.** We must ensure that our priests are practicing what the Church teaches on chastity, lest people learn by what they do. This has been part of the fruit from our previous generations. They were taught by the sins of their fathers and many never learned to live virtuous lives. Secondarily, they may provide prevention training, but they have forgotten the first and most effective way to prevent abuse is to have virtuous communities.

A virtue is an habitual and firm disposition to do the good. It allows the person not only to perform good acts, but to give the best of himself. The virtuous person tends to ward the good with all his sensory and spiritual powers; he pursues the good and chooses it in concrete actions.

The goal of a virtuous life is to become like God.

CCC 1803[13]

Because parents are the primary educators of children, it is a parent's role to protect their child. The Church may assist by helping parents teach virtue, but they should never scandalize a child by providing too much information about sexual sin. Only the parent knows when this information might be appropriate for their child. Children should never be put in the situation of policing adult behavior. This is the role of a parent. The Church could improve their prevention programs greatly by beginning with the solid teachings of chastity and the meaning of our sexuality. This is the time to reform misguided understanding on sexuality and build up the virtue of chastity in our communities.

Compassionate Leadership

The Church needs to be compassionate towards the victims and desire their complete healing and the fullness of the Christian life. The Church should, at a minimum, remove the offender from any ministry or place of honor within the Church. Plaques or pictures honoring the offender should be removed or marked with information on their crime, much like Christ's wounds are still visible in His resurrected body. Information should also be posted providing victims with the information on how to get help. Inform the community of what happened, without identifying the victim, and seek out other victims to offer compassion and healing to them also. The community needs to heal from learning of the fact that one of their trusted spiritual leaders committed such a grave evil to someone in their parish family. This focus should be primary for the Church, but, unfortunately, this rarely happens today. We need and deserve strong, authentic, spiritual fathers to lead our Church.

The civil authorities should apply the law and the diocese should be representing and protecting the victim, and in so doing, protect the Church from further harm and abuse. The Church, via her priests and bishops, must listen to the victim and make sure to acknowledge and validate their pain. The victim should never be further traumatized when they report their abuse or come to the Church for aid. Healing takes a long time and is different for each person. The Church should be protecting the victims, offering assistance and an advocate to walk with them. When the case goes to court, the Church must continue to stand by the victim and provide an advocate to be with them as much as possible. This kind of effort on the Church's part will be a visible sign of a protective father, a father who stands by his children and shelters them from the worst of the storm. These consistent actions will help the Church to reclaim its role.

Feed My Sheep

> "Seeing Peter warming himself, she looked intently at him and said, "You too were with the Nazarene, Jesus." But he denied it saying, "I neither know nor understand what you are talking about." So he went out into the outer court. [Then the cock crowed.] The maid saw him and began again to say to the bystanders, "This man is one of them." Once again he denied it. A little later the bystanders said to Peter once more, "Surely you are one of them; for you too are a Galilean." He began to curse and to swear, "I do not know this man about whom you are talking." And immediately a cock crowed a second time. Then Peter remembered the word that Jesus had said to him, "Before the cock crows twice you will deny me three times." He broke down and wept."

> Mark 14:67-72

Peter made a horrible mistake out of fear and failed to keep his gaze fixed on Christ. The Church is acting like Peter during his denial of Christ in fear of persecution. They are trying to hide their connection to the cover up. The victims are coming to the Church to identify Her as an accomplice with the abuser. It wasn't until Peter saw Christ's eyes that his sorrow was able to overcome his fear, and he was given the strength to weep. The victims deserve this same contrition and the apology of leaders in the Church, who made wrong decisions in the past, and their vow to handle things differently in the future.

*When they had finished breakfast, Jesus said to
Simon Peter, "Simon, son of John, do you love me more
than these?" He said to him, "Yes, Lord, you know that
I love you." He said to him, "Feed my lambs." He then
said to him a second time, "Simon, son of John, do
you love me?" He said to him, "Yes, Lord, you know
that I love you." He said to him, "Tend my sheep."
He said to him the third time, "Simon, son of John, do
you love me?" Peter was distressed that he had said
to him a third time, "Do you love me?" and he said
to him, "Lord, you know everything; you know that I
love you." [Jesus] said to him, "Feed my sheep."*

John 21:15-17

It wasn't enough for Peter to feel sorrow in his heart, Christ gave him a command to nurture and heal the Church. The victims need the Church's response to be like Peter's after his denial. Will the Church begin to weep as Peter wept? Victims are crying out, "Church, do you love me?" Will the Church say yes? Will the Church say yes three times? Leaders of the Church need to say yes like Peter. You must "feed the lambs," by **preaching the Truth.** You must "tend the sheep," by **advocating with victims for justice and healing**. You must "feed my sheep," by **healing the brokenhearted.**

Endnotes

1   "Dysfunctional Family." Gale Encyclopedia of Psychology. . Encyclopedia.com. 26 Jun. 2019 <https://www.encyclopedia.com>.

2   Shawn Rain Chapman https://bethanyhangout.com/2019/06/13/wearblacktomass/

3   https://news.gallup.com/poll/247571/catholics-question-membership-amid-scandal.aspx

4   http://www.usccb.org/bible/matthew/21

5   Shawn Rain Chapman https://bethanyhangout.com/2019/06/13/wearblacktomass/

6   The 1992 Ad Hoc Committee on Sexual Abuse "Five Principles" Regarding Allegations of Sexual Abuse

7   http://www.usccb.org/issues-and-action/child-and-youth-protection/resources/upload/Promise-to-Protect-Pledge-to-Heal-Brochure.pdf

8   APOSTOLIC LETTER ISSUED MOTU PROPRIO BY THE SUPREME PONTIFF FRANCIS "VOS ESTIS LUX MUNDI" http://w2.vatican.va/content/francesco/en/motu_proprio/documents/papa-francesco-motu-proprio-20190507_vos-estis-lux-mundi.html

9   Receding Waves: Child Sex Abuse and Homosexual Priests Since 2000

10   To Protect and to Prevent - Catholic Medical Association

11   Safe Environment Training: The Effectiveness of the Catholic Church's Child Sexual Abuse Prevention Programs page 27

12   https://1in6.org/get-information/the-1-in-6-statistic/

13   Catholic Church. "Duties of Parents 1803" Catechism of the Catholic Church. 2nd ed. Vatican: Libreria Editrice Vaticana, 2012. Print.

ABUSE *of* TRUST

Fortress of the Family

Denae and Allen Hebert

Healthy, Holy Families are the solution to preventing and healing from the trauma of sexual abuse.

My life was saved by two families. The first one was my grandmother, MaMa, and the second was my wife's family. MaMa was twice widowed and only had one child, my mother. Her life was filled with prayer, family, and her parish. She attended daily Mass and her friends were her parish community. Her husband, Allen Broussard, died shortly after her daughter got married. She remarried, and her second husband died within a year. Her life had its share of challenges, but her faith, family, and community helped her through those tough times.

When my parents got married, both of their parents were married, but within a couple of years, my paternal grandparents divorced and my maternal grandfather died. I remember spending quite a bit more time with my maternal Grandmother than with my paternal grandparents. MaMa had a much more stable influence in my life. I remember her often telling me how she had two very good husbands, and she wasn't going to take a chance on another one. She devoted the rest of her life to her daughter's family. My brother and I were the primary beneficiaries of that decision.

The foundation of a loving family was set solid; I was for the most part protected from the effects of my paternal grandparent's divorce. I knew it happened, but the primary influence in my family was from MaMa. Her selfless love for me and my family was enough to protect me from the sin of divorce that was traumatizing my Dad's family. This healthy, faith-filled environment provide a solid foundation, which would ultimately help me to survive the trauma of sexual abuse by a priest.

I met the second family many years after I was abused. I was living in an objectively immoral lifestyle. When I encountered my wife and her family, I saw something beautiful, something familiar that I once had, but had since lost. God presented me with a great gift, and because of my solid foundation of family life before the abuse, I was willing to accept it and even be drawn to it. Most victims of abuse engage in risky, destructive lifestyles for years before crashing. While I still didn't recognize my abuse for many years or even accept all the moral teachings of the Church, especially those related to human sexuality, I desired to have what they had and to choose this way of life for my own family because it brought joy to my life. It was more attractive than the life of sin that Fr. Andy tried to convince me to live.

> *God created us to engage and sanctify the*
> *world, not withdraw from it. Forming community*
> *of life and love is the best cultural contribution*
> *Christian families can offer society. Christian*
> *families working together can change the world.*
>
> *Archbishop Charles J. Chaput*

I experienced this when I encountered a Christian family living according to God's plan. This encounter changed my world, corrected my course, and brought me into a closer relationship with God.

The Domestic Church

The family is the first school of formation for every human being. Each person is born into a family, be it healthy or unhealthy. The circumstances, conditions, and family makeup will vary. The extent to which we make this family healthy and holy affects the entire life of this human being. To say that parents have a huge responsibility is an understatement. But never fear, for Jesus tells us, "For human beings this is impossible, but for God all things are possible." (Matt. 19:26)

God designed the family to be a place of refuge, a place of unity, and a place of safety. Jesus prayed that His Church would be one. In *Lumen Gentium*, the family is given the title of the domestic church and is a place where unity should be taught and embraced.[1] The better we can achieve these lofty goals, the better our family, our parish, our society, our country, and our world will be. It is from these families that our future priests, parents of the next generation, business owners, politicians, lawyers, doctors, teachers, mechanics, etc., come from. If we don't get the family right, the basic cell of society, our communities, cities, countries, and our world will suffer the consequences. Parents play a vital and irreplaceable role in the formation of our Church.

Leader of My Domestic Church

Over the course of several months after I decided to share my witness, there were many fears that I had to deal with. What would other people think about me? How would my Bishop and Pastor treat me after they knew that I had been abused by a priest. In the end, the fear that I remember most vividly occurred after I did an interview with Charles Collins of Crux. In this article, I answered some fairly predictable questions:

- Tell me about the priest that molested you
- When did you first report the abuse?
- How were your dealings with the Diocese?
- What changes would you like to see in Church policies?
- How did you feel about the release of names of credibly accused priests?

I responded to these questions while volunteering at a weekend Diocesan youth event. The article was published a couple of days later. Crux publishes their articles according to the time in Rome, Italy, so it was published at 1 AM on a Monday morning. For some reason, I woke up around that time and read the article. Even though I was exhausted from volunteering all weekend at the youth conference, I couldn't go back to sleep after reading it. The part that kept me awake was the advice I gave on what the Church should do differently to protect children from being sexually abused.

*"Hebert would like to see the Church return
to a model of parents being the primary educators
of their children when it comes to religion.*

*"The hierarchy, through their rules and
attitudes towards the laity have convinced parents
that they need to turn over their children to the
Church to learn the faith," he explained.*

*"Overnight retreats away from their families, drop
off religious education requirements to receive the
sacraments all reinforce that the home is not where
the faith is passed on and the parents are not the
most important person to teach them. If the parents
are not equipped to pass on the faith, then we should
fix that problem, not bypass the parents and teach
the kids from a warm body and a book," he said.*

*"My parents thought there was nothing better for
me in my faith life than to spend a lot of time with a
priest, because priests are holy and they can surely
teach me the faith better than they could ever hope
to. This attitude still exists today," said Hebert."*

I was so worried what my Bishop, Pastor, and other friends who work for the Church would think about how I felt. The comments were from the heart, and we had raised our children with a determined attitude to pass on the faith to them and protect them from harm. That meant asserting our authority as their primary evangelizers and protectors. We caught a lot of flack for many of our decisions in these areas. I had personal meetings with more than one Bishop about our right to prepare our children for the sacraments and even had to write to Rome to have them tell our local Diocese that they couldn't deny the sacraments to our children because we chose not to enroll them in the parish religious education program. But even after standing firm in this belief for over twenty-four years of parenting, I was mortified to see my thoughts on this subject printed in a widely read Catholic publication.

After sharing the article on social media, many of my friends commented on it, and one person even praised the section that kept me awake all night. What I found was that many of my friends and fellow Catholics felt the same way, but they chose to just do what the Diocese told them that they had to do. Therefore, this chapter is dedicated to my fellow parents and to the children who deserve to be evangelized and protected by parents that love them. These children are entitled to receive the faith from their parents. God designed it that way, and it is truly a beautiful plan. This doesn't mean that this method is fool-proof. The Peytons took their job seriously, and their son was still abused. However, I have a feeling that their son's healing has been quicker and will be more complete. Clericalism feels like being bullied, and makes parents feel like they are incapable of passing on the faith to the children that God gave them. Clericalism harms the family and the Church.

Clericalism arises from an elitist and exclusivist vision of vocation, that interprets the ministry received as a power to be exercised rather than as a free and generous service to be given. This leads us to believe that we belong to a group that has all the answers and no longer needs to listen or learn anything.[2]

Pope Francis

The Primary Evangelizers

If the parents are capable, they should be evangelizing and protecting their own children. If they are not capable, then the Church should be equipping them to carry out this job. Subsidiarity is an organizing principle that matters ought to be handled by the smallest, lowest, or least centralized competent authority. In the case of forming and protecting children, that is the parents. For too long parents have expected the Church to be the one teaching their children all about faith and morals.

> *Through the grace of the sacrament of marriage,*
> *parents receive the responsibility and privilege of*
> *evangelizing their children. Parents should initiate*
> *their children at an early age into the mysteries of*
> *the faith of which they are the "first heralds" for*
> *their children. They should associate them from their*
> *tenderest years with the life of the Church. A wholesome*
> *family life can foster interior dispositions that are*
> *a genuine preparation for a living faith and remain*
> *a support for it throughout one's life.[3] CCC 2225*

If we return this duty to the parents, it will have the following positive effects on our Church:

- If parents are actively involved in the spiritual life of their children, there will be fewer parents dropping off minors at the parish. Therefore, the opportunity for the formation of inappropriate relationships will be reduced.
- If more parents are able to effectively pass on the faith to their own children, the parish will not need to provide as many supplemental programs. Parishes will be able to refocus their resources (money and volunteers) to the evangelization of adults.
- The faith will be passed on more effectively. Our young people will be surrounded by the faith throughout the week, instead of one night a week of instruction during the school year, which is typical of a parish religious education program.
- The basic cell of society, the family, will be strengthened.

However, youth ministry is more than catechesis. It is an opportunity for maturing teens to begin to interact with their peers in the parish. Ideally, parents would take an active role in the youth program to help their child in this exciting exploration of the Catholic world outside of their immediate family, while also contributing to the safety of the parish youth program.

Where are Children Safe?

Children are considered safe when they are under the watchful eye of a parent or upstanding adult. They are considered safe when they are in a location that is monitored by trusted members of society, be they teachers, coaches, doctors, youth ministers, or priests. There was a time when children were always safe when in the presence of one of these upstanding adults, but now it has become apparent that this assumption of trust was misplaced. We can no longer rely on titles or locations. Sometimes, even our own experiences will fool us into feeling safe, when the reality is that we are not. The Church was a place that was supposed to be safe, these were people we were taught could be safe, and we have discovered that we were wrong. How can we restore this place and these people to the rightful level of trust and image of safety that they should be?

Who Protects Your Children?

I attended the FBI Citizen's Academy, which is a six week program to educate citizens about all the different activities that the FBI is involved with in the community. On the night that the Cyber Division gave a demonstration on how an attacker can easily break into a smartphone and a laptop, the audience of twenty-five community leaders was universally shocked that this attack could be so easily carried out. Each of the attacks relied on the trust and willingness of the victim to visit a website, open an email, or execute a program on their device. I would suggest that the clerical sexual abuse crisis within the Catholic Church is very similar.

The sexual abuse crisis in the Church is still alive and well; there are still members of the faithful who trust and are willing to go along with whatever their diocese or pastor asks them to do. They do not even question it, largely because the Church has certified that the Church environment and the volunteers are properly vetted.

I am a Catholic. I intend to be a Catholic until the day I die. I love the Church and would die to defend her, and I hope my witness causes my children to learn to love the Church as much as I do. Concerning trust, Michael Vanderburg said in his chapter on the Suffering Church, "I don't trust anybody … I am vulnerable in various degrees to [people], [but everyone] will fail me at some point." Therefore, our guard should always be up, we can only place our complete trust in the Lord.

How can someone be a faithful, engaged Catholic and still protect their family from abuse? Our family is very active in the Church. We live across the street from our parish. We have good friendships with our pastor and many priests in our Diocese and elsewhere. We volunteer in our parish youth group and with our annual Diocesan Youth Conference. Our children participate in many youth focused events, but we are very involved with them in these activities. We get to know the leaders, and we make prudential judgements about the interactions our children have with them. We try to weigh the risk and benefit for each activity in which our children may participate. Life is full of risks, and there are times that we say no to something. It isn't that we are looking for evil at every corner, but we need to protect our children from the potential of abuse. The costs are too high to be lax in this area.

We know we are the primary protectors of our children, and, as such, we do not easily transfer that right to people who we do not highly trust. It requires that we have a strong, trusting relationship with our children. We also spend a lot of time getting to know members of our parish community, our youth leaders, our priests, and our bishop. We desire for our children to have appropriate relationships with other faithful Catholics, but we are always on guard watching for any signs that a healthy relationship is turning into one that could lead to abuse. That is what we signed up for when we became parents, and we hope and pray that our vigilance will be enough. Even with all this vigilance, we may still fail. We hope that if one of our children is abused, that the unconditional love and strong relationship we have worked hard to have with them will help them to overcome the trauma they have experienced. Just as the Church adopted rules in 2002 to Protect and to Heal, so must the families that make up the Church.

*"I personally do not trust anyone other than
myself to protect my children. Abuse can come from
just about anywhere. It's my responsibility to teach
my kids virtue, this is the first defense, and this will
empower them to setting their own boundaries."*

Becky Saucedo
*Theology of the Body Speaker and Educator,
Mother of 11*

Failed Efforts to Protect

The efforts to prevent sexual abuse of children within the Catholic Church mostly rely on catching a perpetrator after someone has already been abused. Teaching adults how to recognize grooming will help prevent some abuse from occurring. But the background checks and zero tolerance policies all rely on an abuser having been reported, prosecuted, and convicted.

The 2002 Dallas Charter for the Protection of Children and Youth was a major step forward, but it stopped short of making systemic changes within the Church. It required:

1. Creating a safe environment for children and young people
2. Healing and reconciliation of victims and survivors
3. Making prompt and effective response to allegations
4. Cooperating with civil authorities
5. Disciplining offenders
6. Providing for means of accountability for the future to ensure the problem continues to be effectively dealt with.[4]

Many of the practical ways in which these new guidelines were implemented impacted the lives of the laity. We were required to attend training and ongoing refresher courses as well as consent to perpetual background checks. If you wanted to volunteer within the Church, these requirements were imposed on lay volunteers in all ministries, not just on those working with children or vulnerable adults. Everyone had to comply or they were not welcome to serve.

There were no exceptions for volunteers who were victims of sexual abuse or for those who found the topics discussed too sickening to endure. You had to attend or give up volunteering in your parish. As a survivor, this response seemed misplaced; it was priests who abused children which gave rise to the Dallas Charter for the Protection of Children and Young People, not sexual abuse by lay volunteers. Yet, lay volunteers bore the brunt of the new guidelines. It felt like the focus was taken off clerics and put onto lay volunteers.

The result was for the laity to suspect one another instead of the priests. We experienced this in our own community. In fact, those members of the laity who chose not to go through the safe environment program were viewed with suspicion as their friends wondered what they had to hide. For my wife and I, this only added to our suffering, because we were hiding something: the fact that I was a victim of clerical sexual abuse. The undesired result of these lay focused safe environment programs was to further breakdown the parish community, to cause suspicion of one another, and the individual members of the community to no longer trust their fellow parishioners. I never noticed a decrease in trust between parishioners and the ordained clergy.

False Sense of Security

The Church didn't attempt to change much within the operations of the parish, they simply implemented background checks and education programs. While there were rules like:

- No full frontal hugs, only side hugs
- No children sitting on laps of adults
- Two required adult volunteers when children are present, which is effectively not enforceable due to lack of volunteers
- No adults going into bathrooms with children, even young ones

- No adults allowed to sleep in youth hotel rooms during overnight outings (picture four teens in their own room with no adult supervision)

The primary message that was communicated to many was that adults were not to be trusted.

Background Checks

Background checks sound like a great idea, but the reality is that only .5% of sexual abuse crimes are prosecuted such that the abuser is convicted. Out of every 1000 sexual assaults, 995 perpetrators will walk free. Background checks only identify abusers who have been caught, but a majority have not been caught and convicted and thus will not be prevented from volunteering.[5]

Educational Programs

Most safe environment training classes seek to educate the attendees about the grooming techniques used by abusers. While this is good information, it will only prevent abuse in a relatively small number of cases. Abusers groom the community, not just the child target. The abuser seeks to ensure that everyone likes them and that they can do no wrong. They are often charismatic and highly manipulative, many are high on the narcissistic spectrum.[6]

Narcissism is a spectrum disorder, which means it exists on a continuum ranging from a few narcissistic traits to the full-blown personality disorder. Narcissistic personality disorder is a mental condition in which people have an inflated sense of their own importance, a deep need for excessive attention and admiration, troubled relationships, and a lack of empathy for others.[7]

They shower not only the child target with gifts and special attention, but also the family and the community. The training programs fail to adequately prepare the community to accept that someone they trusted would be capable of committing this crime. Even if someone witnesses evidence of grooming or worse, they now have to have the courage and fortitude to rely on the evidence and disregard their own feelings of trust in the alleged abuser. Often the internal struggle is too great and the witness avoids, for a period of time, reporting the suspected abuse until it is too late. What is needed is a class on how to guard your heart so that you won't be taken in by an abuser's attempts to groom you.[8]

Holy Families Heal

The family can and should be a place for healing. My own personal story is a witness to how the unconditional love of a holy family can help bring about healing. In searching for a solution to the evil of clerical sexual abuse, we can see that God in His infinite wisdom has tried to reveal it to us in Scripture. It was through the grave evil of Adam's family that sin first entered the world. Our first parents had a dysfunctional family, and the world continues to suffer greatly from it. The Holy Family of Jesus, Mary, and Joseph provide us with proof that it is possible to redeem the world through the family. It is this witness that we should use to show us the way forward. Our families are called to sanctify and bless the world, to be a light to others demonstrating that love can conquer all evil. It is possible to trust God and each other and to love even when life is difficult.

We, too, have experienced a great evil in our family, the Church, and it will be through the great witnesses of holy families that we will heal. Families must begin again to follow God's original plan to transform the world through holiness. Holiness has always been the key, and it is the only thing that can give balm to all the ills of our world. Scripture confirms that there will always be evil in our world, for it is the place of Satan's realm. But, we still have the opportunity to relieve much suffering and live with our eyes fixed on Christ to be in the world, but not of the world.

We can learn much from the Holy Family, the family through which God chose to bring salvation to the world. Both Mary and Joseph loved the Lord with all their mind, heart, and strength. They welcomed the Lord into their home, and their whole lives revolved around Him. They were poor by human standards but were filled with joy and surrounded by family and friends. Their highest priority was serving the Lord and living virtuous lives. Our Church is hurting; our families are hurting; and we can be a force for bringing in the healing of Jesus to remedy the sickness of sexual abuse that has infiltrated not only our society, but our Church as well. This is a time for heroic families to rise up and imitate the Holy Family.

We are called to have Jesus at the center of our family and have Mary as our Mother. Without God, family life lived in holiness is impossible, but with God at the center of our family life, we can do all things and be the light that this dark world needs. Pope St. John Paul II tells us that "the Mission of the family is to guard, reveal, and communicate love,"[9] and by the love of God, we can change the world one family at a time. Families are the design of God to pass on the knowledge of life, faith, and love.

Your Holy Family

So what is God's plan for the family that will help to protect and heal? God's plan for your family is holiness. Each of us, married or single, is part of a family. We all have a part to play to redeem the world. The writings of Pope St. John Paul II provide a beautiful description of what it looks like to be a family after God's own heart.

God's plan for family life consists of setting your priorities with God at the center, cultivating a healthy family prayer life, engaging in family recreation, loving unconditionally, building community with other families, and evangelization.

Priorities

God's plan for family life has a very distinct order of priorities. We are to place God first, spouse second, children third, and everyone else after that.

> *"But seek first the kingdom [of God]*
> *and his righteousness, and all these things*
> *will be given you besides." Matt. 6:33*

Our lives should reflect these priorities. For example, we plan our week to ensure that we nurture our relationship with God by placing Him on our calendar: Sunday Mass, daily prayer, monthly confession, and study of Scripture should be prioritized over work and play.

In a family that isn't committed to this order of priorities, conflicts can arise when work, out of town guests, or a child's sporting event cause us to consider skipping Sunday Mass. If we choose to value the opinion of our parents over that of our spouse, choose to override our spouse's desire and give in to our children's nagging, or believe that our relationship with our children is more important than our relationship with our spouse, each of these errors will lead to disorder and disharmony in our families.

God's priorities may not always make sense, but when kept consistently, they will bring us joy and peace and equip us to weather the storms of life. God's plan is for harmony within the family. This doesn't mean the absence of difficulty, but the promise that God will see us through those tough times and that we will come out stronger afterwards.

> *Thus they will fulfill their task with*
> *human and Christian responsibility, and,*
> *with docile reverence toward God, will make*
> *decisions by common counsel and effort.*

> *- Guadium Et Spes #50*

Family Prayer

Fostering prayer within the family is the most important of all the steps that can be taken. It is the lifeblood of the family, because it takes the family outside of itself and brings it into union with God. An individual prayer life for each parent is a prerequisite, and prayer between the married couple is important as well. All forms of prayer acknowledge that God is important, that we cannot do it alone, and that our relationship with God is an essential part of our lives. We pray to God for ourselves, for our marriage, and for our family.

> *If then my people, upon whom my name*
> *has been pronounced, humble themselves and*
> *pray, and seek my face and turn from their evil*
> *ways, I will hear them from heaven and pardon*
> *their sins and heal their land. 2 Chr. 7:14*

Some would say that a strong marriage is the most important foundation for a happy family, but a strong marriage is the result of a strong prayer life of the husband and wife and their shared prayer together. If there are troubles in the marriage, who should they turn to? They should turn to God in prayer and ask for His help. Family prayer is no different. The center of our family is not a new baby; it is not our children; it is not mom or dad. It is God. When He is placed at the center of our family life, all family issues, disputes, and struggles can be overcome. The surest way to place God at the center of our family is through frequent and sincere family prayer time. Prayer is to the soul like breathing is to the body. Without it, your soul will die.

> *"Family prayer has its own characteristic qualities.*
> *It is prayer offered in common, husband and wife*
> *together, parents and children together…by reason of*
> *their dignity and mission, Christian parents have the*
> *specific responsibility of educating their children in*
> *prayer, introducing them to gradual discovery of the*
> *mystery of God and to personal dialogue with Him…"*
>
> *- Familiaris Consortio #59-60*

Recreation

> *"Having fun together is one foundation of*
> *authoritative parenting. Kids won't value time with*
> *you above time with same age peers if they rarely*
> *spend any time with you doing fun stuff."*[10]
>
> *- Dr. Leonard Sax*

Playing games together is a very powerful way to bond with someone. On the surface, playing games provides an opportunity to be together and interact with other people all around a common set of rules that constitute a given game.

On a deeper level, when we play with others, for a moment, we are on the same level, even if that person is a bit older or younger. Partaking in a game changes the normal rules of life and takes us into an alternate environment where everyone has an equal chance to win. When we play with someone, we are saying that we like to spend time with them, that we enjoy their company, that we share similar interests, and that we can have fun together regardless of differences in age, physical or mental abilities, or interests. The choice of the play activity is pretty important: for little kids it is easy to pick an activity, but as our children grow up, we have to become more creative. Some families might enjoy playing sports together, making music, or even role playing games. The idea is to find something that all are able to participate in and enjoy. Some things we do with the entire family, and other times, we subdivide the children and do things with just the younger kids or just the older ones. The goal is to create lasting memories of being together, to build the bonds of trust, and open the lines of communication. The time invested in your child(ren)'s relationship will prove to be very helpful when life gets hard and they need someone to talk to. We, as parents, want our children to believe that we are there for them, and playing with them helps to communicate that message.

> *"Play is the gateway to vitality. By its nature*
> *it is uniquely and intrinsically rewarding. It*

*generates optimism, seeks out novelty, makes
perseverance fun, leads to mastery, gives the
immune system a bounce, fosters empathy and
promotes a sense of belonging and community."*

- The National Institute for Play

*"Play isn't just about imagination; it is about rest and
rejuvenation. It shapes our brain, fosters joy, creativity
and innovation, and is essential to our health."*

- Brené Brown, PhD

Unconditional Love

*"The family has the mission to guard, reveal and
communicate love, and this is a living reflection of
and a real sharing in God's love for humanity and the
love of Christ the Lord for the Church His bride."*

- Familiaris Consortio #17 Pope St. John Paul II

What God has joined, let no one divide: your family was started
on the day you got married. After you took your vows, the presider
may have uttered words similar to the ones above. It not only applies
to you and your spouse, but also to your entire family. The world
seeks to separate what God has joined together. A strong relationship
between parents and each child will assist them through the difficulties
and struggles they encounter along their journey through life. St. John
Paul II called this the communion of persons. A family is a community
of persons, the first and most important community for every human
being. The family can be a community where the members love one
another unconditionally, or not; a place where the members feel safe,
secure, and loved, or not; a place where they know people care about
them, or not.

Parents have the most influence in defining the culture within their
family. This culture should be healthy, loving, and life giving. This
culture is fragile--it needs to be cultivated and constantly monitored.

It is easy for excessive activities, negativity, sarcasm, the media, and unhealthy friendships to have an undesired effect on the culture of the family and on each member of the family. We need to instill in our children the confidence to truly know and believe that our love for them is unconditional. At the core of the family culture is the unconditional love between family members. The primary relationship is between the husband and wife and secondarily between parents and their children. If you get these right, the relationships between siblings will follow suit. Your family is a great gift from God, be sure to nurture and care for it.

> *"If I speak in human and angelic tongues but do not have love, I am a resounding gong or a clashing cymbal. And if I have the gift of prophecy and comprehend all mysteries and all knowledge; if I have all faith so as to move mountains but do not have love, I am nothing. If I give away everything I own, and if I hand my body over so that I may boast but do not have love, I gain nothing."* 1 Cor. 13:1-3

Community of Families

Healthy relationships between spouses, between parents and their children, and between siblings are prerequisites to the creation and building of holy families. Out of this healthy family life, centered on the Lord, comes the building of strong, supportive, and holy relationships between families. These family to family relationships are essential for the success of a family's quest for holiness. If a family encounters another family at their parish that possesses a family life which they desire, evangelization and knowledge transfer can take place organically through these human interactions. The greatest tool of evangelization is not what we teach with words, but seeing the authentic happiness that pours forth from the life of the community of persons: the family.

*"It is important that families attempt to build bonds
of solidarity among themselves. This allows them to
assist each other in the educational enterprise: parents
are educated by other parents, and children by other
children. Thus a particular tradition of education
is created, which draws strength from the character
of the "domestic church" proper to the family."*

- Familiaris Consortio #27

The fact that so many people have had to suffer the damage
from abuse alone, for so long, is a tragedy that indicates our loss of
community. We must restore the parish to the community of families
that it is supposed to be. This should be the place where we meet each
other and become friends, but all too often only the women or men
know each other, or the children know each other from taking religious
education classes together. We have to restore relationships to their
proper order. The best way to truly know someone is to get to know
the family that they were raised in or the family that they are raising.
To remove the family from an individual is to actually miss out on
learning about someone.

Evangelization

*"The 'Good News' of the family is a very
important part of evangelization, that Christians
can communicate to everyone through the witness of
their lives; and they already do so – this is evident
in secularized societies ... We therefore propose to
all, with respect and courage, the beauty of marriage
and the family, illuminated by the Gospel!"*

- Pope Francis

How often have you seen something working for a friend, a
neighbor, or another family and attempted to implement that same
behavior or activity into your own life? Sometimes we tweak other's
ideas or simply copy it straight out to see if it will work for us. This is

what emulating the lives of the saints is all about. We, too, are called to be saints, and hopefully people will want to emulate us. You will know you are a family that evangelizes when other parents ask you for advice. They see the grace of God shining through your family, and now, you have the opportunity to share the conscious choices you have made to live the life of faith within your family.

We are to make God's invisible love visible: this is the essence of evangelization.

Conclusion

In our Church today, a great evil has been identified. Leaders in our Church have broken the trust we placed in them; not just the priests who abused our children, but the leaders who protected the abusers. We, as a community, have experienced a secondary trauma, and we, like the victims, also go through the feelings of disbelief, anger, and grief. We may feel like sheep without a shepherd. We are looking for strong leadership in the Church. We are looking for saints. Saints are formed by families, holy families, that pray, work, and play together. The saints we are looking for may, in fact, be you and me, our children, and our grandchildren.

> *"Not all can become rich, wise, famous... Yet, all of us — yes, all of us — are called to be saints."*[11]

> *- St. Josemaria Escriva*

The Church must provide support and equip families in this effort. A healthy, holy family is a place of safety and security, where a child is protected and nurtured and the process of discipleship is most effective. Now is the time for the Church to become a family of families that follow the model that Jesus, Mary, and Joseph gave us.

Endnotes

1   http://www.vatican.va/archive/hist_councils/ii_vatican_council/documents/vat-ii_const_19641121_lumen-gentium_en.html Lumen Gentium 11

2   Pope Francis' Address to the Synod Fathers at Opening of Synod 2018 on Young People, the Faith and Vocational Discernment https://zenit.org/articles/pope-francis-address-to-the-synod-fathers-at-opening-of-synod2018-on-young-people-the-faith-and-vocational-discernment/

3   Catholic Church. "Duties of Parents 2225" Catechism of the Catholic Church. 2nd ed. Vatican: Libreria Editrice Vaticana, 2012. Print.

4   http://www.usccb.org/issues-and-action/child-and-youth-protection/charter.cfm

5   https://www.rainn.org/statistics/criminal-justice-system

6   Gilgun, J.F. Contemp Fam Ther (1988) 10: 216. https://doi.org/10.1007/BF00891614

7   https://www.mayoclinic.org/diseases-conditions/narcissistic-personality-disorder/symptoms-causes/syc-20366662

8   https://www.amazon.com/Let-Us-Prey-Narcissist-Pastors-ebook/dp/B073X79X1T/

9   http://w2.vatican.va/content/john-paul-ii/en/apost_exhortations/documents/hf_jp-ii_exh_19811122_familiaris-consortio.html #17

10   Dr. Leonard Sax, *The Collapse of Parenting* page 28

11   Furrow 125 http://www.escrivaworks.org/book/furrow-point-125.htm

The Truths; The Lies Abuse victims believe; How to combat the lies with Scripture.

Attribute of God: Love

Description	Common Lies Created By Abuse	Truth About This Attribute	How to Combat the Lie
God's love is the entirety of his goodness toward his creation.	God loves other people but he couldn't love me.	God loves his children unconditionally and eternally.	**Scripture:** Exodus 3:7; Deut. 7:7-8; Psalm 136: Psalm 145:8-9, 14-17; Isaiah 54:8; Hosea 11:9; Matt. 9:36; Rom. 5:8, 8:31-39; 1 John 4:8-10
It includes compassion and mercy.	God's love must be earned. How can God be a loving father if my own father hurt me?	All people are created in the image of God.	
God's love is everlasting.	I deserved this.	Sinners are not loved by God because they are beautiful; they are beautiful because they are loved.	
God's fatherhood is merciful and all loving.	God does not care about human suffering.	God is deeply grieved by human suffering.	**CCC:** 270, 272, 311, 312
God understands human suffering.			

Adapted from *Mending the Soul* by Steven Tracy. Zondervan. 2005

The Truths; The Lies Abuse victims believe; How to combat the lies with Scripture.

Attribute of God: Wisdom and Truth

Description	Common Lies Created By Abuse	Truth About This Attribute	How to Combat the Lie
God knows all things: past, present and future. "God's truth is his wisdom, which commands the whole created order and governs the world."	I can't be honest with God or his people. God is disgusted with me because he knows all of my secret sins. I can't trust God because he let the abuse happen.	God loves me in spite of knowing everything about me. God knows and cares about all of my hidden struggles. No abuse is ever hidden from God's sight or escapes his justice.	**Scripture:** Deut. 7:9; 1 Sam. 16:7; Ps. 37:18; 139:1-6; Isaiah 40:12-14, 27; 42:9; Jeremiah 1:5; Eph. 3:9-11 **CCC:** 270, 272, 311, 312

The Truths; The Lies Abuse victims believe; How to combat the lies with Scripture.

Attribute of God: Almighty/Omnipotence

Description	Common Lies Created By Abuse	Truth About This Attribute	How to Combat the Lie
God is Almighty .	God is a heavenly despot who cannot be trusted.	God can and will bring good out of human and satanic evil.	**Scripture:** Gen. 50:20; Psalm 103:19; Isaiah 40:26; Jeremiah 29:11;32:27; Romans 8:28; Revelation 19:11-21
God has absolute, unhindered rule over all of creation.	Where was God?	I can trust God's work in my life	
All of creation is subject to him.	God abandoned me.	God is bigger than my abusers and the damage they created.	**CCC:** 269
	God isn't good because he didn't prevent my abuse.	God can heal me.	
		God will ultimately triumph over evil.	

The Truths; The Lies Abuse victims believe; How to combat the lies with Scripture.

Attribute of God: Merciful and Gracious

Description	Common Lies Created By Abuse	Truth About This Attribute	How to Combat the Lie
Despite man's unfaithfulness, God demonstrates the fullness of mercy and graciousness in becoming man and giving his life to free us from sin. He is the sinless lamb slain for the sinner.	God is too pure to ever want someone like me as His child. God could never love me. God could never forgive me. I'm dirty. I'm impure and can never be loved or forgiven.	God is different from and greater than anything in creation. God has nothing in common with an abuser. He is the font of all mercy. His mercy is an ocean of mercy, greater than all abuse.	**Scripture:** Ex. 34:5-6; Leviticus 20:23,26; Isaiah 6:1-7,40:18-22; Habakkuk 1:13; 2 Cor. 6:16-17; 1 Peter 1:15-16; Rev. 4:8; Phillip. 2 **CCC:** 210

The Truths; The Lies Abuse victims believe; How to combat the lies with Scripture.

Attribute of God: Righteousness and Justice

Description	Common Lies Created By Abuse	Truth About This Attribute	How to Combat the Lie
God is morally perfect. He always conforms to what is right (based on hHis perfect character), His justice is perfect.	There is no justice in the universe. Look what my abusers got away with. Those with the most power always win by crushing the weak. God will eventually crush me. I deserve to burn in hell.	No one can ever condemn God's children because Christ's perfect sacrifice satisfied the justice of God. God is a just judge; He will never allow unrepentant evil to go unpunished.	**Scripture:** Psalm 58:10-11, 119:137, 145:17 Ps. 35, Ps. 75 Romans 2:9, 8:32-34; Hebrews 10:1-18; Rev. 16:5 **CCC:** 62, 2577

The Truths; The Lies Abuse victims believe; How to combat the lies with Scripture.

Attribute of God: Steadfast and Faithful

Description	Common Lies Created By Abuse	Truth About This Attribute	How to Combat the Lie
God is absolutely loyal and dependable. He fulfills all his promises. God is trustworthy, and constant	No one can be trusted, not even God. Everyone lies. The Bible works for some people, but not for me. God won't keep being patient with me. He will eventually give up on me like everyone else has.	God will never give up on his children. No matter how many people betray me, abuse me, or don't believe me. I can trust God. God always does what he says. I can trust his promises.	**Scripture:** Psalm 25:10, 119:89-91; Hosea 11:8-9; Philippians 1:6; 1 Thess 5:14, 24; 2 Thess 3:2-3; Hebrews 10:23 **CCC:** 214

The Truths; The Lies Abuse victims believe; How to combat the lies with Scripture.

Attribute of God: Eternal

Description	Common Lies Created By Abuse	Truth About This Attribute	How to Combat the Lie
God transcends the world and history .	There is no hope.	I can trust God because He always sees the big picture.	**Scripture:** Exodus 3:14; Psalms 90:2, 102:12; Isaiah 46:10; 2 Peter 3:8; Rev. 4:8, 22:13
He sees everything, past, present and future, with perfect clarity.	I could never have anticipated this horrible abuse, and I can't deal with it.	I can trust God to fulfill His promises according to His timetable, not mine.	**CCC:** 212, 213
He has no beginning or end.	I will never heal.	No trial in my life catches God by surprise.	
God is the source of all hope.	I can't trust God's promises; they haven't worked yet and they never will.	He has a perfect plan for my healing.	

Fifteen New Gospel Meditations for the Holy Rosary
Jim Field

Each year during Lent, I ask God to show me a "project" I can do for Him. Instead of giving up something for Lent, I started thinking a couple years ago, what might I give to God during Lent? I still consider it a sacrifice of time and effort. I can make little sacrifices all year long and sometimes do so daily. I was thinking about how difficult it is for me sometimes to pray the Rosary. I usually pray it everyday, even if I have to force myself.

I started thinking about the Luminous Mysteries and how they came about. I had no idea. I thought of how we repeat the Mysteries on Mondays, Tuesdays, and Wednesdays. Then, I became curious about three new sets of Mysteries for those days. What mysteries could be added to the Holy Rosary to meditate on more of the Holy Gospel?

I had no idea, and that's when I started searching the Gospel for 15 new Mysteries. I called on the Holy Spirit for assistance. I informed my spiritual director, and he said it was fine to do that. I had become a little nervous I could be doing something offensive. Now, after reassurance, I started to find some really amazing - never included Mysteries!

So, here's what I began to organize. Of course, I kept rearranging, etc. Most of the time it was fun. Kind of like a "Holy Puzzle". Then, at other times, I would wonder, "WHAT AM I DOING?". But, I became absolutely devoted to this project.

I love praying the Holy Rosary and the Divine Mercy Chaplet every day. Since I love the Rosary so much and love reflecting on the life of Christ in Scripture, I selected 15 Scripture passages to meditate on using rosary beads. I call these three new Rosary meditations the Ministerial, Merciful, and Angelical mysteries.

Mondays: The Ministerial Mysteries of Jesus

The formation, or birth, of our Church is the core of these mysteries.

1. Jesus gathers His Apostles

Matthew 4:18 - 22, Mark 1:16 - 20, 3: 13 - 19, Luke 5:1 -11, John 1:35 - 51, Acts 9:15 - 18
Our Lord gathers 12 men, from varying states of life, to carry the message to all corners of the earth for the glory of the Kingdom of God.

2. Jesus teaches through parables

Matthew 13:1 - 53, Mark 1 -33, Luke 13:18 - 20, John 10:1 - 5, 7 - 18
With simple humility, our Lord tells 46 stories as tools for His followers to grow in holiness and become closer to God.

3. Jesus appoints Peter as the Rock

Matthew Chapter 16:16 - 19, Luke 22:32, John 21:15 - 19
Perhaps because of Simon Peter's great love, recognition of Christ as the Son of God, and sincere humble desire to devote his life of service to Jesus, our Lord chose this man as the head of our Church - the Body of Christ on earth.

4. Jesus preaches the Beatitudes

Matthew 5:3 -12, 11:6, Luke 7:23, John 20:29
Our Lord displays unfathomable promises of mercy to His children who appear to be in a state of hopeless circumstance.

5. Jesus continues to minister to His Apostles and appears to many after His Resurrection

Matthew 28:18 - 20, Luke 24:13 -53, John 20:15 -18
Our Lord continues to teach His Apostles and followers for forty more days with a promise of the Holy Spirit. His request to them is to go out into the world and teach through His Holy Sacrifice, and His Resurrection, that death is conquered for eternal salvation.

Tuesdays: The Merciful Mysteries of Jesus

Divine love and compassion is the core of all these mysteries.

1. Jesus heals the sick and raises the dead

Matthew 9:35 - 36, 10:8, Mark 5:21 - 43, Luke 7:11 - 16, John 4:46 - 54, 5:1 - 15
The merciful heart of Jesus flows with compassion for all who are afflicted or mourn.

2. Jesus forgives sin

Matthew 6:14 - 15, 9:1- 8, Mark 2:10, Luke 5:20, 7:47 - 48, 19:41 - 44, 23:24, John 8:3 - 11, James 5:16
God has granted authority for His Son to forgive sin; however, Jesus weeps on the Mount of Olives over the transgressions of the Jews, for their hearts were hardened.

3. Jesus offers salvation to all mankind

Matthew 19:16 - 30, John 21: 24, Luke 10:1 - 7, Romans 10:9 - 10, Philippians 3:4 - 11, Revelation 22:17
God desires that all who have faith in Him and repent shall have salvation, which is found within the Sacraments of the Holy Apostolic Roman Catholic Church.

4. Jesus feeds the multitudes

Matthew 14:13 - 21, Mark 6:30 - 44, Luke 9:10 - 17, John 6:5 - 14
Our Lord fills the desire of hunger and thirst for all children of God.

5. Jesus calms the storms

Matthew 8:23 - 27, 14:24 - 32, Mark 4:35 - 41, John 6:16 - 20
    As the King of the Universe, King of Kings, and Lord of Lords, all of our trials and tribulations are under the full knowledge of our Lord. He offers us peace!

Wednesdays: The Angelical Mysteries

Heaven's merciful intervention is the core of all these mysteries.

1. An angel explains about Mary to Joseph in a dream

Matthew 1:18 - 25
God mercifully sends His heavenly angel to explain to Joseph that he is
to be husband of Mary and the earthly father of Jesus.

2. Angels appear to the Shepherds

Luke 2:8 - 20
A host of heavenly angels appear to the most humble of men, shepherds, about the birth of the Saviour. They faithfully trusted as they
went to visit and worship the newborn Christ, the Savior, born unto the
world.

3. Angels guide the magi in their visitation to baby Jesus

Matthew 2:1 - 12
Guided by a heavenly star the magi seek out the newborn King to adore
Him, and an angel warns them about their departure.

4. An angelic dream warns Joseph to flee with his Holy Family to Egypt

Matthew 2:2 - 13
Joseph faithfully obeys the heavenly being's warning as the protector of
the Holy Family.

5. Angels appear at the tomb of Jesus

Matthew 28: 2 - 7, Mark 16:5 - 7, Luke 24:4 - 7, 19:44, John 20:11 - 13
At the sacred site on the Mount of Olives, Heaven's angels intervene
to console and remind the women, who so loved our Lord, what was
foretold by our Lord's own words, fulfilling many prophecies of the Old
Testament.

Crisis Response Plan

Each Bishop should consider creating a Crisis Response Plan for dealing with current or past allegations of clerical sexual abuse. The following specific steps were provided by a former rector of a minor seminary in which a previous rector was credibly accused of sexual abuse. Hopefully, this list of actions can be used as a foundation on which to build your own plan.

1. Don't look to your superiors or peers for help. They don't know what to do either. If you wait for everyone else to come up with a plan, you're already too late. You need to act promptly, as in today, not months or years from now. At least for the beginning.

2. Put together your own counsel. These should be people that you know, respect, and trust. They will be clergy and laity that are experts and, most importantly, love the Church and are trustworthy.

3. Get in touch with regular folks in the pews as well. Put together at least one committee of these people, both regular church-goers as well as parish staff members, to find out what the issues and concerns are from them, not just from the diocesan offices.

4. Be vulnerable. This sets the tone for everything else. If you didn't ask for this crisis and it sickens you, then say it. And keep saying it to everyone you talk to. But show your emotion, your humanity. It's not time to be a robot, even if your feelings are still raw and it hurts to talk about it.

5. Be open and honest about what you know and what you don't know. When in doubt, over-communicate. This does not touch on internal forum issues. When it comes to protecting the flock, the bishop has the responsibility to let all the faithful know what has and hasn't happened, so that they can make the best decisions for themselves and their families.

6. The fear that knowledge leads to greater scandal is common but unfounded. "The truth will set you free," said the Lord. It's

preferable that people choose to stop reading about the truth because it's uncomfortable, than that they are stopped from reading because it is "secret". Then, they go away with the perception that something is being hidden.

7. As much as possible, do the communication yourself, but if you can't get to all the people interested, then send others in your stead. This is not because you don't want to go, but because you want to communicate across as many levels as possible IN PERSON as soon as possible.

8. Every accusation of abuse should be reported to law enforcement immediately.

9. Investigate each allegation quickly, the same day or within a few days. Be sure that the definitions of abuse are clear. Create a solid investigative team that is made of professionals, hiring outside consultants if necessary. Their process should be clear, simple, and as transparent as possible.

10. Talk to the victim(s) in person, whether it's confirmed or only alleged abuse. Do this quickly and personally, outside of the investigation, to offer spiritual support.

11. Talk to the accused, again outside of the investigation, to offer spiritual support.

12. Although rare, if the victim's claims are not able to be substantiated, and the accused is proclaimed innocent, be sure that this is made public and they are able to return to their work place if they want to.

13. When a proper internal investigation proves that abuse has taken place, compare this with the civil process, and decide based on that situation what the spiritual good for all those involved is. For the abuser, if clergy, it might be laicization, but it might also be ex-communication based on the level of repentance. If the person receives a criminal punishment, such as jail time, then be aware of

their spiritual needs. Discipline needs to be directed towards the salvation of the soul.

14. Offer proper therapy and psychology for all those involved.

15. Use money with Christian stewardship, primarily for those services that are needed that lead to the most healing, such as those mentioned above: retreats, spiritual direction, job training, and so forth. Money should never be used to silence victims nor to appease them but rather for services that lead to deep healing.

16. Healing takes time. Visit the parishes where abuse has taken place and invite any others who were abused to come forward, with a safe way to report accusations. Statues of limitations, whether legal or not, should have no place within the Church's treatment of accusations and abuse.

17. Build up preventative measures that teach the truth about human sexuality and reproduction. Catholic theology about sexuality, marriage, and celibacy are based on fundamental biology, not the other way around. Encourage priests to be unafraid in proclaiming the truth on these topics from the pulpit, the confessional, and all other opportunities.

18. Provide priests with proper support in their specific roles. This means community and self-care for all priests and management training for pastors and the laity helping them. Don't leave priests alone in rectories with little support structure.

19. Communicate all that is happening. Many times dioceses go to extraordinary lengths to fix problems yet no one knows about them. As much as possible, build up relationships with media so as to be able to provide them proper information, both the negative and the positive.

Resources

A week-long retreat program facilitated by mental health professionals and centered on Jesus Christ, Grief to Grace, a Catholic program open to people of all faiths, helps those who have endured physical, emotional, and/or spiritual abuse find healing. Grief to

A spiritual & psychological program for Healing the Wounds of Abuse

Grace has served thousands across the United States and around the world since 2005.

Professional therapeutic staff will engage you in a program of Living Scripture exercises, therapeutic facilitation, cognitive restructuring, and grief work. By traveling the Paschal Mystery of your own life and uniting your suffering to Christ's, Grief to Grace can help you to share also in Christ's Resurrection—finding love, tenderness, belonging, safety, joy, and peace.

For more information visit grieftograce.org, send an email to info@GrieftoGrace.org, or call 610-203-2002.

JOHN PAUL II Healing Center
Transformation in the Heart of the Church

To promote and inspire transformation in the heart of the Church, by healing and equipping God's people for the New Evangelization.

This mission is fulfilled in the very heart of the Church, helping people activate the fullness of their sacramental graces, while transforming their lives.

jpiihealingcenter.org

Maria Goretti Network
For Recovery and Forgiveness

A Ministry to Survivors

The Maria Goretti Network family reaches out to abuse victims, their families, and to those who support our recovery, with God's love as witnessed in the life of Maria Goretti.

"I started attending Maria Goretti Network meetings about 4 years ago. This group is so different than seeing counselors, psychiatrists, or even psychologists. You are not a patient being analyzed or studied. I am not there to seek mental health advice. Witnessing other men and women experience healing as I have is very gratifying. Telling others that I am not perfect but I am perfecting myself, is a comfort to me. Saying this to other members holds me accountable and wants me to do and be better." - Dr. Deb Rodriguez

If you have questions about our organization or would like more information about our network, please contact the Manager of the Network, Miguel Prats, at miguel@mgoretti.org or call him on his mobile phone anytime (24/7) @ (713) 851-3708.

mgoretti.org

Fullness of Truth
Catholic Evangelization Ministries

Fullness of Truth strives to deepen and enrich the faith of thousands of Catholics and non-Catholics each year. We organize Catholic family conferences throughout the state of Texas and beyond. Fullness of Truth is a 501 (c)(3) non-profit lay apostolate relying on the prayers of all those who wish to promote the work of the New Evangelization.

fullnessoftruth.org

The Midwest Catholic Family Conference is held in early August in Wichita, Kansas. It is an annual event for the whole family providing an enticing mix of presentations by world-renown speakers for Adults, College-aged, Young Adults, and religious. Special programs address the needs of Faith for students in High School and Middle School as well as children in the elementary grades.

catholicfamilyconference.org

At the Apostolate for Family Consecration® (AFC), our mission is to empower you to create experiences that make your family's Catholic faith come alive for your children. As a result, your family can become what God wants you to be—a family on fire for Him—and then share that light with others.

afc.org

Further Reading

- *My Peace I Give You: Healing Sexual Wounds with the Help of the Saints* by Dawn Eden. An essential book for those wishing a book on healing from a Catholic perspective.

- *Hurting in the Church: A Way Forward for Wounded Catholics* by Father Thomas Berg. Along with his own story, Fr. Berg intertwines the stories other Catholics who have themselves experienced life-changing hurts, but who, in Jesus, found healing.

- *Veronica's Veil: Spiritual Companionship for Survivors of Abuse.* Another helpful book from T. Pitt Green and Rev. Lewis Fiorelli.

- *Marriage 911* by Greg and Julie Alexander. They thought divorce was the only way out of their lifeless, loveless marriage. Quite unexpectedly, a faithful priest guided them back to the truths of the Church, and as they began to incorporate these truths into their lives, they were able to restore the love they once had for each other. *Marriage 911* chronicles their journey back from the brink of divorce to marital happiness built on a strong Catholic faith.

Eye Movement Desensitization and Reprocessing

Getting Past Your Past, by Francine Shapiro. We are all influenced by memories and experiences we may not remember or don't fully understand. Shapiro, the creator of EMDR (Eye Movement Desensitization and Reprocessing), explains how our personalities develop and why we become trapped into feeling, believing and acting in ways that don't serve us.

EMDR is a therapy based on the concept that every experience we have governs how we respond to future experiences. We connect what is happening right now in the context of what we learned from prior experiences.

We make these connections all the time without being conscious of it. We have automatic responses to external 'triggers'. PTSD is just one example of these automatic responses.

The problem is when we've experienced trauma, situations we find ourselves in can trigger the same or similar emotions, potentially causing us to overreact or respond in an inappropriate way.

EMDR activates the brain's subconscious so the memories can be processed in a controlled environment. It helps one explore memories that can lead to anxiety, depression, addiction, relationship issues, and the inability to resolve conflicts.

Your Holy Family Ministries

Renewing the Church One Family at a Time

YourHolyFamily.org

Your Holy Family Ministries supports parents in their mission to build a family of Joy, united in Faith, which reflects the Love of God to our world through programs and resources designed to enable families to grow closer to each other and closer to the Lord. The programs seek to guide families to the vision of St. John Paul II by teaching families "to guard, reveal, and communicate love" through family prayer and family play that builds a ministry of presence in the home and seeks to build community with other Catholic families as well as becoming a family that gives witness to the Faith.

Your Holy Family Ministries was founded in October 2013 by Allen and Denae Hebert in response to the call of St. John Paul II in Familiaris Consortio (#54) for families to evangelize the world.

33 Day Family Consecration

A Guide for parents to lead their family in total consecration to Jesus through Mary.

Prayer provides the solid foundation on which to build your holy family.

Ages 7 and Up

33 Day Family Consecration Coloring Book

Over 40 original coloring pages matching the theme of each day of the family consecration.

"Little hands are kept busy so that little ears can listen."

33day.org

About the Authors

Allen A. Hébert

Allen Hébert is an Information Technology professional who has worked as a Sales Engineer at various companies. He has been married to his wife Denae for almost 29 years and they have been blessed with nine children. In his spare time he volunteers his time and talent in varying capacities within the Catholic Church. He attended Catholic Schools from Kindergarten through College, and was a member of the Capital Campaign committee and led the technology committee at Holy Family Catholic School in Austin, TX. He was a member of the Speakers Bureau for the Office of Pro-life Activities in the Diocese of Austin, a member of the Adult Faith Formation core team and frequent presenter and Master of Ceremonies in both RCIA and the Jesus is Lord adult faith formation programs at St. William Catholic Church in Round Rock, TX and a former board member of the Central Texas Fellowship of Catholic Men and the Alexander House Apostolate. In 2013, Allen and his wife Denae founded Your Holy Family Ministries.

Denae L. Hébert

Denae Hébert is a homeschooling mother of 9. She has been married to her husband Allen for 28 years. Denae is an educator by trade and holds a Masters in Educational Administration. She served on the Development Board for Holy Family Catholic School in Austin, TX, and is currently on the Board of FISCHETeen, (Families in Support of Catholic Homeschool Education Teen). She helped to develop the FISCHETeen program and has been coordinating their monthly retreats for 9 years Denae also developed a family retreat with her husband Allen and has been planning and coordinating Family Retreats with the Community of St. John since 2012. She and her husband Allen are the cofounders of Your Holy Family Ministries.

Jim Field

From the time he was a little boy, he'd always loved making things. Often, especially with carpentry, it would involve using old salvaged wood, or with lighting, recycled lamp parts. He became obsessed with using discarded stuff—most of it of little value in and of itself— and making it into something beautiful. The joy he found in creating something out of nothing continued into adulthood.

After years of learning various skills—carpentry, electrical, finishing— and mastering the use of different construction materials, he launched out on his own, opening a retail store in the 1980's in Los Angeles. He began selling his creations—antiques and collectibles— and taking orders for custom furniture and lighting. At the time, he never imagined that this new design concept of creating with reclaimed materials would become so popular.

As a builder, he filled the needs of countless customers both in Los Angeles and Lafayette, building most of his products out of "worthless junk". It was always his goal to create something of beauty. To himself, he often marvelled at what could be rearranged and repurposed into something valuable.

In other areas of his adult life, he has cared deeply for others, especially those afflicted in one way or another. The wide array of work he has done in this area has almost always been done anonymously.

Now semi-retired, he continues to work part time in a dining hall kitchen at Purdue University. When he isn't working, he enjoys being involved with church activities in Lafayette, In.

Jess McGuire

I am a single mom who lives in Massachusetts. I'm doing my best to create a loving home environment for my family of two wonderful kids and two dogs, one of whom welcomes the company of family and friends. Our fenced backyard is a delight where we love to garden, and my son is free to run around with the dogs, to laugh, and act a little silly and most of all to experience the joy of being an innocent child of God. I work as a nanny and try to help others, especially those who have been impacted so greatly by abuse.

Deacon Bob Henkel

Deacon Bob J. Henkel Sr. served as a HR Professional in the role of Senior Staffing Consultant for the largest energy producer in the world, recruiting highly talented professionals for the last 11+ years. Prior to this, Deacon Bob worked as a Senior Financial Planner Analyst at The Vanguard Group – Investment Management Company, traveling around the country teaching Financial Planning Concepts.

He earned his Bachelor's Degree in Social Science and also holds designations as a Certified Financial Planner™, a Certified Employee Benefits Specialist, a Retirement Planning Associate, and the recruiting designations of ACIR, CSSR, CIR and the PRC. However, officially on September 30, 2019, he will retire from his current position with August 30, 2019 as his last office day. He will then follow what he believes is God's plan for the next part of his life and enter a full time Master's program at the University of Saint Thomas in Houston, Texas for Clinical Mental Health Counseling. He believes the crosses he carried through his younger life will help him relate to those hurting today. He prays God will use him in this new endeavor to help others carrying crosses to lead to their resurrections.

Deacon Bob was ordained in the Camden Diocese of NJ on June 11, 2005, and he now serves at St. Maximilian Kolbe Parish in the Archdiocese of Galveston-Houston. He has been happily married to the love of his life, his beautiful wife Dana, for almost 34 years, and together they have a 31 year old son, Bobby, and a 29 year old daughter, Jennifer.

Deacon Scott Peyton

Deacon Scott Peyton is the husband of Letitia Peyton, and together they have six children. Scott is a permanent deacon in the Catholic Church and is currently assigned to Sacred Heart Catholic Church in Ville Platte, LA. Scott is the State Director of Louisiana for Right On Crime. Scott serves in various ministries as a deacon for his church parish and diocese. In his capacity as Director of Right On Crime, he can be found at the State Capital or traveling across Louisiana, writing articles and advocating for criminal justice reform.

Letitia Peyton

Letitia Peyton is the wife of Scott Peyton and mom to six children. She is a dedicated homeschooling mom continuing to homeschool her four school-aged children. She is a member of WINE: Women In the New Evangelization and a Regional WINE Specialist for Ville Platte's CajunWINE. She is also a member of Everyday Missionaries, a local women's ministry. When she is not homeschooling or spending time with her family, Letitia is often speaking on Catholicism, leading Bible studies and Catholic book studies for women, or working on some aspect of Catholic women's ministry.

Valarie Brooks

Valarie currently lives in Southwestern Idaho, but she grew up in the oil fields of Southeastern New Mexico, attending grade school at St. Helena's Catholic School in Hobbs, New Mexico. She and her husband Gaylon were married in 1986. They worked together as 12-Step Drug and Alcohol Counselors for the Palmer Drug Abuse Program in New Mexico until Valarie realized God was calling her to be a stay-at-home mom and to homeschool their three children, who are all now grown. She and Gaylon were blessed with their first grandchild in 2018.

Valarie has volunteered with various organizations over the years. She has served as treasurer and newsletter editor for La Leche League of Henderson County, North Carolina, as a Peer Counselor for the Henderson County WIC (Women, Infants and Children) program, as yearbook editor for the Henderson County Homeschool Association, and volunteered with the Leaders In Training 4-H Club. She was the President of the Staff-Parish Relations Committee at East Flat Rock United Methodist Church for two years. She has served as yearbook editor for Families in Support of Catholic Education in Austin, Texas. She is a trained midwife and lactation consultant and is a member of the Association of Texas Midwives. She is currently a member of St. Paul Catholic Church in Nampa, Idaho and of the Treasure Valley Latin Mass Society. Both Valarie and Gaylon love attending the Traditional Latin Mass!

Her passions include quilting, sewing, genealogy research, writing poetry, gardening and canning, crochet, cross stitch, and desktop publishing.

Elizabeth Terrill, LPCC

Elizabeth Terrill, LPCC is an independently licensed mental health counselor in Gallup, NM. She has also been the Victims' Assistance Coordinator for the Diocese of Gallup for the past six years. She earned her bachelor's degree in Psychology and a master's degree in counseling from the Franciscan University of Steubenville. Elizabeth specializes in trauma informed therapy with child and adult survivors of sexual abuse in her mental health practice and utilizes those skills to serve the Diocese by offering support to survivors of clergy abuse. She and her husband have two young children and have been foster parents to many other children. She has made a commitment to improving the health and well-being of children in her community through her professional practice and personal life.

Dr. Deborah Rodriguez

Deborah Rodriguez is a general pediatrician in Tacoma, WA. She has a special focus on working with children, families, and adults who have experienced trauma in their lives. She is a member of the

American Academy of Pediatrics Committee on Child Abuse and Neglect. She also works with survivors of human trafficking using a model of long-term healing and restoration. She has a ministry to adult survivors of abuse and has spoken to groups on the science of trauma and toxic stress and on human trafficking awareness and prevention.

Michael Vanderburgh

Michael Vanderburgh is executive director of the Society of St. Vincent de Paul in Dayton, Ohio. A native of Dayton, Michael's career path included police officer and corrections officer positions, ownership of a life insurance agency in northern Ohio and northwestern Illinois, and, since 1999, nonprofit leadership in financial development and executive positions in Iowa, Kentucky, and Ohio.

Michael is a graduate of The George Washington University (M.A.), Wright State University (B.A), and Sinclair Community College (A.A.S.), and attended law school at Ohio Northern University and the University of Dayton.

Over a decade of service for the Archdiocese of Cincinnati, Michael planned and led the historic One Faith, One Hope, One Love capital campaign, which raised over $165 million in pledges to benefit regional ministries of the Catholic Church in western and southwestern Ohio.

In 2017, a feature article about Michael's life appeared in the *Cincinnati Enquirer*, and the story received a first place award by The Press Club of Cleveland.

Michael resides in Oakwood with his wife Ann Marie and four children.

Christopher West

Christopher West serves as Senior Lecturer of Theology and Christian Anthropology at the Theology of the Body Institute. His global lecturing, best-selling books, and multiple audio and video programs have made him one of the world's most recognized teachers of John Paul II's Theology of the Body. As Founder and President of The Cor Project, he leads an international outreach devoted to helping others learn, live, and share this liberating teaching. His work has been featured in the New York Times, on ABC News, MSNBC, Fox News, and countless Catholic and Evangelical media outlets.

Joanne Schmidt - Editor

Joanne C. Schmidt has contributed articles to a dozen consumer and religious publications, including *Current Biography* and *National Catholic Register*. She was managing editor of *Argosy Magazine* and Editor-in-Chief of *Houston Town and Country* before founding her own magazine, *Inside Texas Running*, which she edited and published for more than twenty-five years. She has a Bachelor of Arts Degree in Magazine Journalism from Syracuse University.

ABUSE *of* TRUST

Acknowledgements

Allen A. Hébert

I want to thank my dear saintly wife, Denae. I had no idea how hard writing this book would be for you and me. To my editors, Emma, Abigail, David, Joanne, Valarie, Fr. Gavin and Vicky, you made all the contributors look good. Thank you for doing the hard work to help us heal and accomplish this work God called me to do. To the many lay evangelists who preached the good news in season and out of season. This book is the direct result of prayer in front of the Blessed Sacrament at our Perpetual Eucharistic Adoration Chapel at St. William in Round Rock Texas; thank you Fr. Dean for your dedication to keeping the Adoration Chapel light on for those of us who so desperately need it.

Denae L. Hébert

To Christ who stretched my heart in order to do this work; to my beloved, Allen, who patiently loved me when my pain made me unlovable; to my children who sustained the home when their mother was unavailable; to Michelle who listened and helped me process this project; to Abigail who edited and organized my disjointed story; to all the friends and family, who were my prayer warriors and without whom none of this would have been possible and to whom I am forever grateful. Thank you for being Christ to me.

Jim Field

Allen and Denae, for having the courage, faith, and desire to help our Church. I'm humbled and amazed by all that has unfolded in only a few short months thanks to them and to all the courageous contributors. This book has been and continues to be an act of tremendous charity.

Thank you Valarie for helping me to get my story into print. The process was much more difficult than I ever imagined it would be.

I'm grateful for all the support I've received from religious and priests—both named and unnamed. For the support I've received in more recent years, I especially thank Father Timothy Combs, who has helped me during the rough days of continued healing. His commitment to spiritual direction has helped me to grow closer to God.

I thank all my family, especially my oldest sister, Jennie Hack. She is the greatest of all my spiritual directors. I also want to acknowledge her amazing husband for his support of her, which has ultimately helped me as well.

I thank all the survivors that I've been connected with over the years of tears and triumphs in the journey toward healing. I especially thank Sheila Boyle in Boston, whom I met through SNAP, for our countless talks in person and on the phone. Her courage and desire to heal carried me through the early days.

Thank you to Elizabeth Terrill for your many hours of counseling me with amazing sensitivity and insight. Over the years, we've created an unseen bond extending from this diocese to your diocese.

And most of all, thank you God for allowing my faith and understanding to grow so deeply, even as my outer life began to disintegrate as my past history of deplorable acts perpetrated by clergy and complicit bishops began to emerge. I believe this is the biggest, most merciful gift of all. I have survived and still believe in the Sacraments and continue to love my Church so much.

Jess McGuire

Thank you all who helped in this journey and putting my story into words: Carol Purtell, Susan Berard-Goldberg, Fr. Francis Signarelli, and, most of all, Allen and his wife, Denae, for their amazing sacrifice in this book. Thanks to editor Joanne Schmidt and, most especially, to Fr. Carl Chudy, SX for his truly amazing support.

I'm grateful for all the support I have received from my family, especially my mother, who is now one of my best friends; Sandra Helena, a wonderful friend and great support for my family and me; Barbara Zino, a caring and faithful friend who complements Fr. Carl's guidance with a woman's perspective as we both strive to be open to Jesus and for me to best live out my calling as mother and friend; and Jean Morrissey for being there no matter what as a support.

I wish to thank my family, especially Nana Kwarteng, I am so happy our family positively impacts your life. To my daughter, who is the most amazing strong and determined woman I have ever met and who will impact the world in amazing ways. Best blessings to my son, who is one of the smartest kids I know and brings so much joy to my life.

I thank all the survivors in my Survivors group, and I'm sorry that it ended. And my childhood counselor, Carl Peterson, who has always been an amazing support to me.

Thank you to the Archdiocese of Boston and our new parish that welcomed my family with open arms. I am thankful for the former Director of the Shrine, Fr. Joe Matteucia as well as the Missionary Fathers for all the support throughout my healing. Most of all, I wish to thank Fr. Carl. Words can never describe the amazing impact you have been and continue to be to my family. As my mother said, "This man has broken down walls no one could break."

Deacon Bob Henkel

I would never be where I am in my faith without many great priests, so many awesome priests truly dedicated to being married to Jesus and living the Gospel. Monsignor Donovan (thank you for bringing us back to the faith), Fr. Mike Signiski, Fr. Mike Mannion, Fr. Joe Ferrara, Fr. Frank Burke, Fr. Charles Conaty, Fr. Rene Canales, Monsignor Peter Joyce, Fr. Dennis Bajkowski, Fr. Art Alban, Fr.

Sean Horrigan, Fr. John Ulm, Fr. Pawel from Bridgeport, Fr. Ignatius Houang, Fr. Denny O'Donnell, Fr. Larry Richards, Fr. Joe Pelligrino, and Daniel Cardinal DiNardo. Cardinal DiNardo is such a servant of God, and he realizes how important and special our youth are to the Church. He dedicates time to our diocesan Youth Ministry at our convention. I have seen him year after year celebrate Mass at the juvenile detention center for incarcerated young teenagers. These amazing men are but a few (forgive me for the names that have been important to me and my family not mentioned). Most of all I want to thank God.

Letitia and Deacon Scott Peyton

To our son, Oliver Peyton, your strength and courage, along with your deep compassion for others, will forever give us the will to stand strong and fight for those who cannot fight for themselves.

To our son, Alex Peyton, your perseverance and dedication to your brother and the love of your family gives us hope that we have instilled in our children the importance of a strong and caring family and a respect for other people.

To our four younger children, we hope that you will one day understand how we tried to protect you from carrying this burden and the sorrows that we carry. Mom and dad know you love your oldest brothers very much and you would have carried their sorrows and agony in your hearts too. We would rather carry them for you until you are older and have a better understanding. Our prayer is that in time there will be healing for our family.

To our families, friends, our counselors, and a handful of priests and deacons who have stood next to us when others left our side, we cannot thank you enough. You have given our family strength through your constant prayers.

Finally, all glory to God for putting those in our path that have helped to make a difference in this fight for justice, healing, and hope in a broken and battered Church.

Valarie Brooks

I would like to thank Allen & Denae Hebert, for their openness to God in being willing to tackle this project and for giving me the opportunity and privilege to contribute in some small way. I know this book has been very challenging for them personally, as well as a tremendous sacrifice for them and their beautiful family. They have given selflessly of their time and effort, forsaking their own comfort, privacy, and personal anonymity. Books like this can only be written by people who care passionately and deeply enough about Jesus Christ and His Holy Church to trust in the grace of the Holy Spirit and step boldly out of their own comfort zone and take a daunting leap of faith in order to help others who are hurting and wounded. I am deeply indebted to both of them for their love, prayers, and support, and for inspiring me and my husband to keep slaying the dragons and to not quit before the miracle!

Dr. Deborah Rodriguez M.D.

Dr. Rodriguez wishes to thank the love of her life, her husband David, and her three beautiful children: Lauren, Erin, and Nathan. Special thanks to Dayle. Also the prayers and support from her Bible study sisters, Rev Jacob Maurer, Rev Edward White, Rev Sean Raftis, her MGN family: Miguel and Rev Gavin Vaverek, Shannon, Rolando, and John.

Michael Vanderburgh

My field hospital priests were Bishop Joe Binzer and Fr. Greg Konerman. I am forever grateful for their selfless care beginning in 2004 and their continuing care and prayers to the present day.

Many other people have encouraged me to share my personal story and witness of faith through my experiences of working in the institutional Church. These include Archbishop Dan Pilarczyk, Fr. Steve Angi, Fr. Len Wenke, Bishop Bob Morneau, Bishop Carl Moeddel, Fr. Tim Fahey, Fr. Tom Schmidt, Fr. Jason Williams, Fr.

Dave Brinkmoeller, Fr. Tom Berg, Fr. Richard Kramer, Fr. Earl Fernandes, Fr. Bob Obermeyer, Fr. Tim Ralston, Fr. Simon Peter Wankya, Fr. Tom DiFolco, Fr. Jerry Bensman, Fr. George Jacquemin, Fr. Marc Sherlock, Fr. Jan Schmidt, and, my best friend, loyal confidant, and colleague, Brian Doyle. I acknowledge the brave witness of other authors here and countless others whose stories may never be told.

I am eternally grateful for my wife, Ann Marie, and her patience and fortitude with me through these many years and our six beautiful children in heaven and on earth. My sons and daughters are special beacons of faith for me and have taught me the love of Our Father.

I commend my small contribution to this effort to announcing the One True Love we recognize in the Holy Trinity — the continually giving and receiving that is God.

Made in the USA
Middletown, DE
11 October 2023

40431185R00208